U0548380

D'AULAIRES' BOOK
OF
GREEK MYTHS

INGRI D'AULAIRE
&
EDGAR PARIN D'AULAIRE

赫尔墨斯
赫菲斯托斯
阿瑞斯
雅典娜
阿波罗
阿尔忒弥斯
狄俄尼索斯
珀尔塞福涅
赫斯提亚
得墨忒耳
赫拉
宙斯
波塞冬
哈得斯
克罗诺斯
厄俄斯
赫利俄斯
塞勒涅
许珀里翁
阿特拉斯
厄庇米修斯
普罗米修斯
伊阿佩托
九位缪斯
谟涅摩辛涅
福柏
忒亚
忒弥斯
瑞亚
克利俄斯
忒提斯
俄刻阿诺斯
科俄斯
阿芙洛狄忒

多莱尔的希腊神话书

[美] 英格丽·多莱尔　爱德加·帕林·多莱尔 著绘

熊裕 译

北京联合出版公司
Beijing United Publishing Co.,Ltd.

Dedication

To our son,Per Ola,
who has helped us so much
in writing and lithographing
this book.

献给

我们的儿子，珀尔·奥拉
在本书写作和刻绘的过程中
他对我们帮助良多

科尔

布柏里尔人
北方的仙女

色雷斯
俄耳甫斯出生地

科尔喀斯

亚马逊

黑海

小亚细亚

野蛮人马兽
逃到了这里

奥林匹斯

蛇髮巨人们从这里进攻奥林匹斯

赫菲斯托斯在此锻造

莱姆诺斯岛

特洛伊

许拉斯
在这里
失踪

约尔科斯

皮立翁山
人马兽的家

塞萨利
拉庇泰人的家

莱斯博斯岛

俄耳甫斯安葬于此

爱琴海

河神阿刻罗俄斯的家

人马兽涅索斯和得伊阿尼拉在此

帕纳塞斯山

卡吕冬
野猪在此

特尔斐的神谕

埃维厄岛

波塞冬的宫殿

开俄斯岛

俄里翁在此失明

金羊毛从这里
飞到科尔客斯

底比斯

赫拉克勒斯
出生地

艾留西斯

珀尔塞福涅在
这里被劫持

雅典

埃伊曼萨斯
山野猪在此

奥革阿斯的
马厩在此

奥林匹亚

科林斯

迈锡尼

赫尔墨斯
出生地

尼米亚
狮子在此

阿戈斯

梯林斯

特罗曾

阿卡迪亚
潘的家

伯罗奔尼撒

怪兽许德
拉在此

狄俄尼索斯在
这里被绑架

伊卡里亚岛

伊卡洛斯
死于这里

德洛斯岛

塞里福斯岛

达那厄
漂流到这里

纳克索斯岛

阿里阿德涅
在这里睡着了

斯巴达

海伦的故乡

爱奥尼亚海

阿芙洛狄忒
升起处

克里特岛

艾达山

克诺索斯
和迷宫

宙斯童年的家

蒂尔

埃及

远古时代
In Olden Times

当人类还在崇拜丑陋的偶像之际，希腊大地上却生活着一群崇尚美与光明的牧羊人和牧主。他们不像他们的邻居那样崇拜黑暗的偶像，而是创造了自己的美丽而光芒闪耀的神祇。

希腊的神祇模样很像凡人，言行举止也像，只是他们更加高大、英俊，完美无缺。喷火的怪物和多头的野兽代表着一切黑暗和邪恶。他们是众神和伟大英雄们要征服的对象。

众神生活在奥林匹斯山（Olympus）之巅。那是一座高而陡峭的山峰，没有人能够爬上去，在那闪亮的宫殿里看见神。但神祇经常降临人间，他们有时会显露真身，有时却伪装成人或动物的样子。

凡人都崇拜众神，而众神则敬仰大地母亲（Mother Earth）。他们都来自大地母亲的恩泽——她是一切生命的初始。

盖亚，大地母亲

Gaea, Mother Earth

大地之神盖亚（Gaea）从黑暗之中生发出来。那是太久以前的事，没有人知道到底是多久以前，也没有人知道她如何孕育而生。那时候大地上还没有任何生物，大地之神年轻而寂寞。深蓝色的天空之神乌拉诺斯（Uranus）从大地上升腾起来，化为布满星辰的天穹，笼罩四方。他看上去壮美无边，年轻的大地仰望着他，爱上了他。天空俯身向大地微笑，数不清的星星也随之闪耀，他们相爱并结合了。很快，年轻的大地之神成为大地母亲，一切生灵之母。所有的孩子都爱他们温暖丰饶的母亲，却害怕那伟大的父亲——宇宙的主宰乌拉诺斯。

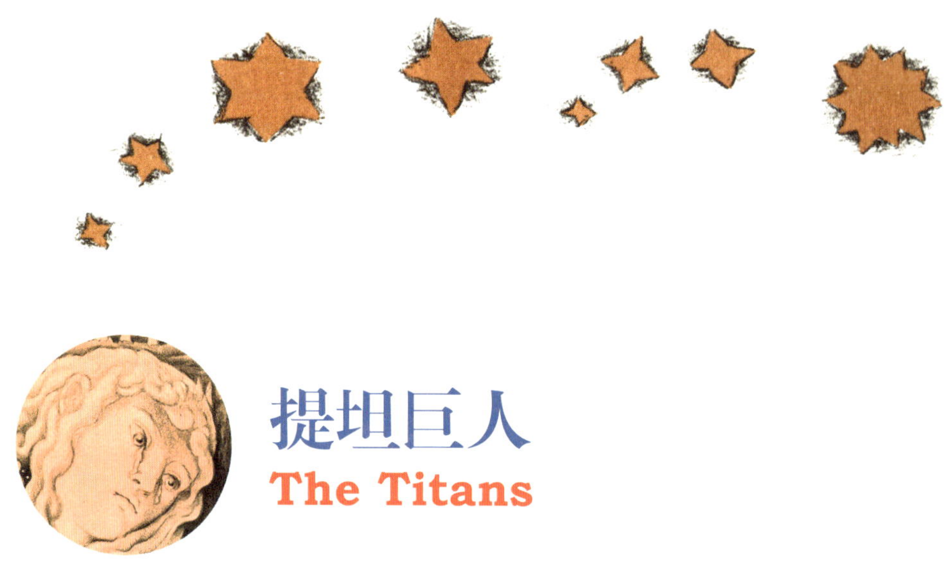

提坦巨人
The Titans

提坦巨人（the Titans）是大地母亲生下的第一批孩子。他们是最初的神祇。提坦巨人的个子比山峰还高，那些山峰是大地母亲为他们打造的宝座。大地母亲和天空之神都为他们感到骄傲。大地母亲总共生了六个提坦巨人。他们有六个妹妹，被称为提坦女神（the Titanesses）。提坦巨人娶了她们做妻子。

当盖亚再次分娩时，乌拉诺斯不再高兴了。这次诞生的孩子同样高大无比，但是每个孩子都只有一只眼睛，亮闪闪地长在额头上。这三个独眼巨人（the Cyclopes）的名字分别叫闪电、雷霆和霹雳。他们不是英俊的神，而是强壮无比的铁匠。他们重重的铁锤敲打出的火花飞迸到天上，映红了天庭，使他们父亲的星星都黯然失色。

大地母亲不久又生了三个孩子。乌拉诺斯一看见他们就觉得恶心。他们各长着五十个脑袋和一百条粗壮的手臂。他讨厌看到这些丑陋的东西在可爱的大地身上走来走去，便把这几个孩子和他们的独眼巨人兄长抓了起来，投进了塔尔塔洛斯（Tartarus）——大地上最深最黑暗的深渊。

大地母亲深爱着自己的孩子，她无法原谅丈夫这样残忍地对待他们。于是她用最坚硬的燧石打造了一把镰刀，对她的儿子，也就是提坦巨人们说：

“拿上这武器，去结束你们父亲的残忍行径，把你们的弟弟们放出来吧。”

有五个提坦巨人害怕了，他们颤抖着拒绝了盖亚。只有克罗诺斯（Cronus）勇敢地接过了那把镰刀，他是提坦巨人当中最年轻的，但也是最强壮的。他向父亲猛

扑了过去。乌拉诺斯打不过挥舞着镰刀的强壮儿子，只好放弃权力逃走了。

大地母亲选择了辽阔无边的海洋——蓬托斯（Pontus）——作为她的第二个丈夫，他们结合之后诞下了水中的诸神。盖亚那富饶的土地上长出了许多树木和花，各种精灵、野兽和早期的人类在她身体的各个角落遍布开来。

克罗诺斯现在成了宇宙的主宰。他坐在最高的山峰上，牢牢地统治着大地和天堂。其他的神祇都服从他的意志，早期的人类也崇拜他。这是人类的黄金时代。人类快乐地生活着，他们与诸神和平共处，彼此之间也没有争斗。人们从不杀戮，门上也不装锁，因为那时候人们还不会偷东西。

但是克罗诺斯并没有把他那些怪物般的弟弟释放出来，大地母亲因此非常气愤，她暗暗地谋划着推翻克罗诺斯。她必须等待，因为强壮到可以打败克罗诺斯的神还没有出世。但是她知道克罗诺斯的孩子当中一定会有一个比他更强，就像克罗诺斯强过他的父亲一样。克罗诺斯也知道这一点，所以每当他的提坦

女神妻子瑞亚（Rhea）生下孩子时，他就把新生的婴儿抢去吞掉。这样，他所有的孩子都在他的肚子里，万无一失，他就没什么好担心的了。

瑞亚却忧伤极了。她那嫁给其他五个提坦巨人的姐妹们都有她们的小提坦巨人环绕膝下，而她却孤零零地独自一人。当瑞亚怀上第六个孩子时，她请求大地母亲帮她把这个孩子从他父亲手里救下来。这正是大地母亲一直在等待的机会。她对着瑞亚耳语，给她出了个主意，瑞亚微笑着离开了。

瑞亚一生下她的孩子——宙斯（Zeus），就把他藏了起来。她在襁褓里包了一块石头，把它交给了丈夫，让他以为这是她的孩子。克罗诺斯上当了，他吞下了这块石头，而小宙斯则被偷偷地送到克里特岛（Crete）上的一个山洞里。老克罗诺斯一点儿都没有听到他小儿子的哭声，因为大地母亲在山洞的外面安置了一些吵闹的大地精灵。他们用剑敲打盾牌，咣咣的声响把其他声音都淹没了。

宙斯和他的家庭
ZEUS and His Family

宙斯由温柔的仙女们照看，仙羊阿玛西娅（Amaltheia）哺育着他。仙羊的角上会流出仙肴和琼浆，那是神所享用的食物和饮品。宙斯飞快地长大了，没多久，这位新生的伟大神祇就迈出了山洞。为了答谢仙女们对他的精心照料，他赐给她们仙羊的角。这是两只永远也不会枯竭的富足之角。他用羊皮给自己做了一副无法刺穿的胸甲，称作宙斯之盾（the Aegis）。这样一来，他变得强大无比，连克罗诺斯也奈何不了他。

年轻的宙斯选择了一个提坦巨人的女儿墨提斯（Metis）作为他的第一位妻子。墨提斯是慎思之神，宙斯需要她的好建议。她提醒宙斯不要试图一个人去推翻他那吞噬自己小孩的父亲，因为所有的提坦巨人和他们的儿子们都站在克罗诺斯一边。宙斯必须先找到自己的强大盟友。

墨提斯来到克罗诺斯面前，巧妙地骗他吃下一种有魔力的草药。克罗诺斯以为这种草药可以让他变得不可战胜，结果这草药却让他感到恶心难受，以至于把自己吞下去的那块石头呕吐了出来，另外五个孩子也一起被吐了出来。他们分别是男神哈得斯（Hades）、波塞冬（Poseidon），女神赫斯提亚（Hestia）、得墨忒耳（Demeter）和赫拉（Hera），这几位强大的神都立刻和宙斯联合起来。当克罗诺斯看到六个年轻的神站出来反对他时，他知道自己大势已去，便交出权力逃走了。

现在宙斯成了宇宙的主宰。他不想自己一个人统治整个宇宙，于是把自己的权力拿出来与哥哥姐姐们分享。但是提坦巨人和他们的儿子们发起了叛乱。他们不愿意被这些新神统治。只有普罗米修斯（Prometheus）和他的兄弟厄庇米修斯（Epimetheus）离开了提坦巨人的阵营，加入宙斯这一边，原来普罗米修斯能够预见未来，他知道宙斯将取得胜利。

宙斯把大地母亲怪物般的儿子们从塔尔塔洛斯放了出来。出于感激，那些百臂巨人竭尽全力地为宙斯作战，独眼巨人们则为宙斯和他的兄弟们打造了强大的武器。

他们为波塞冬打造了一支三叉戟。这支戟威力巨大，波塞冬把它往地上一顿，大地便随之震动，在海里一搅，便掀起山一样高的巨浪。

他们为哈得斯做的是一顶隐身帽子，这样他便可以悄悄地打击敌人。他们为宙斯打造了霹雳。有了这些霹雳，宙斯便成为众神中最强大的，什么都无法阻挡他和他的雷霆万钧之势。经过一场苦战，提坦巨人们最终还是投降了。宙斯把他们锁进了塔尔塔洛斯，派百臂巨人们在门口看守，让他们永远无法逃脱。最强壮的提坦巨人阿特拉斯（Atlas）被发配到世界的尽头，永远矗立在那里，用他的肩膀扛起天穹。

大地母亲因为宙斯把她的孩子——提坦巨人关在塔尔塔洛斯的黑暗深渊而感到愤怒，于是她创造了两只可怕的怪物——堤丰（Typhon）和他的妻子厄喀德那（Echidna），让他们去反抗宙斯。他们的样子十分可怕，众神看到之后都吓得变幻成各种动物四散逃去。堤丰长着一百个令人恐怖的脑袋，那些脑袋都可以碰到天上的星星，凶恶的眼睛滴着毒汁，血盆大口中喷吐着岩浆和火红滚烫的岩石。他像一百条毒蛇发出咝咝的声响，像一百头狮子发出吼叫，把一座座山整个儿地搬起来，朝众神砸去。

但是，宙斯很快便重拾勇气，掉转身来。其他神祇见他摆出架势，也都跑了回来，同他一道与怪物搏斗。一场惨烈的战斗开始了，大地上生灵涂炭。但宙斯注定要获得胜利。当堤丰搬起巨大的埃特纳山（Mount Aetna），准备向众神扔去时，宙斯一下子掷出一百个瞄准精确的霹雳，击中了埃特纳山，山峰落回去，把堤丰压在底下。这个怪物从此就被压在下面，直到今天还不断地从山顶喷出火焰、岩浆和浓烟。

堤丰那丑陋的妻子厄喀德那逃过一劫。她躲进一个山洞里，保护着堤丰的后代——他们也是令人恐惧的怪物。宙斯让他们活了下来，留给后来的英雄们去挑战。

现在，大地母亲终于放弃了斗争。没有叛乱，战争的创伤很快平复。山峰稳稳矗立。海洋有了崖岸。河流在河床中流淌，牛角河神看管每一条河流。每一棵树、每一处泉水也都有仙女守护。大地重新披上了绿装，处处都长满果实，宙斯终于可以在和平中主宰万物了。

独眼巨人们不仅会当铁匠，也会当石匠。他们在希腊最高的山——奥林匹斯山上为众神建造了一座高耸的宫殿。宫殿隐藏在云里，当有神祇要到人间去时，四季女神们便把云门翻卷起来。除此之外，谁都无法穿过云门。

埃尔利斯（Iris）是众神中的飞毛腿信使，她有一条自己的去往人间的通道。她穿着一件七色水珠做的袍子，踏着彩虹，在奥林匹斯和人间忙碌地来回奔跑。

在宫殿辉煌的大厅里，光明永不消逝，众神分坐于十二个金色宝座之上，统治着天堂和人间。宙斯不仅把他的权力分给了他的哥哥姐姐们，也分给了他的六个孩子和爱神，所以奥林匹斯山上一共有十二个主神。

宙斯自己坐在最高的宝座上，旁边摆放着一个装满霹雳的桶。在他的右手边，坐着他最小的姐姐——赫拉。宙斯从他所有的妻子当中选择了赫拉作为他的王后。赫拉旁边坐着她的儿子——战神阿瑞斯（Ares）和火神赫菲斯托斯（Hephaestus）。爱神阿芙洛狄忒（Aphrodite）坐在他们两个中间。再旁边坐的是宙斯的儿子，诸神的使者赫尔墨斯（Hermes），以及宙斯的姐姐收获女神得墨忒耳，她的女儿珀尔塞福涅（Persephone）坐在她的膝上。宙斯的左手边坐的是他的哥哥海神波塞冬。他的身边依次坐着宙斯的四个孩子：雅典娜（Athena）、孪生兄妹阿波罗（Apollo）和阿尔忒弥斯（Artemis），以及最年轻的神——狄俄尼

索斯（Dionysus）。雅典娜是智慧女神，阿波罗是光明与音乐之神，阿尔忒弥斯是狩猎女神，狄俄尼索斯是酒神。

宙斯最年长的姐姐赫斯提亚是炉灶之神。她没有宝座，在大厅的火堆旁照看圣火。人间的每一个火堆都是她的神坛。在奥林匹斯山的众神之中，赫斯提亚是最温和的。

宙斯最年长的哥哥哈得斯是冥王。他喜欢待在地下世界幽暗的宫殿中，从来都不去奥林匹斯山。

神祇永远都不会死，因为他们体内流淌的不是血液，而是神族的元液。大部分时候，他们快乐地生活在一起，品尝甜美的仙肴和琼浆，但是当意愿冲突时，他们也会激烈地争吵。这时宙斯便会伸手去拿霹雳，这令奥林匹斯山上的众神都战栗不已，俯首听命，因为宙斯比其他所有神加在一起还要强大。

赫拉
Hera

赫拉，奥林匹斯山上美丽的王后，是一个善妒的妻子，连无所畏惧的宙斯对她的脾气也要顾忌三分。她讨厌宙斯所有其他的妻子，当宙斯一开始请求她做他妻子时，她拒绝了。后来，宙斯狡猾地制造了一场暴风雨，并把自己变成一只布谷鸟，装出可怜的样子飞入赫拉的怀抱去寻求庇护。赫拉怜惜这只被淋湿的小鸟，将它紧抱怀中帮它取暖，却猛然发现自己抱着的不是小鸟而是无所不能的宙斯。

这样一来，宙斯赢得了赫拉。他们结婚时，大自然中的万物都绽放出花朵。大地母亲送给新娘一棵小苹果树，树上结着的金色苹果是永生之果。赫拉很珍视这棵树，把它种在赫斯珀里得斯（Hesperides）花园里。那是她在遥远西方的秘密花园。她让一条长着一百颗脑袋的龙在树下看守树上的苹果，还命令赫斯珀里得斯的三个仙女给这棵树浇水并照看它。

宙斯很宠爱赫拉，但也很喜欢多岩的希腊大地。他经常变身后偷偷地溜到人间，和凡间女子结婚。他的妻子越多，孩子也就越多，这对希腊很好！他所有的孩子都会继承他的一些过人之处，从而成为伟大的英雄或统治者。但是赫拉妒火中烧，想方设法折磨他的那些妻子和孩子，即便宙斯也无法阻止她。她知道宙斯很狡猾，所以总是紧紧地盯着他。

有一天，赫拉往人间看去时，窥见在一个不应该有云的地方飘着一小片乌云。她马上冲下天庭，直奔那片乌云而去。正如她所料，宙斯就藏在那团乌云里面，但是只有一头洁白的小母牛和他在一起。原来宙斯看见赫拉怒不可遏地冲过来，为了保护他的新娘伊娥（Io），就把她变成了一头母牛。天啊！这头母牛简直和那位少女一样可爱。赫拉没有上当，她装作什么都不知道，假意恳求宙斯把这头漂亮的母牛送给她。宙斯不能揭穿自己，又无法合理地拒绝赫拉这样一个小小的愿望，只好把母牛送给了她。赫拉把可怜的伊娥拴在一棵树上，还派她的仆人阿耳戈斯（Argus）去看着她。

阿耳戈斯浑身上下长着一百只明亮的眼睛。他体形巨大而且力大无比，用

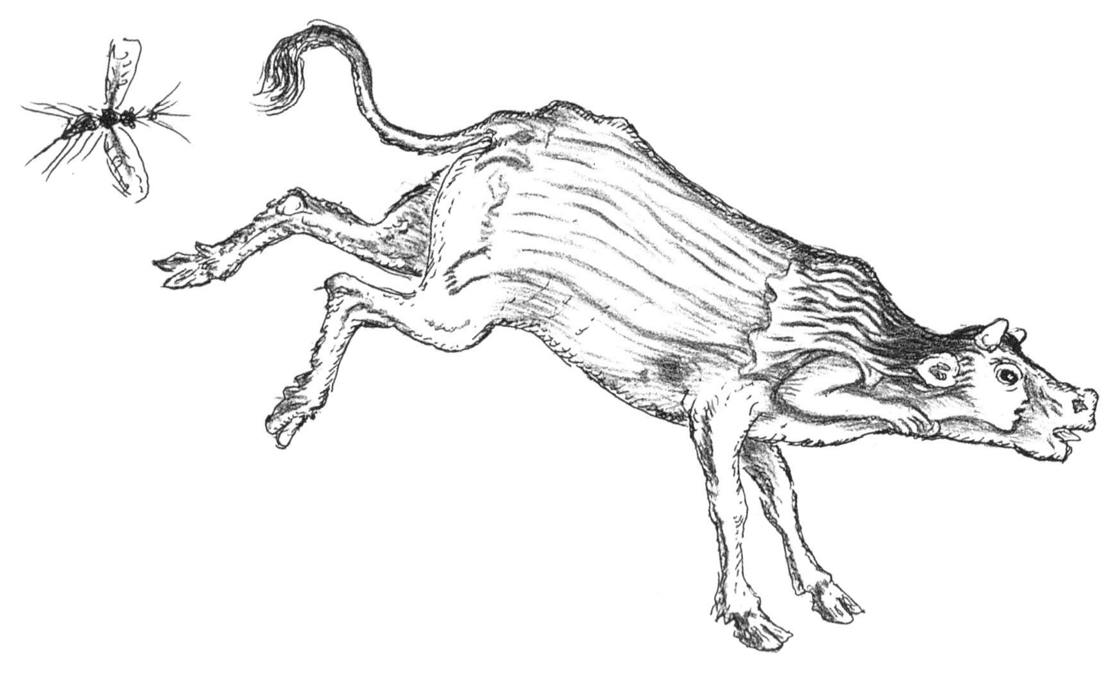

一只手就杀死了怪物厄喀德那——她住在一个山洞里，吞吃了所有经过那里的人。阿耳戈斯是赫拉忠实的仆人，也是最好的看守者，因为他睡觉时顶多只闭上一半的眼睛。

阿耳戈斯坐在母牛旁边，一百只眼睛都看着她，可怜的伊娥只能用四蹄行走，啃吃青草。她抬起忧伤的眼睛望着奥林匹斯山，但是宙斯太害怕赫拉了，他不敢来解救她。最后他实在不忍心让伊娥这样受苦，便派儿子赫尔墨斯——众神中最机智的一个——去凡间搭救她。

赫尔墨斯把自己扮成一个牧羊人，走到阿耳戈斯的身边，用牧人的笛子吹奏起曲子。阿耳戈斯每天除了全副精力盯着一头小母牛之外别无他事，正感到无聊，这会儿听到乐曲的声音，又得了个同伴，自然非常高兴。赫尔墨斯在他身边坐下来，吹奏了一会儿曲子之后，开始讲一个又长又乏味的故事。这个故事既没有开头也没有结尾，阿耳戈斯闭上五十只眼睛睡觉了。赫尔墨斯继续讲啊讲啊，慢慢地，阿耳戈斯另外五十只眼睛也一一闭了起来。赫尔墨斯飞快地用魔棒在他所有的眼睛上都点了一下，让它们在永恒的沉睡中永久闭合，因为阿耳戈斯已经无聊而死了。

赫尔墨斯接着解开了母牛身上的绳子，伊娥便一路跑回了家，回到了她的父亲——河神埃纳克斯（Inachos）的身边。他没有认出这头母牛就是他女儿，而伊娥也无法告诉他到底发生了什么事情，她所能说的就只有“哞”。但是当她抬起自己的小牛蹄在河滩上写出她的名字“伊娥”时，她的父亲顿时明白了是怎么回事，因为他知道宙斯一贯的行径。埃纳克斯从河床中翻腾起来，奔涌着向伟大的雷神复仇。面对扑面而来的愤怒的河神，宙斯为了保护自己，不得不掷出一个霹雳，从此以后，阿卡迪亚（Arcadia）的埃纳克斯河就枯竭了。

看到阿耳戈斯死了，伊娥也被放走，赫拉非常恼怒。她放出一只恶毒的牛虻，去叮咬并追逐那头母牛。为了让人们永远记得她那忠实的仆人阿耳戈斯，她把他一百只亮晶晶的眼睛安在了孔雀的尾巴上——那是她最喜欢的鸟。虽然这些眼睛再也看不见什么东西，但是它们的样子十分华丽。长着小脑袋的孔雀意识到这一点，便成了所有动物中最骄傲自负的一个。

伊娥被牛虻追得跑遍了希腊。为了躲避叮咬的折磨，她一下子跳过了横亘在欧洲和小亚细亚之间的海峡，从此这个海峡就被称作博斯普鲁斯海峡，意思是“母牛跳过之处”。

但是牛虻仍旧一路追着她来到埃及。埃及人看到这头雪白的母牛，都跪了下来对她顶礼膜拜。她成了埃及的女神，赫拉也因此允许宙斯把她变回人形，但前提是宙斯必须保证再也不看伊娥一眼。

作为埃及的女神和女王，伊娥活了很长时间，她为宙斯生下的儿子继她之后成为埃及的王。她的后代后来重返希腊，成为伟大的君主和美丽的女王。可怜的伊娥总算没有白白受苦。

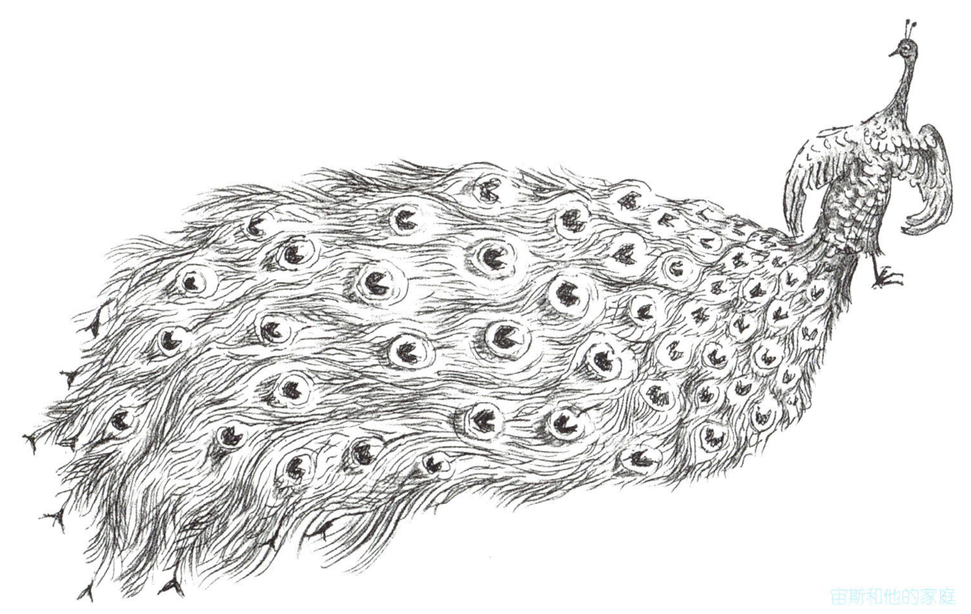

赫菲斯托斯
Hephaestus

铸造之神和火神赫菲斯托斯是宙斯和赫拉的儿子。他是一个勤于劳作、热爱和平的神。他很爱自己的母亲，经常以温和的话语平息她的怒气。一次他甚至敢于介入父母的争吵，站在赫拉一边，气得宙斯抓起儿子的脚，把他扔出了奥林匹斯山。赫菲斯托斯在空中飞了一整天，到夜里才砰地掉在莱蒙诺斯岛（Lemnos）上。他摔得很重，整个岛都震动了。温柔的海洋女神西蒂斯（Thetis）发现了浑身是伤口和瘀青的他。她帮他包扎了伤口，并照顾他直到痊愈。

宙斯原谅了赫菲斯托斯，让他重新回到了奥林匹斯山，但是从那以后，他走起路来就像一团火焰，一跳一跳的。他身材高大壮实，双手也灵巧无比，但孱弱的双腿无法持久站立。于是，他用金子和银子打造了两个机器人来帮他。这两个机器人有机械大脑，会自主思考。它们那用银子打造成的舌头甚至能说话。它们还在奥林匹斯山上赫菲斯托斯的作坊里帮他干活。就是在那里，赫菲斯托斯为众神打造了十二个金色宝座以及各种神奇的武器、战车和饰物。

大地上的火山里也藏着他的熔炉。在那里，独眼巨人都是赫菲斯托斯的帮手。他们帮他鼓动风箱，挥动沉重的铁锤。当赫菲斯托斯开工时，铁锤敲打出的“叮叮”声可以传出几英里，山顶上会迸溅出火花。

奥林匹斯山上所有的神祇都喜欢赫菲斯托斯，他们经常跑到他的作坊里去欣赏他的作品。当赫菲斯托斯那漂亮的妻子阿芙洛狄忒到作坊里来看他为她打造那些无与伦比的首饰时，她会优雅地拎起长长的裙裾，以免沾上炭灰。

阿芙洛狄忒
Aphrodite

美丽的爱神阿芙洛狄忒是奥林匹斯山上唯一既没有父亲也没有母亲的神。没人知道她来自何方。第一个看见她的是西风之神。在清晨那珠辉般的光芒中，阿芙洛狄忒脚踩一团泡沫浮出海面，随着温柔的海浪缓缓飘移。她是那么迷人，看得西风之神几乎屏住了呼吸。他用和煦的风儿将阿芙洛狄忒吹到了鲜花盛开的基西拉岛（Cythera），在那儿，美惠三女神正等着迎接她上岸。作为美丽之神的美惠三女神成了她的随从，她们给她穿上闪闪发光的衣服，戴上炫亮的首饰，还让她坐上由白鸽拉着的金车。她们带着阿芙洛狄忒来到奥林匹斯山。诸神欣喜于她的美貌，让她坐上金色宝座，成为他们当中的一员。

宙斯担心众神为了得到阿芙洛狄忒而大打出手。为了避免出现这样的情况，他很快就为阿芙洛狄忒选了个丈夫。他让她嫁给最稳重的神——赫菲斯托斯。赫菲斯托斯几乎难以相信这从天而降的好运，他费尽心思为阿芙洛狄忒打造最为奢华的珠宝。他用精纯的黄金为她做了一条腰带，还在这条金丝饰品上嵌入魔法。这并不是一个明智的做法，因为阿芙洛狄忒本身就已经让人难以抗拒了，一旦系上这条有魔力的腰带，就根本没人能抗拒得了她了。

阿芙洛狄忒有个淘气的小儿子叫厄洛斯（Eros），他整天拿着把弓，背着满满一囊箭到处游荡，那些箭是爱情之箭，他喜欢将它们射向毫无防备的人心。任何人只要被他射中，都会深深地爱上他所看到的第一个人，这时厄洛斯就会在一旁嘲弄地大笑。

阿芙洛狄忒每年都会回一次基西拉岛，跳进她出生的大海。当她再从水中升起时，就会变得年轻而充满活力，如露珠般清新，就像她第一天被西风之神看到时那样。她喜欢欢闹与浮华，一点儿也不愿意做那满脸黑灰、只知埋头苦干的赫菲斯托斯的妻子。她宁愿嫁给他的兄弟阿瑞斯。

阿瑞斯
Ares

战神阿瑞斯长得高大英俊，却傲慢虚荣。他的兄弟赫菲斯托斯有多好心，他就有多残忍。纷争精灵厄里斯（Eris）是他形影相随的同伴。厄里斯阴险又刻薄，她最大的乐趣就是制造事端。她有一个金苹果，这个苹果闪闪发亮、光泽迷人，所有人都想得到它。她把苹果丢到朋友中间，这些朋友间的友谊很快便会破裂；她把苹果丢到敌人中间，战争便会爆发。因为厄里斯的这个苹果是纷争之果。

每当听到兵戈相交的声音，阿瑞斯便会乐呵呵地戴上锃亮的头盔，跳上战车。他冲入稠密的战阵，把自己的剑挥舞得如同火炬，他想看到的只是血流成河的场面，不关心谁胜谁负。一群邪恶的家伙紧跟在他后面，给人们带去痛苦、恐慌、饥饿和湮灭。

有时候，阿瑞斯自己也会受伤。他虽然是不死之身，却忍受不了疼痛，他的号叫声几英里外都听得到。受伤的阿瑞斯会冲回奥林匹斯山，宙斯会厌恶地骂他是自己最不争气的孩子，并喝令他停止号叫。他的伤口在涂上神药之后很快就痊愈了，他又安然无恙地坐回到他的宝座上——高大、英俊、不可一世，金色头盔上的翎毛骄傲地点动。

阿芙洛狄忒爱慕他光鲜夺目的外表，但其他的神都不喜欢他，尤其是他同父异母的姐姐雅典娜。她憎恶阿瑞斯的虚荣和嗜血。

雅典娜
Athena

智慧女神雅典娜是宙斯最喜欢的孩子。当她从父亲脑袋里跳出来时，就已经完全长大了。

她的母亲——慎思女神墨提斯，是宙斯的第一个妻子。宙斯需要她那高明的建议，所以很依赖她，但是大地母亲警告过宙斯，如果墨提斯给他生了个儿子，那么这个孩子将取代他，就像他取代其父克罗诺斯、克罗诺斯取代其父乌拉诺斯一样。宙斯心想绝对不能让这样的事情发生，但是他又离不开墨提斯的建议，最后他决定把她吞进肚子里去。狡猾的宙斯向墨提斯提议说来玩一个变形游戏，墨提斯没想那么多，就尽情地玩了起来，把自己变成各种或大或小的动物，当她将自己变成一只小苍蝇时，宙斯就张大他的嘴巴，深吸了一口气，一下子把这只苍蝇吞了下去。从此，墨提斯就坐在他的脑袋里，在那儿指点他。

后来，墨提斯要生的是个女儿，她坐在宙斯的脑袋里为自己将要出世的孩子打造了一个头盔，还织了一件华美的长袍。不一会儿，宙斯就感觉到头部剧

烈地疼痛，痛苦地叫喊起来。所有的神都跑来帮他，能干的赫菲斯托斯抓起工具敲开了父亲的头颅。雅典娜身着长袍、戴着头盔跳了出来，一双灰色的眸子眼波流转。雷声隆隆，众神伫立在惊愕中。

胜利精灵奈克（Nike）是雅典娜忠实的伴侣。雅典娜只指挥那些为正义而战的军队，奈克总是紧随其侧。和平年代里，雅典娜会帮助希腊的能工巧匠，教给他们精妙而又实用的技艺。她一直对自己纺织和制陶的技艺感到非常自豪，但是只要她的学生们给她以适当的尊重，她也乐于见到她们青出于蓝。

她有个学生叫阿拉克尼（Arachne），是个普通的乡下姑娘，织布的手艺相当精湛。人们从四面八方赶来欣赏她的织品。她却愚蠢地吹嘘她从雅典娜那儿什么也没学到，她的技艺其实比女神还要好。

这可伤了雅典娜的自尊。她化装成一个老妇，来到那个姑娘面前，想让她明白一些事理。

“你手艺真好，”她说，“但是为什么要拿自己跟女神比呢？做凡人中的最好不就行了吗？”

“让女神雅典娜自己来跟我比试比试吧。”阿拉克尼不可一世地回答说。

雅典娜气愤地现出了真身，神圣庄严地站在了这个女孩面前。

“自大的女孩，”她说，“就如你所愿吧。在你的织布机前坐下，让我们来比一比。”

雅典娜织出了最华丽的挂毯，针脚严密，颜色鲜艳。挂毯上描绘的是无比庄严、拥有无限荣耀的奥林匹斯山众神。

阿拉克尼的挂毯织得也很漂亮；雅典娜自己也不得不承认这个女孩子的手艺无懈可击。但看看她在挂毯上都织了些什么呀。那是一幅取笑宙斯和他的众多妻子的渎神之作。

怒火中烧的女神将挂毯撕得粉碎并且用梭子击打阿拉克尼。阿拉克尼立即就感觉到自己的头缩下去，几乎都没有了，她那灵活的手指也变成了很多细长的腿。她被雅典娜变成了一只蜘蛛。

“不自量力的姑娘，继续纺你的线，永远去织你那张空网吧。”雅典娜对变成了蜘蛛的阿拉克尼说。雅典娜是正义女神，她有时会非常严厉。她知道，只有当神被凡人适当地崇拜时，神才是伟大的。

雅典娜非常喜欢希腊的一个城市，而她的伯父波塞冬也喜欢这个城市。他们都宣称这个城市为自己所有，争吵很久之后，他们决定：谁能送给这个城市一份最好的礼物，谁就能够拥有它。

这两位神领着一大群市民，登上了阿克罗波利斯（Acropolis），那是耸立在这座城市外围的一块平顶岩石。波塞冬用他的三叉戟在悬崖上一击，一股泉水就从那儿流了出来。人们都欢呼着，但这水像波塞冬掌管的海水一样是咸的，不是很有用处。然后，雅典娜拿出了她给这个城市的礼物。她在岩石的裂缝中栽下了一棵橄榄树。这是人们看到的第一棵橄榄树。在这两件礼物中，雅典娜的礼物被认为是更好的，因为它可以为人们提供食物、油和木材。于是，这个城市属于她了。在阿克罗波利斯之上美丽的雅典娜神庙中，雅典娜和她肩上那只聪明的猫头鹰一起守望着她的城市——雅典（Athens），在她的引导下，雅典人也以他们的艺术和各种手艺著称于世。

波塞冬
Poseidon

海洋之神波塞冬是个喜怒无常而且非常暴烈的神。他凶狠的蓝眼睛能够穿透迷雾，海蓝色的头发飘扬在身后。他被称作“撼地之神”，因为他只要用三叉戟往地上一顿，大地便会颤抖并开裂。他把它在海里一挥，便会搅起如山的巨浪和怒号的狂风，船只都会被毁坏，住在岸边的人也会被淹死。但当他心平气和时，又会伸手抚平大海，从水中抬升出新的陆地。

在克罗诺斯和提坦巨人统治时，大海是由涅柔斯（Nereus）掌管。涅柔斯是大地母亲和大海蓬托斯的儿子。他是一个老海神，长着长长的灰色胡须和一条鱼尾巴。他还是五十个海洋仙子的父亲，这些可爱的仙女被称作“涅瑞德斯”（the Nereids）。当奥林匹斯山上的主神波塞冬前来接管海底王国时，善良的老海神涅柔斯把他的女儿安菲特律特（Amphitrite）嫁给他做王后，并且让位给他，自己住到海底洞穴里去了。他把自己在海底的宫殿送给了新王和王后。这座宫殿用最浅色的金子砌成，坐落在一个由珊瑚和闪烁的珍珠构成的花园中。安菲特律特被她的四十九个涅瑞德斯姐妹包围着，快乐地生活在那里。她唯一的儿子名叫特赖登（Triton）。他像他外公涅柔斯一样，下半身长的不是腿，而是一条鱼尾巴。他骑在一头海怪的身上四处游走，拿着一只海螺做号角。

波塞冬很少在家。他是个坐不住的神，喜欢驾着自己雪白的马队追波逐浪。据说他按照激荡的海浪的样子创造了马。波塞冬像他的兄弟宙斯一样，有很多妻子，也生了很多孩子，但是安菲特律特不像赫拉那样善妒。

波塞冬抬出海面的一个岛叫作德洛斯（Delos）。因为小岛刚刚被造出来，所以还漂浮在水上。小岛很荒凉，寸草不生，除了一棵孤零零的棕榈树。就在这棵棕榈树下，人们将迎来两位伟大神祇——阿波罗和阿尔忒弥斯的诞生。

宙斯娶了女神勒托（Leto）。当赫拉发现勒托怀了一对双胞胎时，便妒火中烧，命令世上所有的土地都不许让勒托栖身。可怜的勒托流离失所，走过一个又一个地方，就是无法停留下来生下她的双胞胎。

最后她来到了德洛斯，这个小岛接纳了她。因为它还在漂浮着，不完全算是一块土地，所以可以不受赫拉的禁令约束。

勒托筋疲力尽地坐在棕榈树下，但她还是无法生下这对双胞胎，因为赫拉不许生育女神伊利赛亚（Ilithyia）到勒托那儿去。没有伊利赛亚的帮助，任何孩子都无法出生。所有其他的女神都为勒托感到难过，她们带了一条漂亮的项链去劝说赫拉。这条由黄金和琥珀打造的项链足足有九尺长，赫拉无法抵御它的诱惑。于是，她让伊利赛亚去了。埃尔利斯带伊利赛亚顺着彩虹飞奔到

了勒托身边。

勒托的第一个孩子是阿尔忒弥斯，一个月亮般美丽的女孩，头发漆黑如黑夜。她将成为狩猎女神和一切新生命之神。接着阿波罗来到了这个世界，他像阳光般明媚，他将成为音乐、光明和理性之神。

宙斯看见这对漂亮的双胞胎，心中满是欢喜。他给了他们每人一把银弓和满满一箭囊的箭。阿尔忒弥斯的箭像月光一般柔和，可以令人没有痛苦地死去；阿波罗的箭则像阳光一样强劲而无往不利。

宙斯赐福于这个小岛，并把它从海底拴牢。青草和鲜花从这块贫瘠的土地上快速地生长出来，德洛斯成了希腊所有岛屿中最富足的一座。朝圣者纷纷来此，他们建造神庙，贡献珍宝，以祀奉勒托和她的双胞胎。

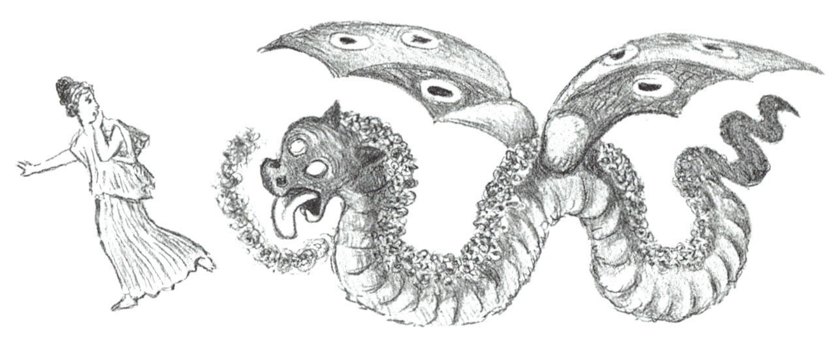

阿波罗
Apollo

像所有的神祇一样，阿波罗长得飞快。当他完全长大之后，宙斯把他送上一驾白天鹅拉的战车，让他独自去赢取特尔斐圣迹（Delphi）。

特尔斐坐落在帕纳塞斯山（Mount Parnassus）一个陡峭的斜坡上，是整个希腊最为神圣的地方。帕纳塞斯山的山腰上有一道极深的裂缝，里面冒出呛人的浓烟。一位西比尔（Sibyl）—— 特尔斐的女祭司——坐在裂缝上面一个三脚祭坛上，烟雾让她陷入了一种神奇的睡眠。在睡梦中，西比尔能听到大地母亲从深处传来的声音，并会把她所听到的那些神秘的词语复述出来。祭司们站在西比尔周围，向那些到特尔斐圣迹来了解探听自己未来的朝圣者们解释她喃喃念叨的预言。

圣迹被一条黑色的巨龙派森（Python）守卫着，它就盘踞在圣迹的周围。过高的年岁使得它自私而且脾气很坏，以至于仙女们都逃离了附近的圣泉，鸟儿们也不敢在树上唱歌。

神谕警告派森说有一天勒托的儿子将会把它杀死。所以，当勒托四处寻找可以生下双胞胎的落脚之地时，它曾经想吃掉她，但是被她逃脱了。这条黑色的老龙看见光芒四射的阿波罗驾着金色的战车朝它驶来，便知道自己的末日到了。但它不肯善罢甘休。它怒气冲天，喷吐着火焰和毒液，庞大的黑色身躯不停地扭曲盘旋，阿波罗将无数支银色利箭射入了它的身体。恶龙身体里的毒液如洪水般在山坡上奔涌而下，特尔斐圣迹就这样属于阿波罗了。

原本阴森冷寂的帕纳塞斯山坡现在充满了光明和欢乐。天空中的鸟儿和圣泉边的仙女又返回这里，咏唱着对阿波罗的赞歌，空气中洋溢着甜美的旋律。在众多的歌声中，年轻神祇阿波罗的歌声是最好听的，因为他同时也是音乐之神。

d'A

阿尔忒弥斯
Artemis

新生的女神阿尔忒弥斯来到父亲宙斯跟前，请求他满足自己的一个心愿。她希望永远做一个在森林里自由自在狩猎的年轻处子，她要求宙斯答应她永远不要将她嫁人。宙斯答应了她。她还向宙斯要了五十个动作敏捷的仙女做随从，还有一群耳朵耷拉下来的猎狗，随她一同狩猎。她的父亲宙斯满足了她所有的要求，她又自己捕获并驯服了四只长着金色鹿角的雌鹿，让它们拉她银色的战车。

当月亮的神奇光芒照进空寂的大山和草木茂盛的山谷之时，阿尔忒弥斯就会带着她的仙女和猎犬开始狩猎。在一番酣畅的狩猎之后，女神喜欢去一个幽静的水潭中洗澡。任何凡人在那个时候看见她都会遭遇不幸！

有一天晚上，一个名叫亚克托安（Actaeon）的年轻猎人在树林中偶然发现了这个水潭，阿尔忒弥斯和她的仙女们正在里面洗澡。他本来应该转身逃命而去，却痴迷地站在那里看着女神。阿尔忒弥斯非常生气！仙女们用衣服遮住她的肩膀，她把手伸到水潭中，掬起一满捧水泼向亚克托安。当银色的水珠碰到他额头时，那里便长出了鹿角，很快，亚克托安整个儿地变成了一头牡鹿。他的猎犬们立刻扑向他，惊恐万分的亚克托安发现自己已经发不出人声去喝止这些猎犬。猎犬们一点儿也不知道这只鹿就是它们的主人，将他扑倒在地。

“任何看见过阿尔忒弥斯洗澡的人都必须死。”女神说完，便拿起她的弓和

箭，和她的仙女们一同狩猎去了。这是一个冷酷无情的女神。

阿波罗和阿尔忒弥斯虽然像白天和黑夜一样不同，却都非常喜欢彼此，而且他们都非常爱戴他们的母亲。任何人只要说了一点点对温和的勒托不敬的话，都会惹恼这对双胞胎。

底比斯（Thebes）有一个名叫尼俄伯（Niobe）的王后，她拥有美貌和财富，而且有十四个孩子。宙斯是她的祖父，她是个非常骄傲的人。

"为什么要崇拜勒托呢？"她对她的臣民说，"为我建一座神庙，供奉我，不要供奉她。我生了七个儿子和七个女儿，她才只有一个儿子和一个女儿。"

阿波罗和阿尔忒弥斯听了这些话后怒不可遏。尼俄伯必须为她的不敬而受到惩罚。

阿波罗把他的箭射向了尼俄伯的七个儿子。这些年轻人自己没有犯什么错，却在大好的青春年华被夺去了生命。阿尔忒弥斯也向尼俄伯的七个女儿射出了她那令人感受不到痛苦的神箭。这七个姑娘悄无声息地倒在床上，死去了。

尼俄伯那颗骄傲的心被击碎了。她不停地哭泣，最后众神都同情她，于是把她变成了一块没有感情的石头。但是，.石头里面仍旧流出一汪水来，好像眼泪一样，顺着坚硬的岩石表面流淌。

阿波罗已经有了许多妻子，但是宙斯始终恪守着他对阿尔忒弥斯的承诺，没有把她嫁出去。只有一次，她答应嫁给一个追求者，但她从一开始就没有打算兑现那个承诺。这个求婚者就是波塞冬的巨人儿子奥特斯（Otus）。

奥特斯和他的兄弟艾菲亚特斯（Ephialtes）长大成人时，个子差不多有六十英尺，而且还在不停地长高。众神担忧地看着他们，因为有一个预言说任何神祇或凡人都无法杀死这对巨人兄弟。大地母亲看见他们却非常欣慰。她仍旧为宙斯把她的儿子——提坦巨人们关在塔尔塔洛斯而感到不快，她希望奥特斯和艾菲亚特斯能够长大到足以推翻宙斯。

有一天晚上，当这对兄弟耳朵贴地而睡时，他们听到大地母亲悄悄地对他们说，像他们这样高大英俊的年轻人不应该甘于被宙斯所统治。这两兄弟心里也正有这样的念头，因为他们像许多强大的人一样，都是自负的家伙。他们把山峰拔起来，一座座地垒在一起，建造了一座和奥林匹斯山一样高的新山峰。他们在山顶上向宙斯喊话，让他交出自己的权力，和奥林匹斯山上其他的神祇一起搬出他的宫殿。奥特斯说，阿尔忒弥斯可以留下来做他的新娘。艾菲亚特斯则希望接收赫拉。

赫拉和阿尔忒弥斯都不屑一顾地把头扭了过去，宙斯则愤怒地向这两个恶棍掷出霹雳。但是宙斯的霹雳只是从他们身边轻轻掠过，没有伤到他们；阿瑞斯又冲出去与他们战斗，他们把他抓住，塞进一个铜瓶子里，并用盖子封住了瓶口。

有那么一会儿，宙斯非常担心，但是理性之神阿波罗说，如果没有人能够杀死他们，那就必须想办法让他们两个自相残杀。他说服了阿尔忒弥斯，让她假装爱上了奥特斯。阿波罗告诉奥特斯，阿尔忒弥斯非常想念他，她已经接受了他的求婚，会在纳克索斯岛（Naxos）上等他。奥特斯得意地笑了。这让艾菲亚特斯非常妒忌。为什么赫拉没有爱上他呢？难道他没有自己的兄弟英俊吗？但是他把这些都藏在了心里，跟着他的兄弟一起去迎接新娘。

阿尔忒弥斯看到这两兄弟到来时，迅速地把自己变成了一只白色的小鹿，跑到了他们要经过的道路上。她在这两兄弟之间跑来跑去。这两兄弟都喜欢打猎，于是都朝这只小鹿掷出了长矛。阿尔忒弥斯灵巧地避开了长矛，而这两兄弟却被对方的长矛给刺穿了，倒在了地上。 不管是神还是凡人都无法杀死这两个巨人兄弟，可这下他们却互相结果了对方。他们被投进了塔尔塔洛斯，盘曲的蛇把他们背靠背地绑在一起。

所有的神祇都感谢阿尔忒弥斯拯救了他们。阿瑞斯还蜷曲在瓶子里，不停地号叫着，众神又把他拽了出来。

俄里翁（Orion）是波塞冬的另一个巨人儿子，但是与奥特斯和艾菲亚特斯不同，他是个非常谦逊的人。他是一个伟大的猎手，什么野兽都逃不出他的棍棒和镶着宝石的剑，但是他从来都不忘夸赞阿尔忒弥斯才是最伟大的猎手。

俄里翁能在水上行走，如履平地。有一天，他来到了开俄斯岛（Chios）。这个岛上有许多狮子、狼和野猪，它们夜里咆哮和号叫的声音很响，吵得开俄斯岛的国王睡不着觉。他对俄里翁许诺，如果他能够驱走岛上所有的野兽，他便把女儿嫁给他。国王的女儿很美，国王将她视若珍宝。俄里翁空前卖力地狩猎。很快，岛上便一只野兽也没有了。但是国王不想和他的女儿分开，于是谎称自己晚上还是会听到狼的号叫。俄里翁非常生气，他威胁说要抢走公主，国王却用好听的话来哄他，派人去拿酒，并不断地把他的杯子注满。俄里翁喝了太多的酒，便睡着了。狠毒的国王偷偷上前挖掉了他的眼睛。

“看你还怎么抢走我的女儿！”他说。

俄里翁双目失明，孤立无援，只好离开了开俄斯岛。他踉踉跄跄地走在海上，要去寻找太阳，因为他知道太阳可以让他重新获得光明。但是他找不到方向。远远地，他听到独眼巨人敲击锤子的声音，便循声来到了赫菲斯托斯在莱蒙诺斯岛上的作坊。这位好心的神可怜他，派了一个小独眼巨人给他领路，带他去东方。

有了小独眼巨人在肩膀上帮他看路，俄里翁一直走，最后终于找到了初升的太阳。太阳用它神奇的光芒照耀着俄里翁失明的眼睛，他的视力便恢复了。他立刻冲回开俄斯岛去找那个背信弃义的国王复仇。但是当他到达时，王宫里已经人去楼空。原来国王在天空中看见了他那巨大而危险的身影，已经带着女儿逃走了。

俄里翁再次出门狩猎，很快便忘记了国王和那个美丽的公主。他走过了一个又一个岛，后来到了一个叫克里特的岛上。他在那里遇到了女神阿尔忒弥斯。女神很高兴遇见他，因为他的狩猎本领和她一样好，而且从不夸耀。他们一起捕猎野山羊，并因为有对方的陪伴而感到快乐。俄里翁是阿尔忒弥斯唯一喜欢过的男子，这令她的弟弟阿波罗心生嫉妒。有一天，趁阿尔忒弥斯不在，阿波罗放出一只巨型蝎子去攻击俄里翁。俄里翁的木棒和威力巨大的宝剑抵挡不住蝎子的毒螯，他只好转身逃跑，但就在他逃跑时，巨蝎叮到了他的脚后跟。

阿尔忒弥斯回来发现自己的同伴死了，很生阿波罗的气。但是她对自己双胞胎弟弟的怒气没有持续多久，阿波罗帮助她把俄里翁的形象变成了一个星座挂在天上，如此一来，这个伟大的猎人便永远也不会被忘记了。

在冬季狂风怒吼的海上，俄里翁的猎户星座闪闪发光，庞大而骇人，乌云在他面前如野兽四散而逃。但是到了夏天，当天蝎座从地平线上升起时，俄里翁的星座便开始倾斜和摇摆，这下轮到他逃跑并消失在海洋中了。

赫尔墨斯
Hermes

赫尔墨斯是奥林匹斯众神中最欢悦的一位神。他是畜牧之神，同时也是旅人、商人、盗贼和其他所有凭借自己的才智生存的人的保护神。

他的母亲迈亚（Maia）是提坦巨人的女儿，住在高高的库勒涅山（Mount Cyllene）的一个山洞里，这个山洞非常深，连赫拉都不知道原来迈亚也是宙斯的妻子之一，也正因为这样，迈亚才能平安地生下赫尔墨斯。

即便对于神来说，赫尔墨斯也算得上是早慧的了。他妈妈几乎还没来得及把他包裹起来放进摇篮里，他就开始想着要淘气了。等妈妈一睡着，他就挣脱襁褓蹑手蹑脚地走出山洞，在黑沉沉的夜色中直奔阿波罗放养白母牛的牧场。阿波罗爱音乐胜过母牛，所以他压根儿没注意到赫尔墨斯潜入他的牧场并盗走

了他最好的五十头母牛。为了不让阿波罗知道究竟是谁，又是以什么样的方式盗走了他的牛群，狡猾的赫尔墨斯拿树皮包住牛蹄以掩饰蹄印，还在牛尾巴上拴上扫帚来扫去前行的踪迹。为了把阿波罗弄得更糊涂些，他甚至将牛群倒着赶出牧场，并在自己的脚上也绑上大捆的树枝，弄得好像是一个巨人曾把什么东西带进牧场，而牧场中却并未走出去过什么似的。然后他就匆匆地赶回库勒涅山，将偷来的牛藏在小树林里，并宰了两头来祭祀奥林匹斯山上的十二位神——居然没有忘记把自己算作第十二位神！然后他又将祭祀用牛的牛肠制成七根弦，紧紧地装套在一个空龟壳上，当他拨动琴弦，这琴就能奏出美妙的音乐，就这样，世界上第一架竖琴诞生了。赫尔墨斯对自己的作品非常满意，他将竖琴藏在胳膊下蹑手蹑脚地返回山洞，然后爬进他的摇篮，闭上眼睛，装出一副熟睡的样子。但即便如此，他也没骗过他的母亲，她知道他都做了些什么。

“羞不羞，”她说，“深更半夜溜出去偷阿波罗的牛。”

“妈妈，那又怎样！”赫尔墨斯说，“我为你和我自己做了该做的事。我们

可不想永远住在这黑黢黢的山洞里吧？要不了多久我就能成为十二位主神之一，住在高高的奥林匹斯山上，而你作为我的母亲也将无限荣耀地住在那儿。”然后他拿出了竖琴弹奏着催眠曲伴着他的母亲入眠。

天亮后，阿波罗怒气冲冲地冲进山洞，而赫尔墨斯却躺在他的摇篮里装作睡大觉，阿波罗可不是那么好愚弄的，一则神谕告诉了他是谁偷了他的牛，他将小赫尔墨斯从摇篮里拉出来，命令他立即把牛还给自己。

“我怎么可能偷你的牛呢？”赫尔墨斯抽抽搭搭地说，“我只是一个刚出生的婴儿，我根本就还不知道牛长的是什么样子。你自己在这个山洞里找找看嘛，哪里有一头牛藏在这里。”

“你可不只是个小偷，还是个骗子呢。”阿波罗气愤地边说边将赫尔墨斯拖出山洞直奔奥林匹斯山而去。

当所有的神祇看到小赫尔墨斯一脸无辜地走在前面，后面跟着盛怒的阿波罗时，都情不自禁地大笑起来。

“让这个小偷加骗子赶紧还我的牛来。”阿波罗对他们的父亲宙斯说。

“可别让哥哥欺负我了。我只是个刚出生的婴儿，无助得很。而且我也不是什么骗子。”赫尔墨斯说，“在我妈妈的山洞里一头牛也没有。”

“如果不在山洞里，那就告诉阿波罗它们在哪里。”宙斯也难掩笑意地说。他对自己的这两个孩子都颇觉得意，很希望他们能成为朋友。

赫尔墨斯必须遵从父亲的话，他不再搞恶作剧，将哥哥带到了他藏牛的小树林里，阿波罗也原谅了他，可是当他数完牛发现少了两头时，又怒火中烧起来。这样的情形赫尔墨斯早就预料到了，只见他飞快地拿出竖琴弹奏起来。阿波罗痴迷地听着这样新乐器发出的美妙声音，完全忘记了愤怒。作为音乐之神，他一定要拥有这架竖琴，于是他提出用他所有的牛群来换这件乐器。

见此，赫尔墨斯起劲地还起价来，最后阿波罗不得不把自己的魔杖也给了他作为交换。不过从此这两兄弟就成了最好的朋友。

虽然赫尔墨斯是盗贼的保护神，但从那次之后他再也没偷过东西。他也从不说谎话，只是也不怎么会把事实真相和盘托出。他的母亲迈亚也再没有任何理由为自己的儿子感到羞愧，作为奥林匹斯十二主神之一的母亲，她和她的儿子一同登上了奥林匹斯的荣耀之巅。

宙斯非常喜欢赫尔墨斯的随机应变，就让他做众神的使者。他给了赫尔墨斯一顶带有翅膀的金色帽子、一双带有翅膀的鞋和一件能把他的魔法宝贝藏起来的短斗篷。他能瞬间从一个地方到另一个地方。他能让那些政客巧舌如簧，也能帮商人讨价还价。在人在神，他都一样的受欢迎。就连赫拉也喜欢他。赫拉真的生他的气也就只有一次，那次是赫尔墨斯杀了她的百眼仆人阿耳戈斯，赫拉当时恼怒非常，一定要惩罚赫尔墨斯，她将所有大大小小的神都召集起来审判赫尔墨斯。她给每个神一块卵石，让他们按自己的决定来投票，那些觉得赫尔墨斯有罪的就把手中的卵石丢在赫拉的脚下，觉得赫尔墨斯无辜的就将卵石丢在赫尔墨斯的脚下。赫尔墨斯当时为自己作了很好的辩护。让一个人无聊至死是犯罪吗？他问。说到底，他对阿耳戈斯所做的不过如此。众神鼓起掌来，许多人把票投给了赫尔墨斯，最后差点儿把赫尔墨斯完全埋在卵石堆里了。

从那以后，旅行者都会在路旁堆上一堆堆的石头，他们相信赫尔墨斯就站在这石堆里，帮他们指明前行的路。这也就是最早的堆石路标。

赫尔墨斯同时也会送将死之人最后一程，他用魔杖合上他们的眼睛，并引领他们去到哈得斯的地府。

哈得斯
Hades

冥王哈得斯是一个性情阴郁、少言寡语的神。凡人都惧怕他，甚至不敢提及他的名字，因为这样可能会让哈得斯注意到他们，派人来索命。作为讳称，人们叫他“富有者”，哈得斯也确实很富有。地下所有的珍宝都归他所有。人们还称他为“好客者”，因为他的幽冥地府总有空余之地来接待下一位亡灵。

混浊的冥河（Styx）环绕地府缓缓流动，赫尔墨斯引导着死者的幽灵来到冥河边上，把他们交给摆渡人卡戎（Charon）。如果他们有钱作为渡资，卡戎就送他们过去。如果没有，他便会拒绝搭载，因为他是个贪婪的人。那些没钱可付的人只好在周围游荡，除非他们找到通往哈得斯地府的乞丐之门。所以，当一个人死去时，他的亲属都会在他舌头下面放一枚钱币。

所有的凡人迟早都要去见哈得斯。一旦进入他的地界，他们就像秋天寒风中的枯叶永远在其中飘荡。地府的三头看门犬刻耳柏洛斯站在大门旁，他放亡灵进入，但一旦从他的尖牙和长满利刺的尾巴旁经过，亡灵们便再也出不去了。

哈得斯和他冷若冰霜的王后珀尔塞福涅一起住在一座黑暗阴森的宫殿里。珀尔塞福涅非常漂亮，却和她丈夫一样沉默而阴郁，因为她不快乐。她不是自己情愿来统治这死气沉沉的地府的，而是被哈得斯劫持来的。

珀尔塞福涅和得墨忒耳

Persephone and Demeter

珀尔塞福涅在奥林匹斯山上长大，辉煌的殿堂中飘荡着她欢快的笑声。她是收获女神得墨忒耳的女儿。她的母亲非常疼爱她，一刻看不见她都不行。当得墨忒耳坐在自己的金色宝座上时，就让女儿坐在自己的腿上；她到凡间照看树木和田野时，也带着珀尔塞福涅。珀尔塞福涅在哪里翩翩起舞，哪里就会长出鲜花。她是那么优雅迷人，连几乎从不见人的哈得斯也注意到了她，并且爱上了她。哈得斯想让珀尔塞福涅做自己的王后，但他知道珀尔塞福涅的母亲根本不会同意和她分开，所以他决定劫持她。

有一天，珀尔塞福涅在草地上东奔西跑采摘各种鲜花时，与母亲和照顾她的仙女们远离了。突然间，大地开裂，几匹黑马拉着一驾幽暗的马车从张口的裂缝中冲出来，手持缰绳的是面无表情的哈得斯。他抓起受惊的姑娘，掉转马头，冲进大地深处。一群正在草地上觅食的猪也跌进了裂缝里。大地就像当时突然裂开一样，又突然合上，珀尔塞福涅的呼救声也随之消逝了。地面上，一个小猪倌站在那里为他丢失的猪群哭泣，得墨忒耳在草地上疯狂奔走，徒劳地寻找凭空消失的女儿。

哈得斯怀里抱着惊恐的姑娘，驾着他那呼哧呼哧的马儿离开了阳光照耀的大地。他们顺着那条黑黢黢的道路不断地向下行驶，来到哈得斯那座阴沉的地

下宫殿。哈得斯领着哭泣的珀尔塞福涅进入宫殿，让她在他身旁的黑色大理石宝座上坐下，给她戴上黄金首饰和珍奇的珠宝。但是这些首饰珠宝并不能给珀尔塞福涅带来快乐。她不需要这些冷冰冰的宝石。她想要那温煦的阳光，想要鲜花，想要她那满头金发的妈妈。

幽灵们从岩石裂缝和罅隙中纷涌而至，来看他们的新王后。与此同时，更多的幽灵在穿越冥河，珀尔塞福涅看到他们在黑杨树下的一条小溪中喝水。那是忘川（Lethe）之水，喝了它，他们就会忘记自己是谁，也忘却人间之事。拉达曼提斯（Rhadamanthus）是亡灵的法官，负责对那些犯下大恶之人的亡灵进行惩处。他们将永远被厄里倪厄斯（Erinyes）复仇的皮鞭抽打。而英雄则被带往极乐世界（Elysian），在那里，他们在永恒的光明中过着永久幸福的生活。

在哈得斯的宫殿周围，有一个花园，那里长着白杨树和垂柳。这些树既不开花也不结果，也没有鸟儿在枝头歌唱。在哈得斯的王国里，只有一棵树能结出果实。那是一棵很小的石榴树。地府的园丁把诱人的果实献给王后，但是珀尔塞福涅拒绝触碰这冥界的食物。

她一言不发地跟着沉默的哈得斯穿过花园，她的心也慢慢地结为寒冰。

地府之外，得墨忒耳在大地上四处奔走，寻找着丢失的女儿，世间万物都与她同悲。鲜花枯萎，树木落尽了叶子，大地变得荒芜而寒冷。冰封的大地让犁尖都无法插入。当收获女神哭泣时，任何物种都无法发芽，也无法生长。人和动物遭受着饥馑，众神乞求得墨忒耳让大地再次恢复生机。但是她拒绝让任何东西生长，除非她找到自己的女儿。

悲伤过度的得墨忒耳变成了一个苍然老妇。她回到珀尔塞福涅消失的那片草地，问太阳是否曾经看见所发生的一切。但是太阳说没有，那天正好有片乌云挡住了他的脸。得墨忒耳在草地上漫无目的地走着，遇到了一个叫特里普托勒摩斯（Triptolemus）的少年。他告诉得墨忒耳，他那当猪倌的哥哥曾经眼见着自己的猪被大地吞没，还听到一个女孩惊恐的尖叫。

得墨忒耳终于明白过来，是哈得斯劫走了她的女儿，她的悲伤转而变成愤怒。她对宙斯说，如果宙斯不命令哈得斯把女儿珀尔塞福涅还给她，她便再也不会让大地重新披上绿装。宙斯可不能眼见着这个世界就此毁灭，于是派了赫尔墨斯下去找哈得斯，让他放了珀尔塞福涅。即便哈得斯也要遵从宙斯的命令，

他只好难过地向王后道别。

珀尔塞福涅高兴地跳了起来。但是，就在她要跟赫尔墨斯一道离开时，花园里传来一声冷笑。哈得斯的园丁站在那里，咧嘴而笑。他指着一颗石榴，里面少了几粒果籽。珀尔塞福涅在走神时吃掉了几粒。他说。

阴沉的哈得斯露出了微笑。他目送赫尔墨斯领着珀尔塞福涅回到地上光明的世界。他知道她还会回到他的身边，因为她已经吃下了冥界的果实。

当珀尔塞福涅再次出现在地面上时，得墨忒耳一下子跳了起来，欢喜地叫喊着，朝女儿飞奔过去。她再也不是那个悲戚的老妇，而是一个光芒四射的女神。她再次赐福于大地，让花儿重新绽放，谷物丰实。

“亲爱的孩子，”她说，“我们再也不要分开了。我们一起给万物带来蓬勃的生机。”然而悲伤很快便取代了欢乐，珀尔塞福涅不得不接受她因为吃了冥界的食物而必须回到哈得斯身边的事实。不过宙斯还是决定不让这对母女永远分离。他裁定珀尔塞福涅必须回到哈得斯那里，她吃了几粒果籽每年就得在地府里待几个月。

每年，当珀尔塞福涅离开时，得墨忒耳都非常悲伤，万物都不能生长，大地上因此有了冬天。但是，一听到她女儿轻快的脚步声，整个大地便会现出勃勃的生机。春天来了。只要这对母女在一起，大地便温暖和煦，处处果实累累。

得墨忒耳是一个善良的女神，珀尔塞福涅离开的那几个月——也就是寒冷的冬天，她不愿见人类忍饥挨饿。于是，她把自己满载谷物的马车借给那个帮她找到女儿的少年——特里普托勒摩斯。她让特里普托勒摩斯把她金色的谷粒撒遍大地，并让他教人类怎样在春天播种、秋天收获，以及如何把谷物储藏起来，度过大地荒芜而寒冷的漫长冬季。

狄俄尼索斯
Dionysus

酒神狄俄尼索斯是奥林匹斯众神中最年轻的一个。在十二主神之中，只有他是由凡间女子所生。他的父亲是宙斯。

好妒的赫拉讨厌狄俄尼索斯的母亲——美丽的塞默勒公主（Semele）。一天，女神趁宙斯不在时把自己化装成一个干瘪的老太婆来拜访公主。她与公主东扯西拉，装出一副十分友好可亲的样子，然后就问塞默勒为什么她的丈夫不在家，还问他是个什么样的男人。

“除了伟大的宙斯，还会是谁呢？”塞默勒骄傲地说。

“你凭什么如此确定呢？”这个老太婆说，“我知道很多人的丈夫都自称是万物之主。你能证明他确实就是宙斯吗？要是换作我，我就会要求他现出他那无限荣耀的真身。”说完她就走了，留下塞默勒一个人在那儿思索。

宙斯回来后，塞默勒要宙斯实现她的一个愿望。宙斯是那么爱她，当即指着冥河发誓说会实现她许下的任何愿望。

“那么就请现出您荣耀的真身吧！”塞默勒说。宙斯请求她换一个愿望，因

为他知道没有一个凡人的眼睛能够承受他现出雷神真身时所放出的万丈光芒，那可比太阳还要亮一百倍啊！但是赫拉已经让塞默勒心里起了很大的怀疑，她拒绝改变愿望。宙斯只有兑现他的承诺，因为他已经对着冥河起了誓。对众神而言，那可是最郑重的誓言。

他把他能找到的最小的暴雨云聚集在一起，拿起他最小的霹雳，在塞默勒面前现出了伟大雷神的真身。即便如此，他还是那样的耀眼，塞默勒着了火，被烧成了灰烬。宙斯一点儿也救不了她。她变成一个飘飘荡荡的幽灵下到哈得斯的地府。宙斯所能做的就只有救下她那尚未出世的儿子，他把这个孩子缝在自己大腿上的皮肤下面，当这个孩子长到足月时，他就蹦了出来——不死的酒神诞生了。

宙斯十分清楚是谁害死了塞默勒，他将她的小毛头交给赫尔墨斯，并且嘱咐他要将这个小毛头藏在赫拉找不到的地方。赫尔墨斯带着狄俄尼索斯来到遥远的奈萨山谷（Nysa），让一群山谷仙子来照料他。狄俄尼索斯就在那儿长大，终日与老虎和豹子为伴。

大串大串的紫葡萄长成在奈萨那洒满阳光的坡地上，狄俄尼索斯及时地发明了用葡萄汁酿酒之法。作为一个年轻英俊的神，他穿着飘逸的蓝紫色长袍到世界各地教人们如何酿酒。仙女们也追随着他，同行的还有那些豹子和老虎，而且有越来越多的追随者加入进来。不管走到哪儿，他都被当成新生的神来崇拜，他的父亲宙斯为此很是欣慰。

狄俄尼索斯回到希腊，游历群岛，教给人们酿酒之法。一天，当他独自躺在海滩上睡觉时，一艘海盗船从旁边驶过。海盗们看到这个年轻人衣着华丽，猜想他一定是个王子，就把他抬到他们的船上，想劫持他以勒索赎金。狄俄尼索斯一直沉睡着，直到这艘船驶到大海深处才醒过来。他温和地与海盗们说理，希望他们能把他送回去。他说，他并不是王子，而是酒神，他的财富不属于这个世界。海盗们轻蔑地大笑并继续航行，丝毫不理会他。

他们的笑声忽然止住了。大海里长出来许多结满葡萄的藤蔓，它们不断地生长，缚住了船桨，又顺着桅杆蜿蜒而上，覆盖了整条船，就好像它是个葡萄架。血红色的酒汁滴落在船帆上，空中回响着老虎的吼叫和驴子的嘶鸣声。狄俄尼索斯好像也在不断生长，直到整艘船上都盈满他的神辉。海盗们惊恐万分，

纷纷跳入海中，但是他们并没被淹死，因为狄俄尼索斯是一位善良的神。他把那些海盗变成了海豚，这也是为什么海豚是所有海洋生物里最通人性的动物的原因。

狄俄尼索斯给人类带来了很多欢乐，宙斯认为是时候在奥林匹斯山上赐予他一个金色宝座了。赫拉气愤地站起来说拒绝与一个凡间女子的儿子共享荣耀，但是宙斯重重地敲了敲他那坚定的拳头，赫拉就一声不吭地坐下了。

但是，神殿里只有十二个宝座。善良的赫斯提亚淡然地从她的宝座上站起来，

说让狄俄尼索斯坐她的位置。她说自己的位置在圣火旁，她不需要宝座。

落座之前，狄俄尼索斯请求去见他一直想念的母亲。宙斯不仅允许他见她，还让他去哈得斯那儿把她带上来分享奥林匹斯的荣耀，因为她现在已经是一位主神的母亲了。狄俄尼索斯高兴地走进神殿，坐到他的金色宝座上。空气中回荡着长笛和铃鼓奏出的乐声。奥林匹斯山上还从未有过这样喧闹欢乐的时刻。宙斯心满意足地环顾四周，并向他的司酒少年伽倪墨德（Ganymede）示意，吩咐他在金樽里斟满甜美的琼浆。

小神、仙女、森林之神、人马兽

MINOR GODS, Nymphs, Satyrs, and Centaurs

除了十二位主神之外，其他的小神也住在奥林匹斯山上。小神当中最有实力的是命运女神——克洛索（Clotho）、拉克西斯（Lachesis）和阿特罗波斯（Atropos）。她们被称为命运三女神，能决定凡人的寿命及众神的统治期限。当一个凡人诞生时，克洛索便会纺出一根生命之线，拉克西斯会衡量出一个长度，阿特罗波斯则负责在生命终结之时将线剪断。她们知道过去和将来，即便是宙斯也无法左右她们的决定。她们的妹妹涅墨西斯（Nemesis）负责让世间万物善恶有报，所有的凡人都畏惧她。

普罗米修斯
Prometheus

提坦巨人普罗米修斯是人类的创造者和最好的朋友。在众神早期的战争中，大地遭到毁灭，宙斯交给普罗米修斯和他的弟弟厄庇米修斯一个任务——让大地恢复生机。他把众多的天赋交给这两兄弟，让他们把这些天赋赋予他们所创造的事物。他们来到凡间，开始用河泥创造人类和各种野兽。聪明的普罗米修斯精心地按照神的模样塑造人类。厄庇米修斯则飞快地造出各种动物，由于缺乏远见，他很快就把好的天赋都用在了这些动物身上。当普罗米修斯把人造好时，却发现好的天赋都已经所剩无几了。动物可以跑得飞快，它们有更好的视力、更灵敏的嗅觉和更敏锐的听觉，也更有忍耐力。此外，它们还有暖和的皮毛，而人类却只能在寒夜中瑟瑟发抖。

普罗米修斯对人类心怀歉疚，便去找宙斯，请求他把一部分圣火赐给可怜的人类。但是宙斯没有答应，圣火只能由神祇专享。

普罗米修斯不忍看到他的人民受苦，于是决定盗取圣火，尽管他知道宙斯会因此而严厉地惩罚他。他来到奥林匹斯山，从圣火中取出了一个燃烧的木块，藏在空心的茴香茎里。他把它带回到大地上，将它交给人类，并告诉他们永远不要让这来自奥林匹斯山的火种熄灭。人类再也不用在寒冷的黑夜里颤抖了，野兽也因为害怕火焰的光芒而不敢攻击他们。

一件奇怪的事情发生了：当人类从地上抬起眼睛望着火堆里的烟袅袅地升上天空时，他们的思想也随之产生了。他们开始好奇和思考，再也不是匍匐在地上的泥土坯子了。他们建造神庙以敬仰天神，他们把最好的肉放到祭坛上去烤，希望与神共享他们所有的一切。

宙斯乍一看到大地上燃起的火焰，非常愤怒，但是当烤肉的诱人香味飘到他鼻子里时，他的怒气又平息了。众神也都十分喜欢肉烤熟之后的香味，这味道和他们天天享用的仙肴和琼浆太不一样了！但是普罗米修斯知道人类的生活是多么艰难，他觉得人类把自己食物中最好的部分烧掉太可惜了。他让人类杀了一头公牛，然后把牛肉分成一样高的两堆。一堆是肋排和嫩肉，藏在腱子肉和骨头下面，另一堆全是碎肉和内脏，上面盖着雪白的肥肉。普罗米修斯请宙斯来到人间，让他从两堆牛肉中挑选一堆作为献祭给他的供品。宙斯当然选了看上去最好的那一堆。当他发现自己被愚弄之后，变得非常愤怒。普罗米修斯不但盗取了圣火，把它给了人类，他还教唆人类欺骗神祇。宙斯决心要对普罗米修斯和人类施以惩罚。

普罗米修斯被永不断裂的锁链缚住，锁在高加索的山顶。每天都有一只老鹰从天上扑下来啄食他的肝脏。因为他是神祇，所以一到晚上他的肝又会重新长出来。但是每天老鹰都会回来，而他也必须再次忍受被啄食的痛苦。

这就是普罗米修斯受到的惩罚。而宙斯惩罚人类的方法则更为诡秘。他派了一个美丽却愚蠢的女人到人间去。她的名字叫潘多拉（Pandora）。

潘多拉
Pandora

潘多拉是赫菲斯托斯仿着阿芙洛狄忒的样子造出来的。他用一块白色大理石雕出了她的模样，用红宝石做她的嘴唇，用晶莹的蓝宝石做她的眼睛。雅典娜对她吹了一口气，她便有了生命，她还给她穿上雅致的衣服。阿芙洛狄忒给她佩上各种首饰，让她鲜红的嘴唇挂上动人的微笑。宙斯在这个漂亮女人的头脑里放入了永不满足的好奇心，然后给了她一个封口的罐子，并且警告她永远不要打开它。

赫尔墨斯把潘多拉带到人间，让她嫁给了与凡人生活在一起的厄庇米修斯。普罗米修斯曾经提醒过厄庇米修斯，叫他永远不要接受宙斯的礼物，但是他经受不住这个漂亮女人的诱惑。就这样，潘多拉与凡人生活在了一起，四面八方的人们赶来看她，都被她异人的美貌给惊呆了。

但是，潘多拉并没有感到十分的幸福，因为她不知道宙斯给她的罐子里装的是什么东西。没多久，她就再也按捺不住自己的好奇心，非要偷窥一下不可。

当她打开盖子的那一刹那，各种苦难便从罐子里涌了出来，它们是：贪婪、虚荣、诽谤、嫉妒，以及各种人类闻所未闻的邪恶。潘多拉被自己所做的事情吓坏了，赶紧把盖子合上，结果希望还在里面来不及飞出来。宙斯把希望放在罐子的最底部，以便释放出来的各种苦难能够很快地将它消灭。正如宙斯所计划的那样，各种苦难开始叮咬人类，但并未如他所希望的是，被苦难叮咬的人类没有变好，反而是变坏了。他们开始说谎，偷盗，并且互相残杀。人类变得如此邪恶，以至于让宙斯都感到厌恶，他决定制造一场洪水，把他们都淹死。

但是，大地上还有一个凡人没有变坏。他是普罗米修斯的儿子，名叫丢卡利翁（Deucalion）。

指责
Scolding
欺骗
Deceit
绝望
Despair
控诉
Accusation
谎言
Lies
嫉妒
Envy
小谎
Fibs
猜忌
Distrust
老年
Old Age
流言
Gossip
阴谋
Scheming
苦役
Drudgery

丢卡利翁
Deucalion

丢卡利翁经常去高加索山上安慰他那受难的父亲。他无法砸开绑在父亲身上的锁链，但是当他在那儿时，他可以赶走那只折磨普罗米修斯的老鹰。丢卡利翁是个好儿子，他的父亲很感谢他的帮助。

普罗米修斯能够预知未来，他知道宙斯正计划制造一场洪水来淹没整个大地。于是，他让儿子去建造一艘方舟，带着他贤德的妻子皮拉（Pyrrha）一起到船上去。

丢卡利翁按照父亲的话去做了。他造了一艘坚固的船。当宙斯发动所有的风，并且把天上的洪水之门打开时，他和皮拉一起坐到了船上。整整九天九夜，大雨一直下个不停，整个大地都被洪水吞没。除了最高山的峰顶还露在水面上外，一切都被洪水淹没了，人类全部被淹死了。只有丢卡利翁和皮拉还活着。

他们坐在方舟中，在一片漆黑深邃的水域里漂泊。

到了第十天，雨终于停了，干燥的陆地渐渐显露了出来。丢卡利翁和皮拉走出方舟，漫无目的地行走在荒凉的大地上。孤单而又凄凉的他们来到一座爬满了水草的神庙，走了进去。祭坛上的圣火已经熄灭了，他们拿出当初上船时一直保存未熄的木柴，重新点燃了圣火，然后举起双手向众神祈祷，感谢众神拯救了他们的性命。宙斯被他们的虔诚感动了，他看到他们如此孤独，心里非常歉疚。于是他对他们说："拾起你们母亲的骨头，把它们从你们的肩膀上抛出去。"

丢卡利翁明白，宙斯所说的母亲，不是指生他们的凡人母亲，而是大地母亲。她的骨头也就是地上的石头。他让皮拉拾起满满一捧石子，朝肩后抛去，他自己也同样向身后抛了一把石头。在丢卡利翁的身后，一群男人冒了出来；而在皮拉的身后，也出现了一群女人。这些新生的人类被称作丢卡利翁的后人。

丢卡利翁的后人是从石头变化来的，他们比从泥土变化而成的人类更坚强。新的人类能够更好地抵御潘多拉释放出来的种种苦难精灵的叮咬。洪水来时，这

些精灵飞到没有水的高处去了，所以直到今天，人类都还深受其害。宙斯发动洪水淹没大地时，风神们肆意横行。这些家伙力大无穷，当他们聚在一起兴风作浪时，混乱和灾难就会随之而来。飞旋的尘土和水柱直逼奥林匹斯山。宙斯决定派一个可靠的守卫去把他们锁住，一次只放一个出来。他选中了丢卡利翁和皮拉的孙子——埃奥罗斯（Aeolus）。宙斯让他负责看管风神，并且让他和风神们一起住在遥远大海上的一个岩洞里。

风神们都讨厌被约束。他们围着埃奥罗斯旋转呼号，想要强行闯出山洞，但是埃奥罗斯非常强壮，他丝毫也不动摇，紧紧地把他们攥在手中。当波塞冬或者其他神祇有召唤时，埃奥罗斯便用他的长矛在峭壁上戳一个洞，放一个风

神出去。然后他又把那个洞堵上，直到出去的风神要回来时再把它打开。

北风之神玻利亚斯（Boreas）受到召唤时，总是呼啸而去，他冰冷刺骨，狂野疾厉，所到之处树木摧折，浪涛翻滚。

南风之神诺塔斯（Notus）被放开时，会从崖壁上的洞口呜呜地钻出去。南风之神身上的水汽很重，那纠缠不清的胡子上都滴着水珠。他让陆地和大海布满浓雾。漫游者迷失了道路，船只无助地漂荡。

西风之神仄费罗斯（Zephyr）比他的兄弟们温和得多。西风刮起时，天上的云都被吹散，万物皆面含微笑。

东风之神欧诺斯（Eurus）是几兄弟中最无足轻重的一个。他很少受到召唤。

厄俄斯
Eos

温婉的黎明女神厄俄斯（Eos）是四个风神的母亲。当万物还在睡梦中时，她就从自己粉红色的枕头上爬起来，宣告新的一天的开始。她用自己玫瑰般柔嫩的手指在一个盛满露水的杯子里蘸一蘸，将那些露珠儿洒向花儿和树木。万物苏醒，欣喜于黎明乍现。

有一天早晨，当厄俄斯俯身看着大地时，她的目光落在了一个刚从睡梦中醒来的年轻王子身上。他是那么英俊，厄俄斯看得着了迷。她想要他做她的丈夫。但是，作为一个女神，她又怎么能嫁给一个只有短暂生命的凡人呢？

一完成自己清晨的使命，厄俄斯便来到宙斯面前，说服他让这个名叫第索纳斯（Tithonus）的年轻王子永生不死。

她把第索纳斯带到她那东方宫殿，他们在一起度过了许多年快乐的时光。

但厄俄斯忘了让宙斯赋予第索纳斯永恒的青春。第索纳斯的力量一点点地从他那灵活的肢体里消失了。他开始起皱纹，并且萎缩下去，他那曾经浑厚而有磁性的声音变得微弱而尖利。他缩成了一个又小又干瘪的老头，但是又无法死去，因为他被赐予了永恒的生命。他变得那么小，那么虚弱，厄俄斯只好把他放到一个小篮子里，藏在她宫殿的一角。在那个黑暗的角落里，他不断地瘪缩，最后变成了一只蚱蜢，永远在那里唧唧地叫着。

但是厄俄斯仍旧娇美而年轻，每当她出去唤醒沉睡的世界，宣告她的太阳哥哥就要升起时，所有的生物看到她仍会满心欢喜。

赫利俄斯和法厄同
Helios and Phaëthon

每当厄俄斯将他东方金殿的大门打开，太阳之神赫利俄斯（Helios）便登上他熠熠生辉的战车，带着夺目的光芒驰骋而去。他的光芒照亮了辽阔的天空。他是如此耀眼，除了众神之外，任何直视他的人眼睛都会瞎掉。他的头被炫目的光芒环绕，他的战车炽烈如熊熊火焰。

赫利俄斯用他有力的手，驾着他那四匹烈马沿着天庭的穹顶一路往上奔驰。那条道路陡峻狭窄，几匹战马也桀骜不驯，赫利俄斯却能把它们驾驭得很好。正午时分，他停在天空正中，环顾四宇，任何事物都无法逃脱他犀利的目光。然后，他继续驾车前行，这时他开始放松缰绳。战马们远远地看见西方那闪闪发亮的夜宫，急切地盼望着回到它们的马厩里去，便顺着下坡的道路奋蹄狂奔，越跑越快。他们超过了一大群朝赫利俄斯的宫殿往回赶的雪白母牛，又遇见了一大群出来去天空牧场的绵羊。因为对应一年中每一个白天赫利俄斯拥有一头雪白的母牛，对应每一个夜晚拥有一头肥硕的绵羊。

当赫利俄斯和他气喘吁吁的战马到达宫殿时，地上的影子变得很长，暮色四合。他的五个女儿——赫丽安德斯们（the Heliades）在等候着他们。她们帮疲惫的战马解下套具，放它们去大海里洗个凉水澡。然后战马们回到马厩休息，而赫利俄斯则开始给他的女儿们讲述他这一天的所有见闻。

夜幕下，赫利俄斯和战马一道登上一艘金色舰船，开始朝世界的另一端进发，他们要回到他在东方的宫殿。因为海上的路程比天空中的路程要近得多，所以他在开始又一天的征程之前，还有时间在晨宫中休歇一下。

赫利俄斯有一个儿子，名叫法厄同（Phaëthon）。法厄同是个凡人，他为自己光芒照人的父亲感到十分骄傲。有一天，当赫利俄斯正准备出发，开始他每天穿越天空的征程时，法厄同来到他面前，央求他满足自己最大的一个心愿。赫利俄斯非常喜爱这个样貌英俊的儿子，便轻率地对着冥河发誓要满足他的任何愿望。但是当法厄同说出他心中愿望时，他便极其后悔自己所立下的誓言了。因为法厄

同想要驾驭一天他的战车，而赫利俄斯深知除了他自己之外没有人能够驾驭得了那几匹烈马。所以，他极力劝说儿子改变心愿，却没有用。

法厄同决意要实现自己的心愿，赫利俄斯只好满足他。他心情沉重地把自己金色的光环戴到儿子头上，在他的身上抹了一层圣油，让他能够抵受得住战车发出的灼热能量。他想提醒儿子要稳稳地跑在天道中央，但是根本就没有时间说，因为宫殿的大门已经打开，马儿也昂首奋蹄要出发了。法厄同跳上战车，抓住缰绳，马儿便冲了出去。

起初，一切都还好，法厄同骄傲地站在熠熠生辉的战车上。但是那几匹烈马很快就察觉出把握缰绳的是个尚不老练的新手。于是它们开始偏离天庭的道路，从道路两旁潜藏的危险的星座边擦身而过。那些天庭的动物被激怒了：金牛冲了过来，狮子发出吼叫，蝎子亮出了含有剧毒的尾巴。马儿受到惊吓，差点儿把法厄同从战车里抛出去。他朝下望去，看见远远的大地，感到头晕眼花，便再也抓不住缰绳。失去控制的烈马开始横冲直撞。它们一会儿跑得离地面太近，大地承受不住战车的炙热，干得裂了缝，河流和湖泊也干涸了；一会儿又朝上跑得离地面太远，大地便开始冻结，变成冰封世界。

宙斯站在奥林匹斯山上，看着直摇头。他必须让疾驰的战车停下来，以免大地遭到毁灭，于是他朝它掷出一个霹雳。一阵火花四溅，战车被劈得四分五裂，法厄同掉进了波河里。他的姐姐们在河岸边久久地悲泣。宙斯同情她们，把她们变成了白杨树，她们的眼泪变成了金色的琥珀。

赫菲斯托斯不得不连夜修理被损坏的战车，以便赫利俄斯可以在第二天继续驾驶它。赫利俄斯深感丧子之痛，他从此再也不许别人驾驶他的战车，只有光明之神阿波罗是个例外。

塞勒涅
Selene

塞勒涅（Selene）是月光女神。夜里，当她的哥哥赫利俄斯休息时，她便会出来照亮世界。塞勒涅驾着她奶白色的马儿慢慢行过天空，那淡淡的月光轻柔地洒在沉睡的大地上，一切都是那么平和与安谧。

有一天晚上，塞勒涅的柔光照在了一个叫恩底弥翁（Endymion）的年轻牧羊人身上，他正在自己的羊群旁睡觉。她停下来看着这个牧羊人。他在睡梦中露出微笑，如此年轻英俊，塞勒涅的心完全沉醉了。她继续驾着马儿穿过夜空，却无法将他从脑海中抹去。

待到使命完成，她便立刻来到宙斯跟前，请求宙斯让恩底弥翁永久地沉睡，这样他就会永远年轻而英俊了。她从姐姐厄俄斯的身上吸取了教训，那就是不要去为一个凡人求取永恒的生命，否则他只会变成自己手中的一只蚱蜢。

宙斯满足了塞勒涅的愿望，于是恩底弥翁便一直沉睡，并在梦里微笑着。

他梦见自己把月亮抱在怀中。但那其实不是一个梦，而是现实——塞勒涅和他生下了五十个女儿，她们都像自己的母亲一样美丽淡雅，也都像她们的父亲一样嗜睡。

在塞勒涅的神奇月光下，河神从银色的水流中起身，去视察河床，而山丘在狂野的人马兽的蹄下颤动。欢笑的仙女和喧闹的森林之神则随着他们的主人——自然之神潘（Pan）的音乐起舞。

潘
Pan

伟大的自然之神潘长得并不英俊。他长着山羊的蹄子、尖尖的耳朵和一对小小的犄角，浑身长满了蓬乱的深色杂毛。他的母亲是个仙女，第一眼看到他那丑陋的样子时就尖叫着跑开了。他的父亲赫尔墨斯却非常喜欢这个孩子的奇特相貌。他把他带回到奥林匹斯山，去取悦其他的神祇。众神看到他都哈哈大笑，并打心底里喜欢他。他们把他叫作潘，派他回到希腊的幽暗森林和怪石嶙峋的山里去，做伟大的自然之神。他是猎人、牧羊人和卷毛绵羊的保护神。

潘是个孤独而情绪化的神。当他忧伤时，会独自走开，躲进一个寒冷的山洞。如果有人碰巧游荡至此，扰了他的清静，他就会发出令人毛骨悚然的尖叫，任何人听到这种尖叫都会吓得掉头就跑，逃得远远的，人们把这叫作“恐惧”（Panic）。

但潘也有心情好的时候，通常是有月光的夜晚。他吹着牧笛，蹦跳着穿越森林和林中空地，走上陡峭的山坡，后面跟着一群手舞足蹈的仙女和森林之神。山谷中仙乐飘飘，十分动听。

森林之神（Satyrs）长得很像他们的主人潘，他们喜欢胡闹，除了追逐仙女之外几乎一无所长。老的森林之神（Sileni）都长得很胖，懒到不愿走路，喜欢骑着驴四处游逛，他们常常从驴背上摔下来，因为他们喜欢喝酒。

脚步轻盈的仙女们看上去总是那么年轻，尽管她们当中有的年纪已经很大了。她们的寿命很长，几乎不会死：她们的寿命比普通人的长一万倍。有的仙女是掌管水的，有的仙女是掌管山和峡谷的。有的仙女生活在树上，有的则生活在泉水边。

当一棵树开始变老并且腐烂时，上面的仙女就要搬到与这棵树同类的另一棵树上去住。伐木人在砍倒一棵健康的树之前，必须记得要请求树上仙女的允许。如果他没有这样做，仙女便有可能放出一群蜜蜂来叮他，或者让他手中的斧子反过来，砍到自己的腿上。

口渴的猎人在未征得仙女的同意之前，决不能喝她的泉水。如果他不把仙女放在眼里，仙女就可能会放一条有毒的水蛇来咬他，或者让水变得有毒，使他喝了之后生病。

人们如果要从河里取水，也要先问问河神。河神们通常对人很热心，也很友善，他们很乐意让人们来分享他们的河水，但谁要是想要带走他们的女儿——水里的仙女，那河神就不会对他客气了。他们会冲出河床，怒气冲冲地朝他扑过去。这些河神可是危险的对手，他们头上长着牛角，可以任意地变幻模样。就连宙斯也不敢惹恼他们。尽管潘喜欢所有的仙女，并对很多仙女心存爱慕，但他和森林之神也对河神敬而远之。

厄科
Echo

厄科（Echo）是潘所爱的仙女之一。她性情欢快，一天到晚喋喋不休，一刻也不肯安静，潘根本没有机会用音乐和诗去打动她。

有一天，赫拉从奥林匹斯山来到人间，寻找宙斯的踪迹。她怀疑宙斯和仙女们混在一起，但是厄科不停地和她闲扯，拖了她很长时间。结果让真的在那里的宙斯趁机溜走了。赫拉一怒之下惩罚了厄科，让她失去了组织语言的能力。可怜的厄科从此便只能重复别人说过的话。

潘心想，这下他总可以用言辞来打动她了。可是，还没等他找到机会，厄科就已经倾心于另一个人。他叫那喀索斯（Narcissus）。他长得非常英俊，每个遇见他的仙女和女孩都爱上了他。不幸的是，那喀索斯除了自己不爱任何人。

那喀索斯去树林中狩猎时，厄科悄悄地跟在他后面，希望从他嘴里听到一句亲密的话，她可以重复给他听。但是那喀索斯几乎没有注意到她。最后，夜幕快要降临时，他们来到一个寂静的池塘边，口渴的那喀索斯俯下身去喝水。突然，他呆住了，像在凝视着什么。原来他在明镜般的水中看见了一张他所见过的最英俊的脸。他露出一个微笑，那人也回他一个微笑。他高兴地点点头，水中那个陌生人也点点头。

“我爱你。”那喀索斯对着那张英俊的脸庞说。“我爱你。”厄科赶忙重复道。她站在那喀索斯后面，很高兴自己终于可以向他表白。

但是那喀索斯既没有看见她，也没有听见她的话：他被水中那个英俊的陌生人给迷住了。他不知道他爱上的人竟是自己在水中的倒影，只管坐在那里对着他微笑，忘记了吃，忘记了喝。他渐渐消瘦，最后死在那里。赫尔墨斯前来带他去往亡灵的归宿。在他坐过的地方，开出了一簇簇美丽的水仙花。厄科站在花丛边，悲伤不已，日益憔悴，也渐渐消逝了。

除了声音，厄科什么也没有留下，这个声音直到今天还在毫无意义地重复着别人说的话。

潘伤心了一阵子，但是没多久他又遇到了一个漂亮的仙女，便把厄科完全忘却了。这个仙女的名字叫作昔林克斯（Syrinx）。

昔林克斯和达弗涅
Syrinx and Daphne

昔林克斯觉得潘实在太难看了，所以一直躲着他。潘在她后面追赶着，为了避开他，昔林克斯把自己变成了一根芦苇。她藏在河岸边无数的芦苇中，潘便找不到她。当他在芦苇丛中穿行，一边叹息一边徒劳地寻找昔林克斯时，一阵风吹过，苇丛摇摆起来，发出萧萧的声音。潘听到便被吸引了。“那你就和我一起歌唱吧。”他说。

他把十根芦苇切成长短不一的形状，绑在一起，做出了第一支排箫。他把这种新乐器称作昔林克斯，因为每当他吹奏起这件乐器时，便仿佛听到了自己所爱的仙女那优美悦耳的声音。潘又一次感到了孤独，他躲进森林深处那个阴凉的洞穴，用他那无与伦比的尖叫吓跑每一个路过的人。

相貌堂堂的阿波罗比潘也好不到哪里去，他爱上了一个叫达弗涅（Daphne）的仙女。达弗涅有一颗冰冷的心，曾经发誓终身不嫁。所以，当阿波罗向她求爱时，她听也不听他那金色竖琴里弹奏出来的音乐，抬脚就跑了。逃跑时，她

金色的头发在身后飘扬，那样子更加可爱了，阿波罗不能失去她。他开始追她，恳求她停下来。达弗涅向河边跑去，那里是她父亲——河神拉顿（Ladon）的地盘。达弗涅边跑边向他呼救，希望父亲帮她摆脱这个追求者。拉顿来不及冲出河床去救女儿，但是达弗涅一踏上河岸边的沙滩，他就把她的脚变成了树根。阿波罗接踵而至，赶上了她，但是就在他伸出双臂去抱她时，她的手臂已经变成了树枝，她可爱的脑袋变成了树冠，达弗涅变成了一棵月桂树。但是，透过坚硬的树皮，阿波罗仍旧可以听见受惊的达弗涅那扑通扑通的心跳声。

阿波罗小心翼翼地折下几根小树枝，用那晶亮的叶子做了一个花环。

“美丽的仙子，”他说，“你不肯做我的新娘，但至少请同意做我的树，让你的叶子成为覆在我额头上的冠冕。”

从那以后，获得一个用阿波罗的圣树——月桂树的枝条做成的桂冠，成了艺术家和英雄的最高荣誉。

达弗涅宁可变成一棵不会动的树，也不肯做主神阿波罗的新娘。但是别的仙女都喜欢坐在他的脚边，听他弹奏优雅迷人的乐曲，当阿波罗或任何一个伟大的奥林匹斯山的神祇选她们做新娘时，她们都会深感荣耀。

人马兽
The Centaurs

人马兽野蛮而粗俗。他们不尊敬任何神祇。这些半人半马的动物，像野蛮人一样狡猾，同时又像未经驯服的马一样狂暴。他们继承了这两者最为糟糕的性情。

第一头人马兽是从云里滚落下来的。人马兽的父亲——拉庇泰（Lapith）王伊克西翁（Ixion）居心不良，妄图得到赫拉。宙斯就弄了一片云来测试他对神是否虔诚。结果伊克西翁误以为这片云是女神赫拉变的，便娶了这片云。由于对神不敬，伊克西翁受到了严厉的惩罚。他被绑在一个燃着熊熊烈焰的车轮上，永远在地府中到处打转，他的后代——人马兽却被留在大地上，祸害拉庇泰的人民。

喀戎和阿斯克勒庇俄斯
Chiron and Asclepius

人马兽的生活毫无秩序和规矩，他们成群地在田野里奔跑，践踏庄稼，抢夺拉庇泰的女人，他们还吃生肉。小人马兽比成年的人马兽也好不到哪里去。他们在父母的虐待中长大，父母对他们拳打脚踢，任他们自生自灭。

半人半马族有一个很善良、充满智慧而且热爱小孩的人物。他的名字叫喀戎（Chiron）。尽管他看上去和其他人马兽差不多，但是他和他们没有任何关系。他是提坦巨人克罗诺斯的儿子，是个神祇。喀戎非常有名，他是希腊最伟大的教师。国王们把年幼的孩子送到他这里来，好让他们养成真正的英雄精神。

喀戎在皮立翁山（Mount Pelion）上有一个安静的洞穴。他在那里教孩子们学习各种富于男子气概的体育运动，还教他们如何用大地上的草药来治病，以及怎样看懂天上的星星。他所有的学生回去之后，无论在勇气还是知识方面都超过他们的父亲。

有一天，阿波罗带着他的凡人小儿子阿斯克勒庇俄斯（Asclepius）来找喀戎。阿斯克勒庇俄斯的母亲是一位拉庇泰公主，已经去世了。阿波罗让喀戎帮他抚养这个男孩。

阿斯克勒庇俄斯得到喀戎精心的呵护，在山洞中长大成人。作为阿波罗的儿子，他的医术很快便超过了自己的养父。

长大之后，他离开喀戎的山洞，下山去帮助希腊的人民，成为第一个伟大的医师。远近的人们成群结队地到他这儿来，许多人来的时候还拄着拐杖，走的时候却都变得活蹦乱跳了。他的病人都喜欢他，把各种珍宝献给他。很快，人们就把他奉为神明，为他修建了庙宇。阿斯克勒庇俄斯在他的每个庙宇里摆上床铺，这就是最早的医院。他手里拄着一根圣蛇缠绕的木杖，从一张床走到另一张床，很高兴看到病人把他当作神一样仰视。圣蛇知道世间所有的奥秘，经常向阿斯克勒庇俄斯透露各种疾病的致病原因和治疗之道。有时，他用一股神奇的微风让病人进入睡眠，然后听他们在梦中呢喃些什么。他们在梦里说的话经常会透露出致病的原因，这样他便可以找到治疗他们的方法。

阿斯克勒庇俄斯有一个妻子和七个孩子，所有的孩子都跟随在父亲左右。他的儿子们成为他行医的助手，女儿们则成为他的护士。他有个女儿叫海吉尔（Hygeia），从早到晚地给病人擦洗身体，这些病人都令人惊奇地很快恢复了健康。在海吉尔的时代之前，人们都认为肥皂和水会害死病人。

阿斯克勒庇俄斯变得非常有名气，非常富有，面色红润，随着年岁日增，他的医术也日益精湛，甚至能够把死人也救活。命运之神开始不高兴了，她们向宙斯抱怨说她们度量和剪断生命之线都变得没有意义了。哈得斯也心存愤懑，因为他那里的亡魂被偷偷地弄了出去。阿波罗向宙斯陈情，说他儿子是在为人类做很好的事情，所以宙斯暂时宽恕了阿斯克勒庇俄斯。但是当他救活死人之后收下人家馈赠的黄金时，宙斯对他掷出了一个霹雳。

世间第一位圣医阿斯克勒庇俄斯就这样被霹雳击中，化成了一撮灰烬。但是他的神庙和关于医药的教谕流传了下来。众神把他的形象变成了星河中的一个星座。

阿波罗因为宙斯杀了他的儿子而非常愤怒，想要报复。他不敢向他强大的父亲举起拳头，便杀了那个为宙斯提供霹雳的独眼巨人。这下又轮到宙斯要为独眼巨人复仇了。他罚阿波罗到人间去当一年的奴隶。

阿波罗找到了一个很好的主人，因此没有吃什么苦头。但是在高耸的奥林匹斯山上，众神想念他和他的音乐，特别是九位缪斯女神（the Muses）。

九位缪斯女神
The Nine Muses

九位缪斯女神是宙斯与提坦女神摩涅莫辛涅（Mnemosyne）的女儿。她们母亲的记忆和她美丽的头发一样长，因为她是记忆女神，知道自创世以来的所有事情。她把九个女儿聚拢在身边，给她们讲各种奇妙的故事。她给她们讲大地的创始和提坦巨人的落败，讲奥林匹斯山上光芒照人的众神以及他们的掌权之路，讲盗取圣火的普罗米修斯，讲太阳和星辰，但她讲的最多的还是她们的父亲，宙斯的伟大和智慧。九位缪斯扑闪着大眼睛听着。她们把这些故事写成诗歌谱成曲子，让它们永远不会被遗忘。

音乐之神阿波罗训练她们，教她们声调和谐地一起歌唱。他带着缪斯女神组成的合唱队穿过奥林匹斯的大厅，走在帕纳塞斯山的山坡上，他们的歌声是那么纯美，连鸣禽也会收声静听。

每位缪斯都有一门自己擅长的艺术。史诗女神卡利俄珀（Calliope）是九位缪斯之首。她有一个人类的儿子，名字叫作俄耳甫斯（Orpheus），他的歌唱得几乎和缪斯女神一样动听。他长大后便离开了母亲和八位亲爱的姨妈，来到了他父亲的王国——色雷斯（Thrace），把欢快的音乐带到了人间。他的嗓音纯净而又真实，就连最彪悍的战士听到也会放下手中的剑，凶蛮的野兽会着迷地伏在他的脚边。树儿把它们的根从泥土里拔出来，挪到他身边去聆听，甚至连坚硬的岩石也会滚到他跟前。

俄耳甫斯的音乐愉悦而欢快，因为他爱上了一个甜美的少女，她叫欧律狄刻（Euridice），她也爱俄耳甫斯。他们举行婚礼的那一天，新娘在草地上翩翩起舞，他情不自禁地唱起了歌，歌声中洋溢着幸福。突然，新娘踩到了一条毒蛇，她被咬中，倒在地上中毒死了。赫尔墨斯轻轻地合上她的眼睛，带她去了地府。俄耳甫斯的喉咙里再也传不出歌声，他的竖琴也弹不出一个音符。所有欢乐都从他生命中消失了。他必须找回欧律狄刻。

俄耳甫斯流着泪，心情悲伤，四处寻找着哈得斯地府的入口。终于，他在世界的尽头找到了地府的入口。他做了一件活人从来没有做过的事情：来到地下王国，乞求哈得斯把他心爱的人还给他。他的音乐能够感动顽石，或许也能够打动哈得斯冷酷的心。希望让他重新打开了歌喉，他一边弹着竖琴，一边唱着歌儿，走上那条黑暗险峻的小路。

他银铃般的歌声如夏日的微风，在黑暗中飘荡着，它的魔力感动了哈得斯地府的铁门。它们徐徐地敞开，让他进去。三颗脑袋的看门犬刻耳柏洛斯匍匐在他的脚下，让他通行。俄耳甫斯一边走进亡灵的国度，一边唱着歌，歌唱他挚爱的情人，哀求欧律狄刻回到他身边。整个黑暗的地府都静悄悄地听着俄耳甫斯的音乐。焦躁的幽灵安静了下来。被无尽的痛苦折磨着的幽灵停止了呻吟，而那些折磨他们的复仇之火和复仇女神们也都放下了手中的鞭子，淌下血红的泪珠。

冷酷无情的冥王哈得斯坐在黑色大理石宝座上，身边是他的王后珀尔塞福涅。他也被歌声打动了，泪水顺着他蜡黄的脸颊流下来，心如寒冰的珀尔塞福涅也在啜泣。她的心被深深地触动了，于是转向自己的丈夫，乞求他让欧律狄刻回到阳光普照的世界。哈得斯同意了这一请求，但是有一个附带条件：在回到地上世界之前，俄耳甫斯不准看他的新娘。欧律狄刻将跟在他的身后，如果他回过头来看她，她就必须回到地府。

俄耳甫斯强抑着内心的喜悦，踏上黑暗的小路，随着他的音乐渐渐远逝，地府又重归沉寂。那条小路很长很长，俄耳甫斯一直向前走着，心里渐渐开始起疑：哈得斯是不是骗他的？他身后的脚步声真的是欧律狄刻的吗？他已经快要走出地府了，前面已经可以看见微弱的光线，但是他再也无法抑制心中的疑虑。他忍不住回头去看欧律狄刻是否真的在他身后。那一刻，他看见了欧律狄

刻那美丽的脸庞，但也就在那一瞬间，赫尔墨斯又出现在她身边，让她转身，把她带回了阴森黑暗的地府。俄耳甫斯听到欧律狄刻幽幽的道别声。由于缺乏信任，他永远地失去了她。

俄耳甫斯回到大地上，他从此再也没有找到过欢乐。他走进荒野，独自悲伤。他开始歌唱，但是他的歌声变得无比忧伤，野兽们听了都淌下泪来，杨柳也忍不住悲泣。

一群野外的仙女从森林中跑过，她们朝俄耳甫斯喊叫着，叫他加入她们的行列。她们呼喊和奔跑的声音很大，所以听不到他银铃般的歌声，也没有被它的魔力所打动。她们叫他和她们一起跳舞，但是他根本无心参加她们的狂欢。这群仙女生气了，一起朝他扑过来。她们把他撕成了碎片，并把他的尸体丢到河里。河水不再发出汩汩的声音，它静听着俄耳甫斯美妙的歌声，原来他的嘴唇一边向大海漂去，一边还在唱着歌。

缪斯女神们为他的死而感到伤心。她们在海上寻找，最后在莱斯博斯岛（Lesbos）的岸边找到了他的尸首。她们为他举行了体面的葬礼，他终于可以作为飘荡的幽灵和他心爱的欧律狄刻在地府中相聚了。

缪斯们不仅歌颂众神和大地母亲所生育的精灵，她们还歌颂那些伟大的君王和英雄，他们都是

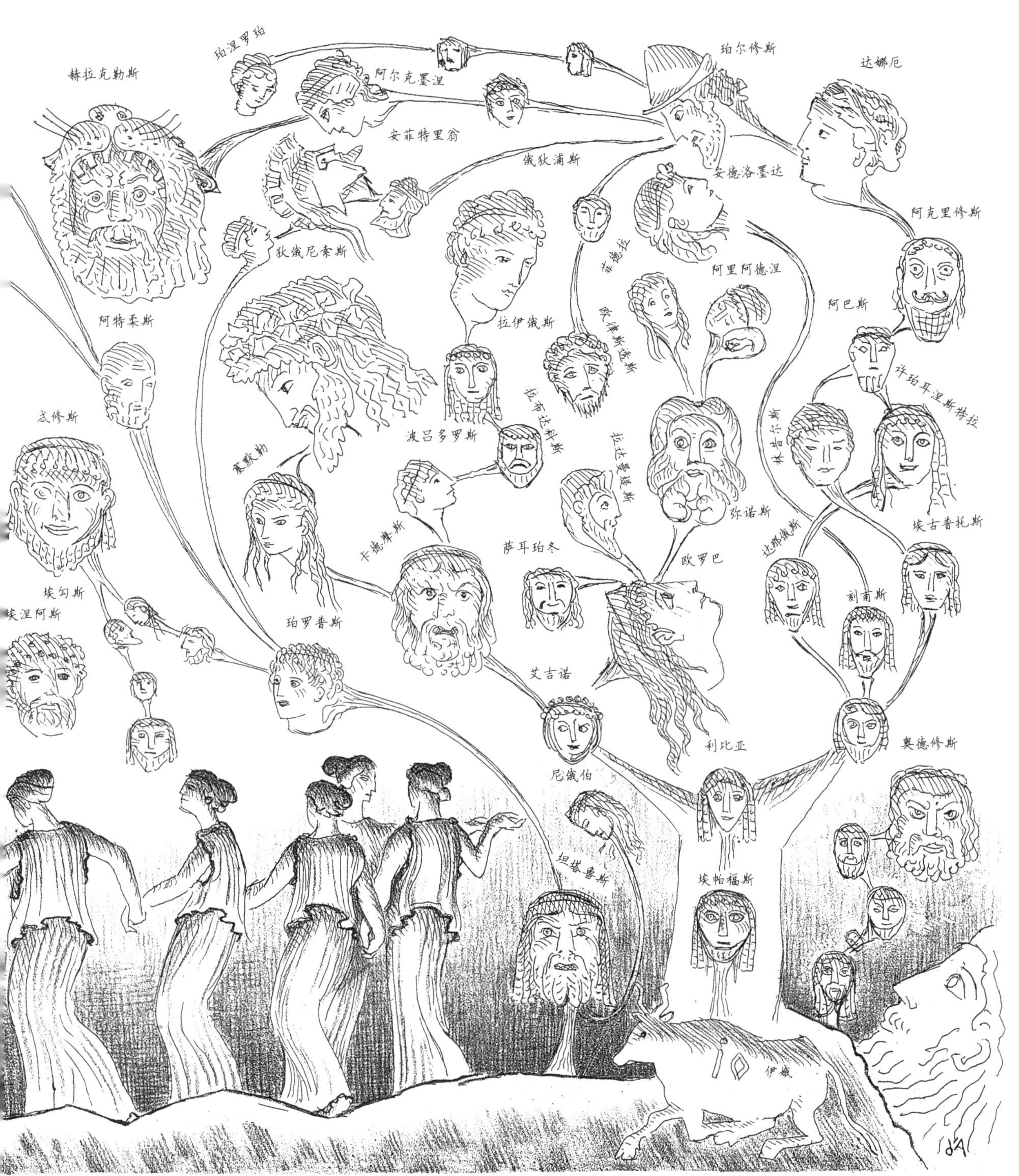

伟大的宙斯的后代。当我们倾听缪斯们歌唱时，那些英雄和勇士的故事还会回荡在我们耳边。

宙斯在凡间的后代
MORTAL Descendants of Zeus

欧罗巴和卡德摩斯
Europa and Cadmus

缪斯们有一首欢快的歌，讲述的是可爱的欧罗巴（Europa）的故事。她是宙斯选中的克里特岛第一位女王。她的父亲，蒂尔（Tyre）的国王艾吉诺（Agenor），是那个被化身为白色母牛逃到埃及的姑娘伊娥的后代。

克里特岛是宙斯长大的地方，他一直在四处寻找合适的少女来做克里特岛的女王。有一天他的目光落在欧罗巴的身上，她的美貌牢牢地俘获了他的心。

他化身为一头雪白的公牛，在欧罗巴和她的女伴们一起玩耍的海边草地上慢跑。一开始，欧罗巴对这头突然出现在自己身边的公牛感到害怕，但是当他用那大大的、温柔的眼睛看着她时，欧罗巴心中的胆怯消失了。她将一个花环套在他宽大的脖子上，温柔地拍打他光滑的身体。公牛在她的脚下跪了下来，她很信任地爬上了牛背，让这头公牛带着她兜风。公牛背着她在海边来回奔跑，欧罗巴开怀地笑着，拍着手喊她的女伴们一起来看她发现的这头漂亮的公牛。但是，公牛突然转身，背着她向海中奔去。她的女伴们惊恐地大叫起来，国王赶忙从宫殿里跑出来，正好看见公牛和他的女儿消失在地平线上。

欧罗巴吓得浑身颤抖，紧紧地抓住牛角。但令她惊奇的是，她的脚上连一丁点儿水也没有沾到，因为海中仙女们在他们周围护航，她们用手将波涛抚平，在海面上开出了一条平坦如砥的大道，这样那头公牛便可以在上面自由奔跑。公牛扭过头来，开口说话了。他告诉欧罗巴，自己并不是一头公牛，而是宙斯，他到人间来是为了娶她为妻并让她去做克里特岛的女王。

宙斯带着欧罗巴来到克里特岛，将一个镶着珠宝的王冠戴在她的头上，这个王冠象征着他的爱，欧罗巴从此在克里特岛上度过了尊荣而快乐的一生。她生了三个儿子：弥诺斯（Minos）和萨耳珀冬（Sarpedon）都成了伟大的君王，拉达曼堤斯则是个非常睿智的人，死后成了地府的法官。

宙斯回到奥林匹斯山，便命令他那做铁匠的儿子赫菲斯托斯制造了一个青铜机器人，让它去守护克里特岛和欧罗巴。那个机器人叫太洛斯（Talos），它每天都要在小岛的海滩上巡视三次，它走路时会发出丁零当啷的声音，只要看到敌人的船只靠近，它就会朝它投掷石块，把它击沉。

蒂尔的国王派了他的三个儿子去寻找他们被拐走的姐姐。其中有两个兄弟很快就放弃了，只有第三个儿子卡德摩斯（Cadmus）带着他的随从一路航行来到了希腊。他们来到特尔斐圣迹前，请神谕指示在哪里能够找到欧罗巴。神谕告诉卡德摩斯，他的姐姐现在安然无恙，并且很快乐，他必须放弃寻找她；他应该待在希腊并建立一个新的王国；一头雪白的母牛将引领他去那个建立卫城的最佳之地。

卡德摩斯离开了特尔斐，而且没多久他还真的遇到了一头白色的母牛。他跟着这头母牛不断跋涉，翻山越岭，最后母牛在一个辽阔平原中央的一座小土丘上躺了下来。卡德摩斯惊喜地发现这是一个建城的绝佳地点。他派了一个随从去附近的山泉取水。不料那个随从一去不回，卡德摩斯又派了另一个人去找他，结果这个人也没有回来。就这样，他的随从一个一个全被派了出去，但是没有一个回来。最后他只好自己前去看看到底发生了什么事情，结果发现有一条龙在守护着那处泉水。这头怪物吞吃了他所有的随从，正显出一副慵懒而昏昏欲睡的样子，卡德摩斯不费吹灰之力便将它杀死了。但是这并不能让他的随从死而复生，他也不可能独自一人把卫城建起来。卡德摩斯把那头白色的母牛献祭给神祇，祈求他们的帮助。雅典娜回应了他的祈求。“去犁一块地，”她告诉卡德摩斯，“把龙的牙齿拔出来，将它们种在垄沟里。”

这个建议听上去很奇怪，但是卡德摩斯照她的话做了。龙的牙齿一种下去，马上就变成了一队凶悍的勇士。他们挥舞着手中的剑，朝卡德摩斯冲了过来。卡德摩斯吓得不知所措。雅典娜又对他说：“朝他们中间丢块石头！”他照办了，勇士们很快便扭打起来，都说是自己身边的人投掷了石块。他们打得很激烈，最后只有五个人活了下来，而且这五个人都受了重伤。卡德摩斯照顾他们，让他们康复，这些人成了他忠实的部下，帮助他建立了底比斯城—— 一座拥有七座城门的伟大卫城。

卡德摩斯成了一代伟大的君王，众神都青睐他。宙斯把阿芙洛狄忒的一个女儿哈耳摩尼亚（Harmonia）嫁给了他做王后。众神给了这位新娘一条神奇的项链，让她永远美丽而年轻。在卡德摩斯和他的后代的统治下，底比斯城成为希腊最伟大的城邦之一。

d'A

坦塔鲁斯与珀罗普斯

Tantalus and Pelops

缪斯们有一首歌咏唱的是被罚在地府永远受苦的坦塔鲁斯（Tantalus）。他站在水中，水一直淹到他的脖子，但他永远都喝不到水，因为只要他一弯腰去喝水，水便会退却。他的头顶上悬着挂满果实的枝条，但只要他一伸手去摘，那树枝便会弯上去，让他够不着。

坦塔鲁斯是宙斯的儿子，众神都很喜欢他，经常邀请他参加他们在高高的奥林匹斯山上的宴会。作为答谢，他也邀请众神来他在小亚细亚的宫殿中用餐。坦塔鲁斯是一位拥有巨大财富的国王，但是他觉得他所拥有的一切没有一样好到可以招待他尊贵的客人。他的儿子珀罗普斯（Pelops）是他最大的财富，他想把最好的东西奉献给诸神，于是决定用他作为牺牲。他把自己的儿子煮熟了呈给诸神享用。但是众神都憎恨用人作为祭品。他们愤怒地把坦塔鲁斯扔到了地府中的受罚之地，并复活了珀罗普斯。但是他的一块肩胛骨不见了，众神于是用一块象牙来替代它。众神还馈赠给他丰厚的礼物。波塞冬给了他一群骏马，叫他出发去赢取一个新的王国。

在希腊，有一个漂亮的公主，名字叫作希波达米亚（Hippodamia）。她是爱

利斯（Elis）国王欧门诺斯（Oenomaüs）的女儿，谁娶了她，谁就将继承他的王国。但是这位父亲非常爱自己的女儿，不舍得和她分开。他有一群马，是他的父亲战神阿瑞斯送给他的礼物。每当有人前来向他的女儿求婚时，欧门诺斯便会提出和他比赛驾车。追求者如果赢了，便可以获得公主的芳心；如果输了，他的头就要被砍下来。凡间的任何骏马都不可能跑得过阿瑞斯的神驹，所以已经有十二颗人头被挂在王宫的大门上了。珀罗普斯来到爱利斯，向公主求爱。国王欧门诺斯不知道珀罗普斯也拥有一群神马，还一心想着把第十三颗人头钉到城门上去呢！但是希波达米亚爱上了这个年轻人，便打算救他的性命。她让国王的马僮在马车上做些手脚，好让珀罗普斯能够获胜。马僮一心想着取悦公主，做得比她要求的还过，他干脆把连接车轮和车轴的木栓拔掉，改用蜡把它们粘在一起。

这是一场盛况空前的比赛！天驹神骏奋蹄齐奔，难分伯仲，令国王惊奇的是不管他怎样用力地挥动鞭子，都无法跑得比对手更快。突然，蜡制的栓子崩开了，马车轮子飞了出去，国王摔在地上命赴黄泉。

珀罗普斯娶到了希波达米亚，成了爱利斯的国王。他把那个不忠的马僮扔到了海里，还给老国王安排了一场隆重的葬礼——他以老国王的名义把希腊的英雄们都请来参加运动比赛。他为胜利者准备了丰厚的奖品，因为他把父亲坦塔鲁斯的巨大财富都带了过来。比赛在爱利斯的奥林匹亚平原上举行，每四年重复一次。这一赛事被称为奥林匹克运动会。

达那俄斯、珀尔修斯和戈耳贡
Danaüs, Perseus, and the Gorgon

缪斯们为达那俄斯（Danaüs）高唱颂歌，他是众多伟大君王和英雄人物中居首的一位。达那俄斯是利比亚（Libya）的国王，他有五十个女儿；他的兄弟埃古普托斯（Aegyptus）则有五十个儿子。这五十个小伙子想娶他的五十个女儿为妻，但他们都是些粗鲁的家伙，达那俄斯国王不想把女儿嫁给他们。他害怕他们会用武力把他的女儿们带走，于是偷偷地建造了一艘有五十支桨的大船，带着女儿们一起逃走了。这五十位公主用力划桨，朝着辽阔的大海驶去。他们来到希腊的阿戈斯（Argos），那里的百姓看到达那俄斯站在一艘巨船的船首，公主们为他划桨，都惊呆了。他们相信达那俄斯一定是神派来的，于是拥戴他做他们的国王。

达那俄斯是一个很好的统治者，阿戈斯一直处在和平和幸福的状态。直到有一天，又一艘大船来到了。划桨的正是埃古普托斯的五十个儿子，他们前来索要自己的新娘。达那俄斯不敢违抗他们，摆下了奢华的宴席。但是他悄悄给了五十个女儿每人一把匕首，嘱咐她们待到左右无人时就把自己的丈夫杀死。四十九个女儿都听了他的话。但他最大的女儿许珀耳涅斯特拉（Hypermnestra）爱上了她的王子林昔尔斯（Lynceus），并和他一起逃走了。达那俄斯想给他的女儿们再找新的女婿，但是没有人敢娶她们了。这四十九个达那伊得斯姐妹（the Danaïdes）从此过着毫无快乐可言的日子，她们死后在地府受到了惩罚，她们要用筛子打水，去灌满一个永远也装不满的浴池，以洗净自己的罪。

达那俄斯国王老了之后，没有人继承他的王位，他只好派人去找许珀耳涅斯特拉和林昔尔斯。他们生活得无比幸福。他们成了阿戈斯的国王和王后。他们死后，他们的儿子继位当了国王。他们的儿子死后，他们儿子的儿子阿克里修斯（Acrisius）又继承了王位。但是阿克里修斯没有儿子。他只有一个长着金色头发的漂亮女儿，名字叫作达娜厄（Danaë）。但是她的美貌并不能给父亲带来欢乐。他想要的是一个儿子和王位继承人。他听到一则神谕，说他将死在自己女儿的儿子手里，于是他把达娜厄关进一个密室，这个密室既没有门也没有窗，只有屋顶上有一扇小天窗。这样追求者便无法一睹她的美貌，她也无法结婚生子。但是阿克里修斯没有防备宙斯。这位天神从屋顶的小窗中窥见了那位孤独的少女。他化身为一瓢金色的雨水，来到她的身边。这下达娜厄再也不孤单了，她成了宙斯快乐的新娘。但是当她的父亲听到密室中传来婴儿的哭声之时，他生气地破墙而入，想要杀死自己的外孙。但他一听说这个孩子的父亲是宙斯，便不敢下手了。他把达娜厄和她的孩子珀尔修斯（Perseus）装在一个箱子里面，扔进大海。如果他们被淹死，那便是波塞冬的罪过。

宙斯轻轻地把箱子推送到一个海岛的岸边，一位撒网的渔夫把它拖上了岸。看到箱子里这一对母子时，他惊呆了。达娜厄向他讲述了自己的身世遭遇。这位好心的老人膝下没有儿女，他把达娜厄和年幼的珀尔修斯带到自己

的茅屋里，像照顾自己的孩子一样照顾他们。

在他简陋的茅屋中，珀尔修斯成长为一个俊美勇敢的少年，他为自己是宙斯和美貌的达娜厄的儿子而深感自豪。但是达娜厄的美貌吸引了岛上一位冷酷的国王的目光。这位国王想让她做自己的王后。达娜厄作为宙斯的妻子，曾经发誓不再嫁人。她拒绝了国王，但是没有用。国王还是紧追不舍，甚至想强行把她带走，幸亏珀尔修斯挺身而出阻止了他。心怀叵测的国王于是决心除掉珀尔修斯，他散布假消息说他将要迎娶一个邻近小岛上的公主。按照习俗，岛上的每个男子都要为他献上礼物。但珀尔修斯实在太穷了，他没有任何礼物好奉献。他只好替国王效劳，以此作为礼物。这正中了国王的下怀。“去把美杜莎（Medusa）这头怪物杀死，把她的头带来见我。”他说。被派去杀美杜莎的人没有一个能够活着回来的，国王心想这下应该可以永远摆脱珀尔修斯了。

美杜莎是可怕的戈耳贡三姐妹（the Gorgon）之一。她们的可怖之处在于任何活物只要一看到她们就会立刻变成石头。她们生活在一个遥远的海岛上，没有人知道它的确切方位。

珀尔修斯告别母亲，踏上寻找美杜莎的征程。他跋山涉水，四处探听，但没有人能够说出戈耳贡怪物到底在哪里。当他站在一个岔路口，不知何去何从时，雅典娜和赫尔墨斯突然出现了。宙斯派他们来帮助珀尔修斯。他们可以告诉他去戈耳贡岛的路，但是他还需要更多的帮助。雅典娜借给他一块被打磨得

像镜子一样闪闪发亮的盾牌。赫尔墨斯借给他一把削铁如泥的锋利宝剑。他们还告诉他，他还需要向北方的仙女借三件宝物，但是连神也不知道这些仙女住在哪里。这个秘密被灰色三姐妹（the Three Gray Sisters）小心翼翼地保守着，她们永远也不会心甘情愿地把这个秘密说出来，因为这灰色三姐妹正是戈耳贡们的姐妹。但是赫尔墨斯答应把珀尔修斯带到她们那儿去，去把这个秘密套出来。他把珀尔修斯夹在胳肢窝里，升到天上，然后开始往前飞，他们的速度比风还快。他们向着西方一直飞，飞了很远，来到一个太阳永远照不到的地方，那里的一切都灰蒙蒙的，就像笼罩在暮色中一样。灰色三姐妹就在那里。她们的头发是灰的，脸是灰的，而且她们三个只有一只灰色的眼睛，她们轮流用这只眼睛来看东西。趁着其中一个将眼睛传递给另一个的当口，珀尔修斯冲上前去把这只眼睛抓了过来。

“现在你们的眼睛在我手上，”珀尔修斯喊道，“告诉我怎样才能找到北方仙女，否则你们休想再得到它。”

灰色三姐妹哀号着，乞求珀尔修斯把眼睛还给她们。但是珀尔修斯坚持不肯，她们只好把路线告诉了他。赫尔墨斯再次把他夹在胳膊下面，向北飞了很远很远，来到北风也吹不到，太阳永远也不会落下的北方之地。北方的仙女盛情款待了他们，珀尔修斯向她们说明来意，她们便爽快地把他所需要的三件宝物借给了他：一双带翅膀的鞋子，让他可以飞起来；一顶可以让他隐身的帽子；一个什么都装得进去的神奇的袋子。赫尔墨斯说，现在你可以去杀掉美杜莎了。他把道路指给他，并祝他好运。珀尔修斯穿着带翅膀的鞋子，飞到了遥远的西方。当他来到戈耳贡三姐妹的岛上时，他没有往下看，而是通过雅典娜的平滑如镜的盾牌看过去。盾牌上映出来的画面让他不禁打了个寒战。戈耳贡三姐妹就躺在岸边，睡得死死的。她们嘴巴咧开着，露出长长的黄色毒牙，她们头上长的不是头发，而是一条条扭来扭去的毒蛇，脖颈上覆着青铜鳞甲。她们四周怪石嶙峋，这些怪石显然都是被变成了石头的人。

珀尔修斯看着盾牌，猛地俯冲下去，手起剑落，割下了美杜莎的脑袋。怪物被割断的脖子里弹出一匹漂亮的飞马——珀加索斯（Pegasus）。它嘶鸣了一声，把其他两只戈耳贡怪物惊醒了。珀尔修斯赶紧把美杜莎的脑袋丢进了神奇的袋子里，飞到了天上。两个戈耳贡姐妹一边哭号，一边扇动沉重的翅膀飞了起来，漫无目的地追赶着。她们无法找到珀尔修斯，因为他戴了一顶能隐身的神奇帽子。

在回家的路上，珀尔修斯飞过了埃塞俄比亚（Ethiopia）海岸，他看见下面有一个美丽的少女被铁链锁在岸边的岩石上。她是那么苍白，他起初还以为那是一尊大理石雕塑，接着他看到有泪珠从她眼睛里滚落。他俯冲下去，试图扯断铁链。

“快逃！”她说，“不然你也会被海怪吃掉的。”但是珀尔修斯不肯离去，于是这位少女把自己悲惨的遭遇告诉了他：她的名字叫安德洛墨达（Andromeda），是刻甫斯国王（Cepheus）和卡西俄珀亚王后（Cassiopeia）的女儿。她的母亲十分虚荣，她不自知地吹嘘自己比海中仙女涅瑞德斯还漂亮。波塞冬无法忍受一个凡人拿自己与海中仙女相比，作为惩罚，他派了一头海怪去袭击埃塞俄比亚王国。为了平息神的怒气，拯救自己的王国，她的父亲不得不将她这个独生女儿做牺牲，献给海怪。所以她被锁在这崖壁上，等着被吞噬。她请求和她订了婚的王子来救她，但那个王子吓得逃走了。

“我来救你，你便是我的妻子。”珀尔修斯说。

他正说着，一只狰狞的海怪从海里蹿了出来，它张开血盆大口要来吞吃安德洛墨达。但是珀尔修斯飞到半空，朝海怪扑了下去，将宝剑刺入它的喉咙。海怪号叫着，猛甩着尾巴，身子不停地打滚。海怪沉了下去，海水被它的血染

得通红。从那以后，那片海就被称作红海了。

海怪一死，安德洛墨达那个胆小懦弱的追求者便带了许多士兵赶到了，他声称安德洛墨达是他的妻子。这会儿他倒是变得大胆而且气势汹汹，刻甫斯国王不敢和他作对。

“安德洛墨达，把你的眼睛蒙起来！”珀尔修斯说道。说完，他便把美杜莎的头从袋子里拎了出来。那位追求者和他的手下惊恐地看着，唰的一下就变成了石头！不幸的是，国王和王后也看到了这颗戈耳贡女妖的脑袋，他们也变成了石头。不过，既然宙斯的儿子将要和他们的女儿结婚，众神出于同情便把刻甫斯和卡西俄珀亚挂到天上，成为了星座。

珀尔修斯抱起安德洛墨达，向家的方向飞去。当他来到渔夫的茅屋前时，却发现达娜厄和渔夫都已经躲了起来。原来国王刚把珀尔修斯支走，就试图前来带走达娜厄。为了救她，好心的老渔夫只好和她一起逃走了。珀尔修斯听到这一切，便径直朝国王的宫殿去了。

“这便是你想要的妖怪的头！”他喊道，同时把美杜莎的头从袋子里拎了出来。国王和他的随从都惊讶地看过去，便立刻僵在那里，变成了石雕像，有的嘴巴还惊奇地张大着。

岛上的人都十分高兴终于摆脱了这位暴君，渔夫和达娜厄从藏身之处走了出来，他们马上拥戴渔夫做了新的国王。国王为珀尔修斯和安德洛墨达举行了最为盛大的婚宴，每个人都喜笑颜开。

珀尔修斯没有保留戈耳贡女妖的脑袋，因为它对一个凡人来说太危险了。他把盾牌交还给雅典娜时，把这颗头也送给了她，其他借来的宝物也都物归原主。

珀尔修斯想，他现在已经成为一个英雄了，那他的外公阿克里修斯应该会很高兴见到他。于是他带着达娜厄和安德洛墨达启程前往阿戈斯。但是老国王一听到他的外孙正在来的路上，便吓得逃走了，因为他还记得那则神谕的警告。这样一来，珀尔修斯便成了阿戈斯的国王。

珀尔修斯是位英明善良的君主，他的母亲和妻子常伴在他的左右。他还是一个运动健将，全希腊的运动会他都参加。有一天，一阵狂风吹来，使他掷出去的铁饼偏离了方向，砸死了一位正在观看比赛的老者。这位老者不是别人，

正是他的外公阿克里修斯！那则神谕最终还是变成了现实。

从那以后，珀尔修斯再也不愿住在他外公的城邦里。所以他在不远的地方建造了一座坚不可摧的新城，叫作迈锡尼（Mycenae）。许多伟大的君王和英雄都是他和安德洛墨达的后代。

珀尔修斯和安德洛墨达最终死去时，宙斯把他们也变成了天上的星座。

聪明的国王和虚荣的国王
Clever and Vainglorious Kings

米达斯国王
King Midas

珀尔修斯把戈耳贡女妖的头给了雅典娜，她把它系在护胸甲上，这让她变得更加强大了。她还取了美杜莎的两根骨头，为自己做了一支双管笛。她对自己吹奏出来的乐曲非常满意，但就是不明白，为什么每当她吹起这支笛子时，赫拉和阿芙洛狄忒便会爆出一阵大笑。有一天，她在光滑的盾牌里看到了自己的样子。她看到自己噘着嘴巴，腮帮子憋得鼓鼓的，那样子根本就不是那个端庄高雅的她。雅典娜一阵厌恶，把那支双管笛丢到了人间，并在上面加了诅咒。

一个叫马尔西阿斯（Marsyas）的森林之神正在弗里吉亚森林（Phrygian woods）里蹦跶，他捡到这支双管笛，便吹奏起来。他发现自己能够同时吹出两种曲调，心里一阵狂喜。他在森林里蹦蹦跳跳，吹着他的双管笛，吹嘘说自己演奏出的音乐比阿波罗的还好听。

阿波罗听说一个森林之神竟然敢将自己与他这位音乐之神相提并论，不禁皱起了眉头。他从奥林匹斯山冲到了弗里吉亚森林。马尔西阿斯正陶醉在自己的音乐之中，他甚至提出来要和阿波罗一比高低。

“你要比，我们便比，”阿波罗说，“我若赢了，就要把你的皮扒下来。”

九位缪斯女神自然是裁判，而马尔西阿斯则坚持要求把弗里吉亚的米达斯国王（King Midas）也请来做裁判。

米达斯是个好心却愚笨的凡人，他和弗里吉亚的森林之神一向相处融洽。有一天早上，他的仆人发现一个老迈的森林之神睡在国王最喜欢的花床上，米达斯却没有惩罚他，而是把他放走了。这个年迈的森林之神是狄俄尼索斯的随从，狄俄尼索斯为了回报这位好心的国王，决定满足他的一个心愿。目光短浅的米达斯国王许了个愿，他希望凡他的手碰过的东西都变成金子。他的点金手让他成了人间最富有的人，但是他也因此差点饿死，因为连他吃的喝的东西都变成了金子。他的小女儿跑过来抱他，也被变成了金子！米达斯只好乞求狄俄尼索斯把他的心愿取消，让所有的东西都恢复原样。

这一次，米达斯国王又显示出了糟糕的判断力。九个缪斯女神都认为阿波罗绝对是更好的音乐家，米达斯却把票投给了弗里吉亚的森林之神。阿波罗轻

蔑地将竖琴倒了过来，并演奏出和之前一样美妙的音乐。他让马尔西阿斯把他的笛子也倒过来，吹出与之前同样动人的音乐。可是不管他怎么用力地吹，那笛子都发不出半点声音。这下，即便米达斯也不得不承认森林之神的笛子比不上阿波罗的竖琴了。就这样，马尔西阿斯输掉了比赛。阿波罗把他的皮剥下来，做了一面鼓。然后，他转向米达斯国王，说道：“像你这么笨的耳朵，应该只有驴子才有。就让你从今往后都长一对驴耳朵吧！”

从此，米达斯国王走到哪里都戴着一顶高高的尖角帽，把他的耳朵藏在里面。他的臣民以为这是国王开创的新潮流，很快弗里吉亚人的头上都戴上了一顶高高的尖角帽。

只有国王的理发师知道米达斯帽子里的真相。国王禁止他向外人透露一个字。理发师心里藏着这么重要的一个秘密，憋得都快爆炸了。有一天，他再也忍不住了，便跑到一片无人的空地，在地上挖了个坑，对着那个坑耳语道：“米达斯国王有一对驴耳朵！”他飞快地把坑填起来，以为这样秘密就不会泄露出去了。岂料附近的芦苇听到了他的话，它们随风摇摆时，便悄悄地耳语起来：“米达斯长着驴耳朵，米达斯长着驴耳朵。”很快，这个秘密便传开了。

国王米达斯羞惭不已，他离开王座，躲进了没人看得见他的密林深处。

西西弗斯
Sisyphus

科林斯的西西弗斯（Sisyphus）是有史以来最聪明的国王。他的机智甚至愚弄了神祇。

有一天，西西弗斯碰见河神埃索普斯（Asopus），河神正在找他的女儿埃伊娜（Aegina）。西西弗斯对自己王国内的所有事情都了如指掌，于是就跟在河神后面说："如果你给我的城里提供一处泉水，我就告诉你你的女儿在哪里。"因为他那偌大的城邦唯一的不足就是缺少清冽的泉水。

埃索普斯讨厌把自己的水分给别人。他扭捏了半天，最后还是在地上敲了敲，一汪晶莹清澈的泉水便从那里汩汩地冒了出来。

"带走你女儿的是宙斯。"西西弗斯说，"我看见他带着你的女儿匆匆地从这儿经过。"说着他还给埃索普斯指出了宙斯的去路。河神满腔怒火地冲了过去，很快便赶上了那对私奔者。宙斯出乎意料地被逮了个正着，手边又没有带霹雳，为了避开怒气腾腾的河神，免得自己和埃伊娜仙女遭殃，他把自己变成了一块石头，把埃伊娜变成了一个小岛。

西西弗斯得到了一汪清泉，埃索普斯却失去了女儿，而宙斯则因为西西弗斯搅黄了他的好事而怀恨在心。他让哈得斯把他抓到地府，严厉地惩罚他。哈得斯很高兴能够为他的兄弟办点儿事情，所以亲自动身去抓西西弗斯。狡猾的国王西西弗斯看到冥王亲自来抓他，便装出一副受宠若惊的样子。他问冥王，为什么不是赫尔墨斯来带他，把亡魂领往地府不是赫尔墨斯的职责吗？就在哈得斯思忖着找个正当理由时，西西弗斯身手敏捷地用一根锁链把哈得斯绑了起来。就这样，冥王像条狗一样被拴在了柱子上。

只要西西弗斯不把哈得斯放开，地上的人就死不掉。命运女神的生命之线都缠作一团，整个世界也一片混乱。最后，众神威胁西西弗斯说，要把他的生活弄得凄惨无比，让他觉得生不如死。这样西西弗斯才不得不把哈得斯放了。人们又可以死了，生命的轨迹也恢复了正常。第一个被索命的，当然就是西西弗斯了。这次来找他的是赫尔墨斯。这个足智多谋的国王早料到了这一点，他嘱咐他亲爱的妻子，让她不要给他办葬礼，也不要在他的舌头下面放钱币。他作为一个身无分文的乞丐来到了地府。哈得斯大吃一惊！西西弗斯毕竟是个国王，照例他应该有一个葬礼，而且舌头下面要含一枚金币，以作为过冥河的渡资。他的妻子必须受到惩罚，否则这就会给别人树立一个不好的榜样。于是哈得斯把西西弗斯送回到地面上，让他去教训自己的妻子，使她有所敬畏。“我又要了他一次！”西西弗斯在和他忠实的妻子重逢之后说。他们在一起快乐地生活了很多年，最后才寿终正寝，来到了哈得斯的地府永久安息。他在地府领到了一个任务，这让他终日忙碌，再也无暇去想什么花招了。他必须把一块巨石推到一座陡峭的山上去，但是每当他快要到达山顶时，巨石便会从他手上滑落，一路滚回山脚。

柏勒罗丰
Bellerophon

柏勒罗丰（Bellerophon）是西西弗斯的孙子，他是一个伟大的驯马者。为了能够骑上珀加索斯，也就是那匹从美杜莎的脖子里蹦出来的飞马，他甚至愿意倾其所有。珀加索斯飞到希腊，被九位缪斯女神发现并照看着。这是一匹迅疾的烈马，只有缪斯女神们能靠近和抚摸它。

有一个夜晚，柏勒罗丰在雅典娜的神庙里睡着了。他梦见女神给了他一个马笼头，用它可以驯服飞马。当他醒来时，手里真的攥着一个金子做的马笼头。

此后不久，珀加索斯飞到了科林斯（Corinth），它看见西西弗斯从河神那里要来的清泉，便停下来喝水。柏勒罗丰踮着脚尖，小心翼翼地靠近了飞马，将马笼头套到它头上。珀加索斯长嘶一声，看着柏勒罗丰，突然变得无比驯服，让他骑到自己背上。飞马和这位骑手配合得天衣无缝。他们在天上疾驰，越过大地和湖海，迅疾如风。

柏勒罗丰骑着飞马，踏上了征服喀迈拉（Chimera）的征程。喀迈拉是一头喷火的怪兽，在小亚细亚的利西亚国（Lycia）祸害一方。她比噩梦还恐怖。她的身体前段是狮子，后段是蛇，中段是山羊。她有三个脑袋都会喷火；她的皮十分坚实，任何武器都无法刺穿。柏勒罗丰手里拿着一支长矛，矛尖上挑着一个铅块，壮着胆子，俯身朝怪兽冲过去，怪兽喷出的火焰几乎要燎着飞马的皮毛了。喀迈拉像毒蛇一样吐着信子，像羊羔一样哀鸣，张大着她的狮口大声吼叫着。柏勒罗丰把铅块丢进了她的喉咙。铅块被怪兽嘴里喷出的火焰熔化了，铅水流到她的肚子里把她杀死了。那些被吓得躲在家里把门闩起来的利西亚国民现在终于敢走出来了，他们的国王感激柏勒罗丰，于是把女儿嫁给了他。老国王去世之后，柏勒罗丰继承了王位。他成了一个伟大的国王，深受人民爱戴，他的邻国和潜伏在四周的各种怪兽都惧怕他。但是随着声名日盛，他的头脑也开始发昏了，他变得不可一世，觉得自己和神一样伟大。他甚至把自己看得和宙斯一样重要。他骑着飞马飞得越来越高，最后甚至想飞到奥林匹斯山去。这下柏勒罗丰可骄傲得过头了。珀加索斯把他掀了下去，他掉到地上，落在异国他乡的蓟棘丛中。他衣衫褴褛，跛着脚，像无名的乞丐一样四处游荡，直到死去。珀加索斯独自来到奥林匹斯山，宙斯让这匹俊美的飞马专门为他背负霹雳。

墨兰波斯
Melampus

柏勒罗丰的一个堂兄墨兰波斯（Melampus）由于对动物仁慈而获得了荣耀、名望和三分之一个王国。当他还是小孩时，在路上发现一条死去的母蛇。他没有把它踢到水沟里去，而是妥善地安葬了它，还把失去母亲的小蛇捡了回来，悉心地饲养它们。小蛇们感激他的恩情，把他的耳朵舔得干干净净，使他可以听懂所有动物的语言，不管是飞禽还是走兽。从动物的谈话中，他知道了人间的许多秘密，变得无比睿智。

有一次他因为偷邻国国王的牛被抓住而进了监狱。一天夜里，他躺在小床上，听到一窝白蚁在房梁里面说话。“兄弟，”一只白蚁对另一只说，“我们这样啃一晚上，这屋顶不到天亮就会塌了。”

墨兰波斯跳起来使劲砸门。他要求给他换个房间，因为屋顶很快就要塌了。狱卒笑了起来，但是他实在闹得太厉害了，狱卒只好给他换了个房间。他刚走出房间，屋顶就塌了个大洞。所有人都惊奇不已，国王把他召去，告诉他如果他能够治好他儿子的病，他就把他原本想偷的那些牛送给他。原来，国王的儿子从小就得了一种病，没有人知道病因。

墨兰波斯杀了一头牛，把肉丢在地上。很快，两只秃鹫就俯冲下来，开始狼吞虎咽地吃肉。吃饱之后，一只秃鹫对另一只说："自从上次国王给天神献祭了一只公羊之后，我就没这么饱过。我还记得当时国王手里拿着一把血淋淋的匕首，小王子看到这一幕，被吓坏了。他哇哇尖叫，国王只好甩掉匕首，跑过去抚慰他。结果，那把匕首刺进了那边那棵树里，伤到了树上的仙女。仙女就对那个男孩下了咒语，打那以后他就生病了。现在树皮已经把匕首包了起来，要是国王知道这些的话，他应该把生锈的刀子挖出来，用上面的铁锈煮汤给王子喝。"

墨兰波斯立刻把树上的刀子挖了出来，煮成了铁锈汤。生病的王子喝下那汤，马上就痊愈了，他甚至可以跳过一片麦地而不弄折一根麦秆。墨兰波斯成了一个鼎鼎有名的医疗圣手，希腊各个地方的国王都来请他去给他们治病。

梯林斯（Tiryns）的国王有三个可爱的女儿，她们突然得了疯病，认为自己是母牛。国王派人去找墨兰波斯。墨兰波斯说，如果国王肯把王国的三分之一给他，他就可以治好这三位公主。国王心想，这也要得太多了，于是墨兰波斯便离开了。公主们的病变得更严重，她们在全国各地乱跑，还像牛一样哞哞地叫。国王只好再派人去找墨兰波斯。墨兰波斯这次带了他的兄弟一起来，而且要求国王也分三分之一的王国给他的兄弟！国王只得答应了，因为他的女儿们到处跑，还喊着，"我们是母牛，我们是母牛！"这实在太令人难堪了。

墨兰波斯雇了一些跑得很快的人，让他们去追回这几个发疯的公主。他们跑了大半个希腊才抓到她们并把她们带了回来。墨兰波斯逼她们喝下了一种神奇草药做成的药剂，治好了她们的病，但还是有一个不幸的公主因为虚脱而死了。

国王这下得把三分之二的王国分出去了，他心想，干脆把两个女儿也许配给墨兰波斯和他兄弟，这样倒更合算。从此，他们便幸福地生活在一起了。

赫拉克勒斯

Heracles

缪斯女神们为赫拉克勒斯唱起颂歌时总是充满骄傲，她们常常称他为大力神。他是世间最强壮的人，也是达娜厄最伟大的后人。他的母亲是珀尔修斯和安德洛墨达的孙女阿尔克墨涅公主（Alcmena）。她的美貌和德行都备受称誉。

赫拉克勒斯是宙斯的儿子，赫拉自然对阿尔克墨涅心存恨意，并把怒气发到赫拉克勒斯身上。当他还是个婴儿时，赫拉就派了两条花斑蛇跑到他的摇篮里去，但是小赫拉克勒斯一下子就用他有力的双手抓住了它们，把它们捏死了。他一天比一天强壮，但是他的麻烦在于他不知道自己有多大的力气。

由于出身高贵，赫拉克勒斯必须学习唱歌和弹奏竖琴，但是他更喜欢摔跤和打斗。有一天，他的音乐教师莱纳斯（Linus）因为他唱歌跑调而斥责了他。赫拉克勒斯一生气，拿起竖琴朝莱纳斯的头上拍了过去，不料下手太重，一下便把那可怜的人打死了。赫拉克勒斯力气太大，让他在宫廷里待着太危险，所以他被派到山里去放牧。在山里，他将一身神力用来对付那些逡巡的野兽。不久，底比斯周围乡村的狮子和野狼都被他杀得绝迹了，他这个大力士的名声也广为传播。赫拉克勒斯作为一个英雄从山里回来了，底比斯的国王十分看重他，甚至把女儿嫁给了他。赫拉可不高兴看到这些，她让赫拉克勒斯发起了疯病。他开始胡言乱语，把自己的孩子也当成野兽打死了。清醒过来后，他被自己的所作所为吓坏了，他来到特尔斐圣迹，询问怎样才能弥补自己的罪过。神谕告诉他，他必须去给他的堂兄弟欧律斯托斯（Eurystheus）当十年的奴隶，并为他办十件事情。

赫拉很高兴，因为迈锡尼的国王欧律斯托斯是个孱弱矮小的人，他厌恶自己这个强壮的堂兄弟赫拉克勒斯。有了赫拉的协助，他想出了一些最难的任务让赫拉克勒斯去完成。

欧律斯托斯让赫拉克勒斯去完成的前四个任务是去杀死附近乡野中危险的野兽和怪物。

在尼米亚（Nemea）山谷中，住着一头可怕的狮子，它的皮坚硬得任何武器都刺不穿。它是厄喀德那那些令人恐惧的后代之一，宙斯让它们活了下来，留给后来的英雄们去挑战。

赫拉克勒斯把它从洞穴里赶出来，赤手空拳抓住它，并把它勒死了。然后他用狮爪把狮皮剥了下来。他把尼米亚狮怪那刀枪不入的皮毛披在头和肩上，去向欧律斯托斯报告他的第一个任务已经完成。

在莱尔娜（Lerna）沼泽里，有一只九头怪兽许德拉（Hydra），它是厄喀德那的另一个后代。这头怪兽身含剧毒，光它呼出来的浓烟就能把靠近它的任何东西置于死地。赫拉克勒斯在他巨大的肺里吸满了气，屏住呼吸，就朝许德拉奔了过去。他挥舞着棍棒，把那怪兽的脑袋都敲了下来，怪兽的脑袋一颗颗都滚到了地上。但是他每打掉一颗脑袋，原处很快又会长出一颗新的。他转过半个身子，大声地叫他的马夫拿火把过来把怪物的颈子烧焦。这样新的脑袋就长不出来了。赫拉看到赫拉克勒斯就要取胜了，便派了一只巨蟹来钳他的脚后跟。赫拉克勒斯一面敲掉怪兽的最后一颗脑袋，一面猛地一脚把那只巨蟹踢飞了。然后，他把自己的箭浸到许德拉的血里，这些箭就变得剧毒无比，只要被它擦着一点儿都必死无疑。赫拉克勒斯回到迈锡尼，他的第二个任务也完成了。

埃伊曼萨斯山（Mount Erymanthus）的山坡上有一只狂野又恐怖的野猪，它长着像剑一样锋利的獠牙。欧律斯托斯派赫拉克勒斯去把这只野猪活捉回来。

赫拉克勒斯大喊着把野猪从洞穴里赶了出来，并在它后面一路追赶，一直赶到白雪覆盖的山顶上。笨重的野猪陷在了雪地里，赫拉克勒斯毫不费力地抓住并制服了它。他一路连推带拉，把野猪滚到了迈锡尼的城门前。欧律斯托斯看见这只可怕的野猪，吓得跳进了一个大坛子，都不敢探头来看。

接着，欧律斯托斯又派赫拉克勒斯去赶走斯提姆菲里安湖（the Stymphalian Lake）里一群危险的鸟。它们身上的铜羽毛非常锋利，只要一根羽毛落下来，都会把它所碰到的东西杀死。但是这些铜羽毛无法穿透赫拉克勒斯的狮皮。赫拉克勒斯还弄出很大的声响，咣当咣当的声音令怪鸟们惊骇万分，它们都吓得飞走了，再也不敢回来。

欧律斯托斯看到赫拉克勒斯这么轻易地就完成了他的头四个任务，觉得很失望。这次，他派赫拉克勒斯去活捉一头阿尔忒弥斯的灵鹿回来。他希望赫拉克勒斯的天生蛮力会伤害到灵鹿，这样女神就会对他发怒了。但是赫拉克勒斯非常有耐性地追随着敏捷的灵鹿翻过一座座山、一道道河谷。他花了将近一年的时间，终于抓到了一头灵鹿。他小心翼翼地把这头灵鹿带回了迈锡尼。

接下来，为了羞辱这个强壮的堂弟，欧律斯托斯命令他去清洁奥革阿斯国王（King Augeas）的马厩。这位国王住在西方，去那儿要翻越崇山峻岭。他有许许多多的马，而且他的马厩和谷仓有好多年都没有清扫过了。一堆堆的粪便积得像山一样高。欧律斯托斯认为没有人能够在一年之内把他的马厩清扫干净。

但是力大无穷的赫拉克勒斯改变了两条河的河道，大水从马厩和谷仓这里流过，不到一天的时间，就把它们冲洗干净了。

在赫拉的指使下，欧律斯托斯又派赫拉克勒斯去遥远的地方完成最后的四个任务。他必须去东方，把亚马逊女王希波吕忒（Hippolyta）的金腰带取来，送到迈锡尼。亚马逊（the Amazons）是一个母系部落，那里野蛮好斗的女人奔跑和打斗起来比任何男人都厉害。欧律斯托斯确信这次连赫拉克勒斯也会被那些愤怒的女人打败。但是当赫拉克勒斯来到亚马逊的地盘，骄傲的女王一看到

他那鼓起的肌肉便被迷住了，根本都不用赫拉克勒斯动手，女王便把腰带给了他。女王还非常愉快地表示愿意嫁给他。但是赫拉伪装成一个亚马逊人，散布谣言说赫拉克勒斯是来绑架希波吕忒的。亚马逊人朝赫拉克勒斯冲了过来，但她们这一次可真是碰到对手了！赫拉克勒斯挥舞着他强有力的棍棒，那些平日里只会纺纱、做饭、照看孩子的弱小的亚马逊男人都惊奇地发现他们那强悍的妻子们被一个单枪匹马的男子打败了。

赫拉克勒斯带着希波吕忒的腰带胜利地回到了迈锡尼。他没能把女王带回来，因为她在战斗中被杀死了。

在遥远的北方，有一位国王，名叫狄俄墨得斯（Diomedes）。他是一个非常不好客的国王，他训练自己的四匹母马吃掉任何进入他地盘的陌生人。

这次，欧律斯托斯派赫拉克勒斯去抓住这四匹吃人的母马，并把它们活着带回来。

赫拉克勒斯来到北方，杀死了狄俄墨得斯国王，并把他扔给他自己的母马吃掉。母马吃了邪恶的国王之后，变得十分温顺，任由赫拉克勒斯驱使着它们回到了迈锡尼的城门前。

欧律斯托斯又让赫拉克勒斯去克里特岛捕捉一头凶恶的、会喷火的公牛。克里特岛上的人都是了不起的斗牛士，但是连他们也捉不住这头牛。当公牛冲过来时，赫拉克勒斯却毫不惧怕它鼻子里喷出的火焰，一把抓住牛角，将它摔在了地上。赫拉克勒斯带着被制服的公牛再次回到迈锡尼。欧律斯托斯又吓得躲到了坛子里。

赫拉克勒斯的第十个任务是要去海上一个遥远的岛屿带回一大群红牛。这群牛的主人是一个长着两条腿三个身子的怪物革律翁（Geryon）。

赫拉克勒斯大步流星地走了，很快便来到了西方陆地的尽头。那里他所能见到的唯一的一条船便是太阳之神赫利俄斯的金色舰船。赫拉克勒斯挽起长弓，瞄准了太阳，他威胁说如果赫利俄斯不把船借给他，就把他射下来。赫利俄斯不敢拒绝，便把金色舰船借给了赫拉克勒斯。出发之前，他拔出来两座巨大的峭壁，分别安放在划分欧非大陆的海峡的两边。今天这两处峭壁还矗立在那里，它们被称作“赫拉克勒斯之柱”。

赫拉克勒斯在海上航行时，周围都是滔天的巨浪，他用一支剧毒的箭对准浪涛，扬言如果它们不立即平息下去便将这箭射向它们。浪涛害怕地平息了下去，赫拉克勒斯扬起风帆继续航行，来到革律翁的岛屿。他一上岸就开始着手把红牛装上船，革律翁的看门人和他的双头狗朝他冲了过来。赫拉克勒斯大棒一挥就把他们都打跑了。随后革律翁自己也冲出来攻击他，他那三个庞大的身躯在两条细腿上直晃悠。赫拉克勒斯不慌不忙地拿起弓，瞄准目标，用一支毒箭一下射穿了怪物的三个身子。由于时间紧迫，赫拉克勒斯带着红牛尽快地往回划。当他抵达大陆时，赫拉派了一群牛虻去叮咬那些牛，

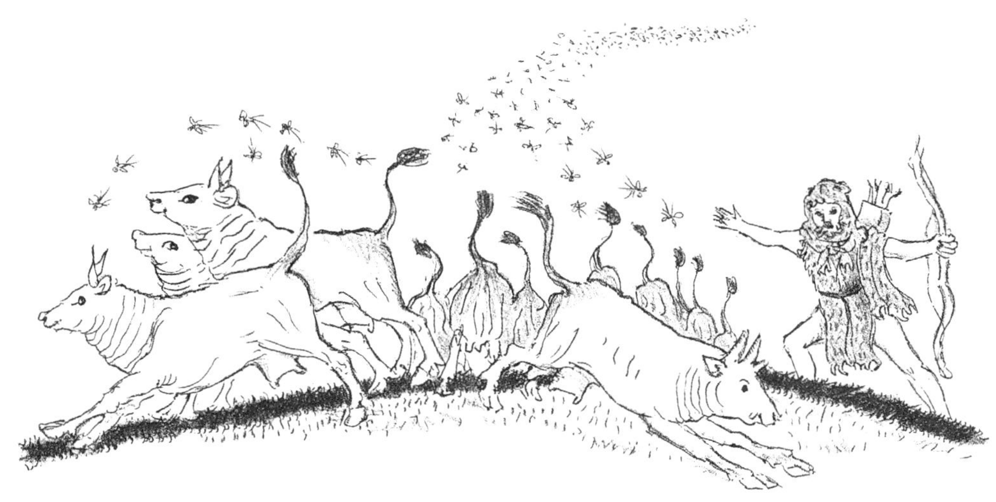

结果红牛四散逃窜，跑到了欧洲各地。尽管如此，赫拉克勒斯还是设法把红牛都拢到了一起。当一年之期将满时，他将红牛带回了迈锡尼。欧律斯托斯把牛献祭给赫拉，为了表示感谢，赫拉悄悄地在他耳旁说，他应该要求赫拉克勒斯再去完成两个任务，因为在杀许德拉时他的马夫曾经帮忙烧它的颈子，而且洗净奥革阿斯的马厩的是那两条河里的水，不是赫拉克勒斯。

赫拉克勒斯很生气，但他还是顺从地鞠了一躬，因为那已完成的十个任务让他获得了很大的荣耀，这会儿他还想赢得更多。

赫拉克勒斯的第十一个任务是找到赫拉的赫斯珀里得斯秘密花园，并从小苹果树上摘下三个金苹果。这棵苹果树是大地母亲送给赫拉的结婚礼物。老海神涅柔斯是世上唯一知道这个花园在哪儿的人，但是他不肯把秘密说出来。赫拉克勒斯抓住他，逼他说出这个秘密，他不断地变幻成各种动物想要逃脱。但是赫拉克勒斯牢牢地抓住了他，最后涅柔斯只好告诉他赫斯珀里得斯花园就在太阳西落之地，离肩扛天穹的提坦巨人阿特拉斯不远。

在去花园的路途中，赫拉克勒斯听到被绑在高加索山上的提坦巨人普罗米修斯在呻吟。尽管急着赶路，但赫拉克勒斯还是于心不忍，就过去帮他扯断了铁链。宙斯惊叹于儿子的天生神力，便任由他扯断了铁链。普罗米修斯心存感激，便提醒赫拉克勒斯，让他不要自己去摘金苹果，不然他会死掉。那金苹果是永生之果，只有天神才可以摘取。

赫拉克勒斯一路跋山涉水，终于来到了赫斯珀里得斯花园。提坦巨人阿特拉斯就站在不远处，赫拉克勒斯主动提出要帮他扛一会儿天，只要他能帮他从赫拉的树上摘下三颗金苹果。阿特拉斯说他很高兴可以放下重担歇息一会儿，但是他害怕巨龙拉顿（Ladon）。那条巨龙就躺在树下，它那一百颗脑袋上所有的眼睛都睁得大大的，看护着那棵树。但是百首巨龙也吓不倒赫拉克勒斯。他拿出弓箭射杀了它。接着，他把天穹扛在肩上，这样阿特拉斯就能腾出手去摘取苹果了。负责照看苹果树的三个小仙女流下了伤心的泪水，但是负责看守的巨龙已经死了，她们也阻止不了阿特拉斯。

天穹实在太重了，赫拉克勒斯的膝盖都要被压弯了，阿特拉斯却还在旁边伸展着四肢，享受着自由。

“我还可以亲自帮你把苹果送到欧律斯托斯那里去。”提坦巨人说着就准备走了。赫拉克勒斯心里很清楚，阿特拉斯压根儿就不打算回来，但他还是假装答应了。

“好呀，”他说，“但你得过来帮我扛一会儿，我要拿我那狮皮做个垫子，这天穹太硬了，压得我肩膀不舒服。”

阿特拉斯心想他说得也是，就放下金苹果，扛起了天穹。

“谢谢你帮我摘苹果。”赫拉克勒斯说完，就快步踏上了归程。

在回迈锡尼的路上，赫拉克勒斯被擅长摔跤的巨人安泰（Antaeus）拦住了。他住在路边的一个小屋里，老是强迫过路的人跟他摔跤。他是大地母亲的儿子，只要不离开大地他就不会死，所以他总是赢，他的屋子就是用失败者的头颅和骨头垒起来的。赫拉克勒斯把巨人安泰摔到地上，以为他已经死了，谁知他却又精神抖擞地站了起来，赫拉克勒斯明白是怎么回事了。他抓住安泰，举在空中，把他拧断了气。

赫拉克勒斯匆匆赶回迈锡尼，把金苹果交给欧律斯托斯。但是欧律斯托斯不敢保留这几个苹果。他把它们给了雅典娜，她又把它们送回了赫拉的花园——它们本来该在的地方。

第十二个任务是要赫拉克勒斯去到地府，逮住哈得斯那条长着三颗脑袋、气势汹汹的看门狗刻耳柏洛斯，并把它带回迈锡尼。

赫拉克勒斯四处搜寻，终于在遥远西方的赫利俄斯夜宫附近找到了地府的入口。赫拉克勒斯怒目圆瞪、大步流星地来到了地府。那些四处飘荡的鬼魂都吓得瑟瑟发抖，连哈得斯也一下就被震慑住了，他让赫拉克勒斯把狗带走，只是不要虐待它就好。刻耳柏洛斯发出低吼，甩着带尖刺的尾巴冲了出来，但是

赫拉克勒斯一把勒住它的脖子，勒得它三条舌头都吐出来了。刻耳柏洛斯呜呜地叫唤着，被赫拉克勒斯拉着来到了地上世界，并跟着他一路回到了迈锡尼。欧律斯托斯看到这条令人恐惧的猎狗，吓得又一次跳进了那个坛子，蜷缩在里面大气都不敢出。赫拉克勒斯不知道怎么处置这条狗，于是又把它一路拽回了哈得斯的地府。

现在赫拉克勒斯终于自由了。他完成的任务可不止十个，而是十二个。赫拉克勒斯的罪过已经得到了赎偿，宙斯为这个强壮的儿子感到欣慰，对赫拉也不怪罪，因为她无意中帮助赫拉克勒斯赢得了世间英雄从来未有过的荣耀和声誉。赫拉克勒斯备受尊崇，他环游希腊，又做出许多英雄壮举，结交了许多朋友。

但赫拉还是不肯善罢甘休，她让赫拉克勒斯再次陷入了疯狂，许多人像苍蝇一样被他拍死了。恢复清醒之后，他不得不再一次为自己赎罪。这次要由他的父亲宙斯来对他进行惩罚，而且可不是让他去赢得什么荣耀。

宙斯判赫拉克勒斯为吕底亚（Lydia）的翁法勒（Omphale）女王做三年奴隶。她给赫拉克勒斯穿上女人的衣服，让这世间最勇猛的男人蹲坐在她的脚下，用他的大手去做些纺纱、缝衣服的活儿。她自己则穿上赫拉克勒斯的狮皮，挥舞着他的棍棒。赫拉克勒斯不停地嘟囔和叹气，但还是照着女王的命令行事。三年期满之后，赫拉克勒斯也学会了谦恭待人。

他又创造了很多英雄事迹，他的朋友高兴地看到他又恢复了当年的样子。塞萨利（Thessaly）的国王阿德墨托斯（Admetus）是他的一位至交。阿波罗当

年被罚在人间做奴隶时就是在他的手下。为了感谢阿德墨托斯对他的善待，阿波罗说服了命运女神，只要阿德墨托斯能够找到愿意代他而死的人，在他的生命之期结束之时她们就不会剪断他的生命之线。国王心想，这还不简单吗？他那些忠心耿耿的臣子们不总是说他的生命比他们自己的还宝贵吗？阿德墨托斯国王一直很害怕早死，因为他和他美丽的王后阿尔刻提斯（Alcestis）生活得很幸福。国王和王后都很喜欢赫拉克勒斯，总是一起热情地欢迎他。但是有一天，当赫拉克勒斯来到王宫时，只有阿德墨托斯一个人前来迎接他。他看上去悲伤而沮丧。赫拉克勒斯问他发生了什么事，他只说家里的一个女眷死了，他得去

参加她的葬礼。说完，他留下仆从自顾自地走了。那些仆从看上去也很悲伤。他们默默地伺候在他身旁，不肯回答他的问题。赫拉克勒斯独自吃喝玩乐，最后终于忍不住抓了一个仆从，逼他说出事情的原委。这个仆从只好告诉他，阿德墨托斯的死期到了，他问他的臣子是否有人愿意替他去死，但那些臣子没有一个愿意的。阿德墨托斯又去找他的父母，他们都已经很老了，对人生都已经感到厌倦了。他问他们是不是愿意替他去死，结果他们也拒绝了。但是，当他回到宫殿时，他看到王后阿尔刻提斯正准备前去地府。她太爱他了，她说，她甘愿为他献出自己的生命。国王太珍惜自己的生命，就让他的王后去了。现在国王和整个王宫里的人都在哀悼阿尔刻提斯。

赫拉克勒斯听完这个故事，流下了大颗大颗的眼泪。他是一个说干就干的人，于是就抓起棍子，大步流星地朝地府走去，他要让哈得斯把阿尔刻提斯放回来。这样一个忠贞的妻子不应该死掉。

赫拉克勒斯根本都用不着使用他的棍子。他一阵风似的冲进哈得斯的宫殿，刻耳柏洛斯立刻给他让开了路。冥王哈得斯的妻子对他冷若冰霜，所以当他听赫拉克勒斯讲了阿尔刻提斯献身替死的故事之后，非常感动，就把她放走了。

赫拉克勒斯把王后阿尔刻提斯带回到阿德墨托斯国王身边，宫殿里悲伤的氛围

变成了狂欢。这下，他们一起吃喝玩乐起来，阿尔刻提斯成了有史以来最忠心的妻子，变得远近闻名。

赫拉克勒斯自己也想要一个妻子，他选中了卡吕冬的公主得伊阿尼拉（Deianira）做他的新娘。得伊阿尼拉已经被许给了河神阿刻罗俄斯（Achelous），但是她一想到要嫁给河神就害怕。因为河神可以变成任何模样，她将永远也不知道丈夫晚上回家时是什么样子。她更愿意嫁给大英雄赫拉克勒斯。两个追求者决定摔跤，胜利者将拥有公主得伊阿尼拉。毫无疑问，获胜的是赫拉克勒斯。河神变成一头公牛朝他冲过来，赫拉克勒斯抓住它的一只角，把它扭断了，河神都来不及变成别的样子，就被他摔在了地上。赫拉克勒斯和得伊阿尼拉结了婚，幸福地生活在一起。

有一天，他们在外面旅行，遇到一条涨水的小河，赫拉克勒斯轻易地就涉水过去了，得伊阿尼拉却害怕地站在岸边。人马兽涅索斯（Nessus）在一旁彬彬有礼地提出要背她过河。但是涅索斯和所有的人马兽一样，都喜欢漂亮姑娘，他还没走到一半，就心生邪念，想把她拐跑。他一到岸边，就背着她飞奔而去。得伊阿尼拉大声呼救，赫拉克勒斯朝人马兽涅索斯射出一支毒箭，他倒在了地上。他临死前悄悄地对得伊阿尼拉说："取一点我的血，把它保存起来。如果哪天你怀疑丈夫不再爱你了，就涂点血在他的袍子上，他就会重新爱上你。”

得伊阿尼拉小心翼翼地把几滴血保存了起来，因为她很清楚许多女孩都想偷走她伟岸的丈夫。

有一天，赫拉克勒斯外出征战，取得了很大的胜利，便派了一个信使回家去把他最好的战袍取来。他想和手下一起好好庆祝一下，但是得伊阿尼拉以为他想要把自己打扮得更英俊，好去吸引别的姑娘。于是，她把涅索斯的血涂了一点在那战袍上。赫拉克勒斯一穿上战袍，便觉得浑身像火烧一般。原来涅索斯给得伊阿尼拉的并不是什么爱情药剂，而是他自己的血，里面混有赫拉克勒斯的箭头上所沾的许德拉怪兽的毒液。赫拉克勒斯非常强壮，毒液要不了他的命，但是那种痛苦令人无法忍受。他让他的手下搭起一个火葬的柴堆，他把自己的狮皮铺在上面，躺了上去。然后，他把他的弓和毒箭作为告别的礼物送给了一个叫菲罗克忒忒斯（Philoctetes）的年轻朋友。当火焰在他周围升腾起来时，人们听到一声巨雷，赫拉克勒斯受宙斯之命，躺在他的狮皮上面，朝奥林匹斯飞去。

众神都欢迎赫拉克勒斯，并且非常高兴他能够加入他们的行列，因为命运女神曾经预言奥林匹斯将受到可怕的敌人的攻击，只有世间有史以来最强壮的人站在他们一边，诸神才能得到拯救。这一预言很快就应验了。为了对万能的宙斯做出最后一击，大地母亲生下了五十个腿像蛇一样的巨人。他们包围了奥林匹斯，并打算攻进奥林匹斯宫。几乎没人能够打得过他们，因为就像赫拉克勒斯在凡间遇到的那个巨人安泰一样，他们只要一触到大地便会恢复元气。赫拉克勒斯知道战胜他们的方法，在他的帮助下，众神打败了巨人，把他们投进了塔尔塔洛斯深渊。赫拉克勒斯现在成了奥林匹斯山上的英雄，受到众神的爱戴。赫拉也来请求他原谅自己，并把她的女儿——青春女神赫柏（Hebe）嫁给他，做他在奥林匹斯的妻子。从此，赫拉克勒斯永远过上了幸福的生活，众神都喜爱他。他的父亲宙斯感到非常高兴。

忒修斯

Theseus

缪斯女神不仅歌颂赫拉克勒斯和他的功绩，她们也歌颂克里特岛的故事。克里特岛的统治者是宙斯和欧罗巴生下的儿子弥诺斯。他的王后帕西法厄（Pasiphaë）是太阳之神赫利俄斯的女儿。和所有太阳之神的后代一样，她也有一双金光闪闪的眼睛，喜欢富丽堂皇的风格。弥诺斯国王希望他的王后住的宫殿和她父亲的宫殿一样宏伟，于是命令代达罗斯（Daedalus）建造了克诺索斯宫（the Cnossus）。代达罗斯是雅典的建筑家，他开创了很多精妙的技艺。

宫殿建了一层又一层，梁柱成林。螺旋形的楼梯和纵横交错的通道连接着厅堂和庭院。大厅的高墙上绘有壁画，庭院中泉水喷涌，就连浴室也有潺潺的流水。屋顶上装饰着纯金的牛角，克里特人对牛有一种崇拜，因为宙斯当初就是化身为公牛把欧罗巴驮到岛上来的。国王、王后和王室成员在这宫殿中过着奢华而快乐的生活，直到有一天波塞冬从海里派了一头白色的公牛过来。因为克里特岛四面环海，那可是他的地盘，所以他想让克里特岛上的人也崇拜他，他命令弥诺斯国王把这头公牛献祭给他。但是帕西法厄王后太迷恋这头漂亮的白色公牛，她央求国王不要杀掉它。她对它喜欢得不得了，甚至命令代达罗斯造了一头中空的木牛，好让她藏在牛肚子里近距离地欣赏这头公牛。

波塞冬非常生气，作为惩罚，他让这头公牛变成了一头疯牛，把整个克里特岛弄得一团糟。尽管克里特人都擅长斗牛，但是他们当中没有一个人能够制服这头怪兽，直到赫拉克勒斯奉命来把它抓去。

为了惩罚国王和王后，波塞冬让帕西法厄生下了一头怪物，叫弥诺陶洛斯（Minotaur）。这是一头半人半牛的怪物，他除了人肉什么都不吃。这样一头怪物可不能让他自由地活动，于是聪明的代达罗斯在王宫的地下给他建造了一个迷宫。迷宫由一些小房间和许多通道组成，没有人能够从里面走出来。弥诺陶洛斯就被关在里面，只要给他吃人，他就安然无事。当他饥饿时，他的咆哮声让整个宫殿都为之颤抖。弥诺斯国王不得不对邻国发动战争，这样他才能将战俘送给弥诺陶洛斯做食物。弥诺斯的一个儿子去雅典时被意外杀死了，他借机威胁要攻陷这个城邦，除非他们每九年进贡七个雅典女子和七个雅典男子到克里特岛，献给弥诺陶洛斯。为了拯救自己的城邦，雅典国王埃勾斯（Aegeus）不得不答应了这个条件，因为弥诺斯比他强大得多。雅典人开始抱怨了，因为埃勾斯国王自己没有子女，也就没有什么好失去的，其他的雅典人却得看着自己的儿女成为残忍的弥诺陶洛斯的牺牲品。

两个九年过去了，埃勾斯国王也变老了。挂着表示哀悼的黑帆的船要第三次出发了，这时国王听到一个消息，说特罗曾（Troezen）有一个叫忒修斯（Theseus）的少年英雄正在来雅典的路上，他一路上杀死了各种怪物和强盗。埃勾斯国王听到这些，心跳加速了。他年轻的时候曾经去过特罗曾，还与公主爱特娜（Aethra）秘密地结了婚。他没有带爱特娜一起回雅典，但是在离开之前，他对爱特娜说："我把我的剑和金凉鞋都藏在这块巨石下面。如果你生下了我的儿子，他长大了能够举起这块巨石，就让他来找我。那时候他就有能力继承雅典的王位了。"埃勾斯国王那个时候正以身强力壮而闻名。

少年英雄忒修斯到达雅典之后直接去了王宫。高大英俊的忒修斯穿着凉鞋佩着宝剑站在那里，国王喜出望外。他终于有了一个儿子，而且还是个英雄。国王高兴地宣布忒修斯就是他王位的合法继承人，当忒修斯提出他将替代一个殉身者前往克里特岛时，他成了所有雅典人心目中的英雄。埃勾斯国王乞求他的儿子不要去，但是忒修斯主意已定。“我们会结果弥诺陶洛斯的性命，我们会平安回来，”他说，“我们会挂黑帆出航，返航挂白帆，那是成功的信号。”

船扬帆起航，来到了克里特，十四个年轻的雅典人被关在地牢里等待着他们的末日。但是国王弥诺斯有一个可爱的女儿，名叫阿里阿德涅（Ariadne），她是人们所见过的最漂亮的姑娘。她不忍心让英俊的忒修斯成为丑陋的弥诺陶洛斯的牺牲品。她找到代达罗斯，求他帮忙拯救忒修斯。他交给阿里阿德涅一个有魔力的线球，告诉她，午夜时分弥诺陶洛斯会睡得很死，她必须在这个时候把忒修斯带到迷宫。这个有魔力的线球会滚在他前面，引他走通迷宫来到怪物的住处，那时候就要看忒修斯是否打得过那只怪物了。

趁着夜色，阿里阿德涅来到忒修斯的牢房，对他耳语道，如果他能够答应娶她并带她走，她就会帮助他。忒修斯爽快地答应了，阿里阿德涅领着他来到了迷宫门口，把线球的一端绑在门上，同时把线球给了他，这样他就可以顺着线找到出来的路了。忒修斯一把线球放到地上，它就开始向前滚，领着他穿过黑暗的回廊，上楼，下楼，穿过盘旋的通道。忒修斯手里紧捏着线，任由线球领着他走，不久便听到了弥诺陶洛斯雷鸣般的鼾声。在一堆骷髅和白骨中间，弥诺陶洛斯躺着睡得正香。

忒修斯扑到弥诺陶洛斯身上。怪物号叫着，整个克诺索斯宫都震动了。但是怪物毫无防备，忒修斯又十分强壮，他赤手空拳便杀死了这头残忍的怪兽。

忒修斯快速地顺着线回到了站在门口望风的阿里阿德涅身边。他们一起释放了其他的雅典人，并跑回停在港口的船上。开船前，他们在弥诺斯国王所有的船上都凿了洞，让他无法追击。阿里阿德涅催促他们赶快出发，因为即便是她也无法帮他们对付那个守护克里特的青铜机器人太洛斯。如果让他看到他们的船要开走，他会扔石头把船砸沉，如果有人想游到岸上，他会投身火堆把自己烤得通红，然后用一个火热的拥抱将幸存者化为灰烬。他们才刚升好帆，一阵轻风把他们送出海港，就听到了太洛斯那咣当咣当的脚步声。仓促之中，他们忘记了用那表示胜利的白帆替换表示哀痛的黑帆。

忒修斯满怀喜悦。他不仅从弥诺陶洛斯那里拯救了雅典人，还带回了一个美丽的新娘。但夜半时分天神狄俄尼索斯出现在他面前对他说："我不许你娶阿里阿德涅。因为我已经选中她做我的妻子。你必须在纳克索斯岛把她放下。"

忒修斯无法和奥林匹斯山上的天神作对。当他们来到纳克索斯岛时，他命令所有人都到岸上去休息。阿里阿德涅在那里陷入了沉睡，就在她睡着时，忒修斯让其他人都回到船上，他们抛下阿里阿德涅自己出发了。

可怜的阿里阿德涅醒来发现自己被遗弃了，伤心地哭起来。当一个英俊的

陌生人向她走来时，她一点儿也不知道他就是天神狄俄尼索斯，也不知道是他命令忒修斯丢下了她。狄俄尼索斯温柔地拭去她的泪滴，又给她喝了手里的杯中之物，她的悲伤马上烟消云散了。她朝狄俄尼索斯露出了微笑，狄俄尼索斯将一个亮晶晶的宝石王冠戴到她头上，让她做了他的新娘。他们在一起快乐地生活了很多年，他们的儿子们成为周边岛屿上的国王。狄俄尼索斯非常爱阿里阿德涅，当她死去时，他把她的王冠放到天上变成一个星座，让人们永远也不会忘记她。

忒修斯沉浸在失去阿里阿德涅的悲伤之中，仍旧忘记了升起白帆。国王埃勾斯看见从克里特返回的船上悬着黑帆，便绝望地跳进了海里。

忒修斯继承了父亲的王位，他和所有的雅典国民一起哀悼逝去的国王，为了纪念他，他们把他跳下去的那片海称作爱琴海（the Aegean）。

弥诺斯国王发现自己的女儿和雅典人一起私奔了，简直气疯了。他知道，除了聪明的代达罗斯之外没有人能够帮助忒修斯破解迷宫之谜，所以代达罗斯成了王宫里的囚犯，所受的待遇十分恶劣。代达罗斯无法忍受被囚禁和才华空耗的生活。于是，他偷偷地制造了两对翅膀，一对给他自己，一对给他的儿子伊卡洛斯（Icarus）。他们用蜂蜡给翅膀镶上了羽毛。他教儿子如何使用这翅膀，并告诫他不要飞得太高，否则太阳的热度会把蜂蜡融掉。然后，他们爬到一座最高的塔上，拍着翅膀，像两只鸟儿一样飞走了。国王弥诺斯和机器人太洛斯都拿他们没有办法。

伊卡洛斯年轻而又愚蠢，他忍不住想在天上飞得更高一点，好让整个世界都在他的俯瞰之下。但是他飞得离太阳太近了，蜂蜡开始融化。羽毛一松脱，翅膀也散架了，伊卡洛斯掉进海里淹死了。伤心的代达罗斯独自往前飞，来到了西西里岛。他的名声早就传到了这里，西西里岛的国王也想拥有一个华丽的王宫和有流水的浴室，所以热情地接待了他。

国王弥诺斯待他的船一修好，就出发去找那个机智的工匠代达罗斯。他先向东，后又向西，当他来到西西里海岸，看见那座拔地而起的奇异宫殿，马上就明白这是谁建造的。但西西里的国王把代达罗斯藏了起来，否认他在帮他做事。诡诈的国王弥诺斯派人送了一个海螺到王宫去，并说如果谁能够将一根线穿过这弯弯曲曲的螺壳，他就送给他一袋金子作为奖励。西西里国王让代达罗斯来解决这个难题。代达罗斯沉思了一会儿，他在一只蚂蚁身上绑了根蚕丝般细的绳子，把蚂蚁放在海螺壳的一端，又在海螺的另一端涂了一点蜂蜜，蚂蚁闻到蜂蜜的味道，就从海螺壳里爬了过去，那根绳子也跟着穿过了螺壳。国王弥诺斯看到穿好绳子的螺壳，立刻要求把代达罗斯交出来，他现在有证据证明是西西里国王把他藏起来了，因为除了代达罗斯，没有人能够给海螺穿上绳子。

西西里国王只好承认这一事实。他邀请弥诺斯赴宴，答应交出代达罗斯。按照惯例，国王弥诺斯要在宴会前先洗个澡。但他一踏进代达罗斯建造的华丽浴池，沸腾的热水就从水龙头里冲了出来，把他烫死了。代达罗斯在西西里国王的王宫里度过了余生。

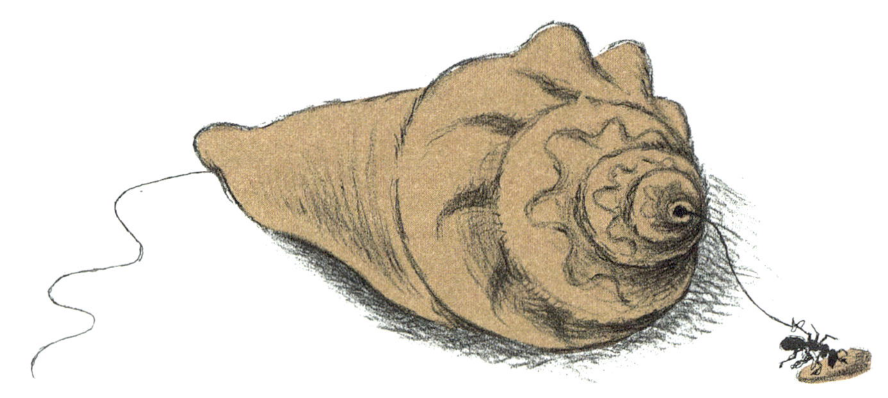

弥诺斯死后，克里特和雅典之间实现了和平，忒修斯娶了阿里阿德涅的妹妹菲德拉（Phaedra）。他成为雅典有史以来最伟大的国王，其英名传遍了希腊。另一个伟大的英雄人物，希腊北部拉庇泰的国王庇里托俄斯（Pirithoüs）是他亲密无间的朋友。两位英雄初次相识是在格斗时，但是他们惺惺相惜，所以最终扔掉武器，立誓结为永远的朋友。他们一起完成了许多英雄事迹。当庇里托俄斯与拉庇泰的一个公主结婚时，忒修斯理所当然地被邀请参加婚宴。人马兽也受到了邀请，尽管粗野无礼，但他们毕竟是国王的远亲。一开始，人马兽们还比较安分，但是当酒坛子传来传去喝到酒酣耳热时，他们开始喧嚣吵闹起来。突然，一只年轻的人马兽站了起来，一把抓起新娘的头发，带着她跑开了。见此情景，其他的人马兽也都各自抓起一个尖叫着的姑娘，向山里奔去。

忒修斯和庇里托俄斯带着他们的人马上追了出去，很快便赶上了那些人马兽。一场酷烈的搏斗开始了，野蛮的人马兽拔起大树当作棍棒挥舞，但是在忒修斯和庇里托俄斯面前，这简直是班门弄斧。他们被赶出了希腊，胜利的英雄带着新娘和其他的拉庇泰姑娘回到了筵席上。

庇里托俄斯快乐地生活了一阵子，后来便成了鳏夫，他请求他的朋友忒修

斯帮助他去赢取一位新的妻子，忒修斯立誓要帮助他，但是当他听说他想娶的不是别人，正是冥后珀尔塞福涅时，他颤栗了。庇里托俄斯说，她和哈得斯在一起并不快乐。忒修斯已经应允了他的朋友，而承诺了的事情不能食言，于是他只好和庇里托俄斯一起下到地府。他们强行通过了刻耳柏洛斯这一关，进入到幽暗的冥宫。哈得斯阴沉着脸看着两位胆敢闯入他领地的英雄，礼貌地听他们阐明来意。“坐这凳子上，”他说，“我们商量一下。”两位英雄一坐下来，哈得斯便阴笑了一声，原来那是一条有魔力的凳子，人一坐下去便休想再站起来。他们只好永远坐在那里，任由幽灵和蝙蝠在他们头上飞来飞去。

很久之后，赫拉克勒斯身负使命来找哈得斯，他看见两位英雄徒劳挣扎想从凳子上起身，便心生怜悯。他抓住忒修斯，用他有力的臂膀一把将他拉了起来。但是当他想把庇里托俄斯拉起来时，大地猛地震了一下。天神不让赫拉克勒斯放他出来，因为他竟然想娶一位女神做妻子，这是对神的大不敬。忒修斯回到雅典，他变得更加睿智，但也更瘦了，原来他的一大块肉还粘在那条凳子上呢。从此之后，雅典人便偏好瘦削的大腿。

俄狄浦斯
Oedipus

有一天，一个双目失明的老人来到忒修斯面前，请求他允许自己在他的王国内住下，并安详地死去。没有人敢让这个老人待在他们的国家，因为他是复仇女神厄里倪厄斯的报复对象。他四处游荡无家可归。这个名叫俄狄浦斯的老人对忒修斯讲起了他的故事。

他的不幸在出生之前就已经开始了。他的父亲，底比斯国王拉伊俄斯（Laius）听到一则特尔斐神谕，说他的王后伊俄卡斯特（Jocasta）肚子里的孩子命中注定将杀死自己的父亲，并娶自己的母亲为妻。国王心想，绝不能让这一切发生。所以俄狄浦斯一生下来，他就命令手下把这个孩子抱走，遗弃到深山里。但是命运另有安排。邻国科林斯的一个牧羊人听到了孩子的哭声。他捡起这个小男孩，把他带到了国王那里。科林斯的国王和王后没有孩子，他们愉快地收养了这个漂亮的小男孩。他们深爱着俄狄浦斯，他一点儿也不知道自己不是他们亲生的儿子。俄狄浦斯无忧无虑地长大成人。有一天，他去特尔斐神庙卜问自己的将来。耳边传来的神谕令他深感恐惧！他命中注定要杀死自己的父亲，并和自己的母亲结婚。

绝不能让这一切发生，俄狄浦斯心想。他要掌控自己的命运，于是便遁入深山，再也不肯见他亲爱的父母。

在一条狭窄的山路上，他与一位贵族的马车遭遇了。“为我主人的马车让开道！”贵族的仆从们一边吼道，一边想把俄狄浦斯推下山路。俄狄浦斯生气地予以还击，在打斗中，贵族和他的仆从都被杀死了，只有一个人得以逃走。俄狄浦斯继续前行，来到底比斯城。但是底比斯的七个城门都紧闭着。有一头名叫斯芬克斯（Sphinx）的怪物盘踞在城外的悬崖上，没有人敢进出城门。这只长着翅膀的女首狮身怪物要求所有路过的人解答她的谜题。如果他们解不出来，就会被她撕成碎片。没有人解得开斯芬克斯的谜题。

她看见俄狄浦斯，便问：“什么动物早晨用四条腿走路，中午用两条腿走路，

晚上用三条腿走路？”说完，她险恶地瞟了他一眼。

“是人。”俄狄浦斯答道，“年幼的时候，他用四肢在地上爬；长大了，他便站起来用两条腿走路；年纪大了，他就得拄根拐棍。”

斯芬克斯发出一声恐怖的尖叫。谜题被解开，她便失去了魔力。斯芬克斯绝望地跳下悬崖摔死了。底比斯的城门敞开，人们蜂拥而至，来感谢这位陌生人让他们获得了自由。他们的老国王不久前被杀死了，国王身后无子，没有人可以继承他的王位。当人们听说俄狄浦斯是科林斯的一位王子，便让他和守寡的王后成婚，并做他们的国王。毫无疑问，伊俄卡斯特王后比俄狄浦斯要老得多，但她依旧容貌美丽，因为她脖子上戴着一条神奇的项链。这条项链是众神送给底比斯的第一位王后哈耳摩尼亚的礼物。任何人只要戴着这条项链，便可以在有生之年都永葆青春和美貌。就这样，俄狄浦斯成为了底比斯的国王，以其公正和睿智统治了这个城邦许多年。

有一天，消息传来说科林斯的国王寿终正寝了，俄狄浦斯一面为父亲的死感到悲伤，一面也为自己逃脱了那可怕的命运而高兴。不久，一场瘟疫在底比斯开始流行，人们大批大批地死去。俄狄浦斯派人找来一位预言家，向他询问拯救臣民的办法。预言家说，瘟疫会一直蔓延下去，直到有人为老国王报了杀身之仇。于是，俄狄浦斯起誓要找到杀死老国王的人，并把他的眼睛挖出来。他派人出去寻访，最后找到了拉伊俄斯国王卫队中那个幸存的仆从。当被带到俄狄浦斯国王面前时，这个仆人立刻认出俄狄浦斯正是那个杀死老国王的人！

可怕的真相完整地浮出了水面，原来这个仆人正是当年把俄狄浦斯丢进深山的那个人，他也一直知道那个孩子被科林斯的国王发现并收养着。

伊俄卡斯特王后绝望地回到房间，结束了自己的生命。俄狄浦斯恐惧之下自抠双眼，离开底比斯，变成了一个可怜的老头。他的女儿安提戈涅（Antigone）跟随在他身边，四处流浪，没有一个城市肯接纳他们。最后，他们来到了雅典。

“你的安息之所应该受到祝福而不是被诅咒。”忒修斯听了他的故事之后说道，“你已经尽了人世间的一切努力去逃避这命运了。”

一直追逐他的复仇女神厄里倪厄斯放下了她们手中的鞭子，俄狄浦斯可以在安宁中死去了。

俄狄浦斯的两个儿子，厄特俄克勒斯（Eteocles）和波吕尼刻斯（Polynices），对他们父亲所遭受的苦难不闻不问。他们留在底比斯，为争夺王位而打了起来。最后他们达成协议，两个人轮流当国王，每年轮换一次。厄特俄克勒斯先当上了底比斯的统治者，一年的期限到了，他却不肯交出王位。

波吕尼刻斯愤然出走，他带走了哈耳摩尼亚的魔法项链，并发誓要带一支军队回来，用武力夺回他的合法王位。

他找到他的岳父阿戈斯国王，试图说服他派一支军队去底比斯。国王有一个姐姐，国王很听她的话。他这个姐姐年纪很大，而且爱慕虚荣。波吕尼刻斯允诺，只要她能够说服国王去攻打底比斯，他便把哈耳摩尼亚的项链送给她——这可以让她重新变得年轻美丽。国王的姐姐果然神通广大，国王和他的手下，还有七支勇士组成的军队都跟随波吕尼刻斯一起出发，去攻打底比斯的七个城门。但是他们大多数都再也回不来了。

七支大军攻不开底比斯的城门，而底比斯人也无法击退来犯的大军。所以，人们决定让这两兄弟单独格斗一次，胜者为王。

厄特俄克勒斯让他的兄弟受了重伤，但是波吕尼刻斯在倒下去之前也回敬给他致命的一击。他们两个并排倒在地上死了，所有的流血牺牲都白费了。

厄特俄克勒斯的儿子成了国王，而带来诸多不幸的哈耳摩尼亚的项链则被悬挂在特尔斐的一座神庙里，再也没有哪个女人会去戴上它。

金羊毛
The Golden Fleece

缪斯女神为英俊的伊阿宋（Jason）和他寻找金羊毛的历险唱起了颂歌。

约尔科斯（Iolcus）的伊阿宋由睿智的人马兽喀戎抚养长大，他的力气和教养都十分出众，这和他英俊的外表相得益彰。伊阿宋的父亲害怕夺走他王位的兄弟珀利阿斯（Pelias）会对他的后代下毒手，所以把他送到人马兽喀戎那里，请他将他抚养长大。在喀戎那空寂的山洞里，年轻的伊阿宋被培养成了一个擅长各种运动的英雄。长大成人之后，他告别了养父，要去约尔科斯夺回本属于他父亲的王位。

这个英俊的年轻人走下山时，正好遇上赫拉来到人间。伊阿宋金色的头发披在肩上，结实的身体裹在一张豹皮里。赫拉被他俊朗的外表吸引了。她飞快地把自己变成了一个干瘪的老太婆，无助地站在一条涨水的小河岸边，装出一副不敢过去的样子。伊阿宋彬彬有礼地提出要背她过河，并把她放在自己坚实的肩膀上。他开始涉水而过，起初她还很轻。但是伊阿宋每前进一步，老太婆就变得更沉一点，当他走到小河中间时，老太婆已经变得很重了，他的脚深深地陷在了河泥里，一只鞋也掉了，但还是勇敢地奋力向前走。当他到达对岸时，老太婆变回了女神赫拉的样子。

“喏，”她说，“你是我所喜爱的凡人，我将站在你一边，帮你从你叔叔珀利阿斯那里赢回王位。”赫拉十分乐意做出这样的承诺，因为她对珀利阿斯心存芥蒂，原因是他有一次向众神献祭时居然把她遗漏了。

伊阿宋谢过赫拉，满怀信心地继续赶路。当他来到约尔科斯时，人们都聚集在他周围，好奇这个陌生的英俊少年是谁。国王珀利阿斯看到他时却吓得面如土色。有一则神谕曾经预言，有一个只穿一只凉鞋的年轻人将会是他的末日克星。当伊阿宋说出他是谁、为何而来时，珀利阿斯还装出一副热情友好的样子，心里却怀着鬼胎，盘算着要除掉这个客人。珀利阿斯设宴款待了伊阿宋，跟他说好话，还许诺只要他能够完成一件英雄壮举以证明他担当得起国王的重任，他便会让出王位。

“在黑海岸边的科尔喀斯（Colchis）王国，”珀利阿斯说，“有一片幽暗的树林，林子里有根树枝，上面挂着像太阳一样闪闪发光的金羊毛。把金羊毛带来给我，王位就是你的了。”

金羊毛本来属于一只会飞的公羊，这只公羊曾被宙斯派去救塞萨利王子弗里克索斯（Phrixus）的性命。地里的庄稼没有收成，弗里克索斯那邪恶的继母就对他的父亲说，必须用他的儿子做祭品，好让他的臣民免于饥荒。伤心的国王建造了一座祭坛，并把自己的儿子放在了祭坛上。但是，宙斯讨厌用活人献祭。就在国王举起匕首之际，一只金毛羊从天而降，背起弗里克索斯飞走了。他们向着东方飞了很远，最后在科尔喀斯停了下来。科尔喀斯的国王知道弗里克索斯是天神派来的，就把自己的女儿嫁给了他，并将金毛羊作为祭品献给了天神。它金灿灿的毛被悬挂在一片神圣的小树林里，成为这个王国里最有价值

的珍宝。

珀利阿斯国王断定伊阿宋没法活着回来，因为他知道好战的科尔喀斯国王绝不允许别人取走金羊毛，而且还有一只永不睡觉的龙看护着它。但他并不知道伊阿宋有赫拉在暗中相助。

“给我木料和人手，为我建造一艘坚固的大船，我就可以出发了。”伊阿宋说。国王满足了他的要求，为他建造了一艘大船，叫作“阿耳戈号”（the Argo）。这是人们见过的最适合航海的船。受赫拉的指示，雅典娜在船首安放了一块神橡木。它在危急关头会说话，告诉伊阿宋该怎么办。

有了这样一艘大船，伊阿宋轻而易举地召集到了一大批英雄作为他的船员。就连赫拉克勒斯也带着他的年轻朋友许拉斯（Hylas）来了。卡拉伊斯（Calaïs）和仄忒斯（Zetes）——北风之神的两个带翅膀的儿子也加入了。俄耳甫斯也随同一道，用他的音乐鼓舞船员。很快，船上的五十支船桨都分别交到了五十位英雄的手里，英雄们立誓要和伊阿宋并肩面对一切艰险。

出发之前，这些自称为阿耳戈英雄的人向众神献上了丰厚的祭品，任何一位神祇都没有被遗漏。波塞冬十分高兴。他唤起了西风，阿耳戈号便挂满风帆向东方进发了。当风吹累了，渐渐停息下来时，阿耳戈英雄们就伸出船桨全力划动，俄耳甫斯拿起竖琴演奏起来，大船便劈波斩浪，快如箭矢。后来，英雄们一个个都力气耗尽，收起了船桨。只有赫拉克勒斯和伊阿宋仍旧坚持着，他们都想胜过对方。最后，伊阿宋昏了过去，但就在他向前倒下时，赫拉克勒斯的桨也断成了两截，所以两个人最终平分秋色。

阿耳戈英雄们在一个树木繁茂的海岸边登陆，好让赫拉克勒斯去砍树做一支新桨。当赫拉克勒斯出去寻找合适的树木时，他那年轻的朋友许拉斯拿了水罐去池塘打水。结果池塘中的仙女看见这美貌的男孩，便爱上了他。她将他拉下水，一起沉入了水底，许拉斯就这样消失得无影无踪了。

赫拉克勒斯找不到他的朋友，难过得发了疯。他在林间奔跑，呼喊着许拉斯的名字，把所有挡在他面前的东西都打倒在地。阿耳戈英雄们虽然勇敢，但他们看到赫拉克勒斯癫狂的样子也感到害怕。他们赶忙上船，丢下赫拉克勒斯出发了。

阿耳戈英雄们继续向东航行，到了一个国家，这个国家的国王因其知识和智慧而声名远播。阿耳戈英雄们上岸探听去科尔喀斯的路线，但是国王虚弱得无法回答他们的问题。他瘦得皮包骨头。每当食物端到他面前时，就会有三只讨厌的长着女人面孔的胖鸟——哈耳庇厄（Harpie）——俯冲下来将食物吃掉。它们吃不掉的就弄得又脏又臭，让人没法吃。王国里没有人能够赶走这三只哈耳庇厄。

阿耳戈英雄们为快要饿死的国王感到难过。他们让国王摆好桌子，当哈耳庇厄再次盘旋而下时，北风之神的儿子卡拉伊斯和仄忒斯便腾空而起，以比哈耳庇厄还快的速度飞过去，抓住了这些恶鸟，并重重地鞭笞它们。三只恶鸟险些丧命，它们逃到南方，再也不敢露面了。饱受饥渴之苦的国王终于可以安心地用餐。他对阿耳戈英雄们感激不尽，便把路线和沿途将遭遇的险阻都告诉了他们。他说，没有船可以到达科尔喀斯的海岸，因为通往黑海的水路被两块会动的岩石挡住了。这两块岩石时开时合，处在它们中间的任何东西都会被撞得粉碎。但是如果一艘船能够像飞鸟一样快速，它就有希望穿过去。他送给伊阿宋一只鸽子，让这只鸽子飞在船前面。如果鸽子能够飞过去，那他们还有可能穿得过去。如果连鸽子也飞不过去，他们最好掉头放弃。

阿耳戈英雄们告别了国王，向着魔岩驶去。他们老远就听到了撞击的声音，英雄们都颤抖了起来。但是，当魔岩分开时，伊阿宋放出鸽子，那鸽子就像一支箭似的从两块岩石中间飞了过去，只是在两块岩石又合并起来时，尾巴上被夹掉了几根羽毛。

“大家快划！”伊阿宋喊道。俄耳甫斯抓起竖琴弹奏了起来，乐曲激励着勇士们以前所未有的速度向前划去。当两块岩石分开时，阿耳戈号如飞矢一般冲了过去，只有船尾被并拢的岩石撞碎了一小块。魔岩再度分开并固定在那里。魔咒被打破了，从那之后船只便可以在黑海中安全地驶进驶出。

黑海是一片危险的航域，为了引导着阿耳戈英雄们度过种种危险，赫拉忙得一刻也闲不下来。在她的帮助下，伊阿宋带着他的船安然无恙地穿越了狂怒的风暴，经过了海盗海岸和食人岛，最终来到了科尔喀斯。

科尔喀斯的国王埃厄忒斯（Aeëtes）是太阳之神赫利俄斯的儿子，他是个一点儿也不好客的国王，事实上他会把所有来到他国家的异乡人都杀死。当他看到阿耳戈号靠岸时，便怒火中烧。伊阿宋带着他的随从来到王宫，说他们都是伟大的英雄，此行是来服务于国王以换取金羊毛的，这时候国王简直气得冒了烟。“好啊，”他对伊阿宋说，“明天，日出之后日落之前，你给我那喷火的公牛套上轭，犁出一块地来，并像底比斯的卡德摩斯那样在地里种上龙的牙齿。如果你做到了，金羊毛就是你的了。但要是你做不到，我将会把你和你们所有这些英雄的舌头都割去，把你们的脑袋都砍下来。”国王埃厄忒斯知道没有人能够受得了他那些公牛鼻子里喷出来的热浪。但是他不知道赫拉正在暗中帮助伊阿宋。

赫拉知道国王的女儿美狄亚（Medea），那个站在父亲身边的低眉顺目的姑娘，是唯一可以拯救伊阿宋的人。她是一个漂亮的年轻女巫师，是巫师女神赫卡忒（Hecate）的祭司，赫拉必须让她爱上伊阿宋。赫拉让阿芙洛狄忒派她的小儿子厄洛斯将他的爱情之箭射入美狄亚的心中。阿芙洛狄忒许诺给厄洛斯一个珐琅球，于是，就在美狄亚抬眼看向伊阿宋时，厄洛斯把箭射入了她心中。她金色的眼睛放射出光芒；她从来没有见过如此英俊的男子。她一心想着用她的法术将伊阿宋从她残酷的父亲那里拯救出来，为了救伊阿宋的命，她什么都可以做。她来到赫卡忒的神庙，祈求这位巫师女神帮助她。在巫师女神的指点下，她调制出一种神奇的药膏。只要涂上这种药膏，一天之内都能够刀枪不入，也不会被烈焰灼伤。

趁着天黑，美狄亚派人去找伊阿宋。当伊阿宋来到神殿时，她羞赧地告诉他，她爱上了他，以至于不惜背叛自己的父亲来拯救他。她将魔法药膏交给伊阿宋，告诉他只管靠近喷火的公牛，不用害怕。伊阿宋把这位年轻的女巫拥入怀中，对奥林匹斯的众神起誓，他要让她做自己的王后，并且永远爱她，直到他死去的那天。赫拉听着他的誓言，赞许地点了点头。

当早晨太阳升起时，伊阿宋径直来到喷火的公牛面前。这些公牛吼叫着朝他喷出烈焰，但是伊阿宋涂上了美狄亚的药膏，变得水火不侵、力大无穷，他给这些公牛套上轭具，来回驱使着它们，将整块地都犁好了。然后，他将龙牙种下，地垄沟里马上长出一群战士。伊阿宋像卡德摩斯一样，朝他们中间丢了一块石

头，并远远地看着他们互相残杀。在日落之前，他们都倒地死了。

伊阿宋完成了他的任务，但是国王埃厄忒斯并不打算信守约定。他把他的手下召集起来，命令他们天亮前去占领阿耳戈号，将这些异乡人杀死。悄悄地，美狄亚来到伊阿宋那里，告诉他现在必须取走理应属于他的金羊毛，并且在天亮之前逃离科尔喀斯。在夜色的掩护下，她领着伊阿宋来到黑树林，像太阳般金光闪闪的金羊毛挂在一根树枝上。那条永不睡觉的龙就盘踞在树干周围。但是美狄亚念起咒语，对那条龙施起了魔法。她用她那金色的眼睛盯住那条龙，用魔法驱使着它，让它陷入了深深的睡眠。伊阿宋迅速地取下金羊毛，带着美狄亚飞奔到正在待命的阿耳戈号上，悄无声息地溜出了海。

破晓时分，国王的人前来攻击阿耳戈号，却发现船已经开走了。一起消失的还有金羊毛和国王的女儿美狄亚。埃厄忒斯气红了脸，他带着庞大的科尔喀斯舰队前去追赶。他想夺回金羊毛，并且惩罚他的女儿。埃厄忒斯的一个儿子驾驶着最快的舰船，很快便赶上了阿耳戈号。

阿耳戈英雄们以为这次必败无疑，但是美狄亚再次拯救了他们。

她向她那站在船舵前的哥哥喊话，假装对自己的所作所为心存悔意。她说如果他能够跟她在附近的一个小岛上单独会面，她就跟他回去。同时，她悄悄地嘱咐伊阿宋埋伏起来，等她的哥哥一来就将他杀死。她知道她的父亲要为儿子举行葬礼，便会停止追赶。

赫拉和其他神惊恐地看着美狄亚，她的身上已经沾染了哥哥的鲜血。凡人所能犯下的最大罪过莫过于害死自己的亲人。宙斯生气地掷出了霹雳。顿时电闪雷鸣，海上怒涛汹涌。阿耳戈号船首上的神橡木说话了。“悲哀啊，”它说，“你们都要大难临头了。你们当中没有一个人能够回到希腊，除非伟大的女巫喀耳刻（Circe）答应洗去美狄亚和伊阿宋身上的罪恶。”

被怒号的狂风和高耸的巨浪弄得颠上倒下的阿耳戈英雄们开始寻找喀耳刻的住所。很久之后，在意大利海岸，他们找到了喀耳刻的宫殿。美狄亚警告阿耳戈英雄们不要离开船，因为喀耳刻是一个危险的女巫，她会把来到她岛上的人变成和他们本性最接近的动物，并以此为乐。有的人变成了狮子，有的人变成了兔子，但是大部分人都被变成了猪和驴。美狄亚拉着伊阿宋的手，好让伤害不要降临到他的头上。他们上了岸。

喀耳刻是美狄亚的姑姑。和太阳之神赫利俄斯所有的后代一样，她的眼睛里闪烁着金光。她看见美狄亚，便认出这是她的亲戚。但是她并不乐意见到她的侄女，因为她已经通过法术知道了美狄亚的所作所为。但她还是答应向宙斯献祭，请求他原谅美狄亚和伊阿宋的罪行。她献祭的鲜肉和蛋糕炙烤出来的香气飘到了宙斯那里，令他心情大悦。他听了喀耳刻的祷词，重新对美狄亚和伊阿宋展开了笑颜。

美狄亚和伊阿宋谢过喀耳刻，飞奔着回到船上。阿耳戈英雄们欣喜异常。现在他们可以向希腊进发了。但是他们还要经过各种险阻和奇怪的海域。不久，他们来到了塞壬女妖（the Sirens）居住的岛屿。塞壬女妖一半是鸟，一半是女人，和令人憎恶的哈耳庇厄不一样，她们是令人着迷的尤物。她们坐在悬崖上，半藏在浪花后面，唱着美妙的歌曲，所有听到她们唱歌的水手都会跳进海里向她们游去，最终却只能淹死在水中，或者精力耗尽而死在塞壬

女妖的脚下。当塞壬女妖们魅惑的歌声传到阿耳戈英雄们耳朵里时，俄耳甫斯拿起竖琴，唱起了响亮而美妙的歌曲，将其他的声音统统淹没，所以没有一个阿耳戈英雄从船上跳下。

不久后，阿耳戈号要经过一个狭窄的海峡，两只妖怪把守在那里。海峡的一边蹲伏着妖怪斯库拉（Scylla）。她的腰部以上看上去像个女人，但是她的屁股下面不是腿，而是长着六只凶狠、咆哮的恶犬，它们将任何靠近的物体都撕成碎片。妖怪卡律布迪斯（Charybdis）住在海峡的另一边。她永远也吃不饱，所有进入到她的水域的船只都会被她吞进喉咙。

阿耳戈号无助地在两只妖怪间徘徊着，阿耳戈英雄们再次陷入了茫然不知所措的境地，就在这时，顽皮的海中仙子涅瑞德斯升出了海面，是赫拉命令她们来的。她们抬起阿耳戈号，在手中传递着把它送过了危险水域，来到宽阔的海面。波塞冬唤起西风，阿耳戈号挂满风帆向希腊驶去。

当他们看见希腊的海岸之时，勇敢的水手们大声欢呼了起来。他们离开很多年，心里充满了思乡之情。但是当阿耳戈号靠近约尔科斯港口时，一名渔翁向船上招手，他警告伊阿宋说，国王珀利阿斯得知他安全返航的消息，已经计划好了要将他杀死。叔父的背信弃义令伊阿宋情绪低落，美狄亚眼睛里却泛出亮光，她要求独自上岸。再一次，她想要拯救他的性命。

她装扮成一个年迈的女巫，来到了约尔科斯，她说自己有一种神奇的草药可卖，这草药可以令老的东西重新焕发青春。人们围着她，想知道这个女巫师是从哪里来的。珀利阿斯也亲自走出王宫，要求她证明自己所说的都是真的，因为他觉得自己正在变老。

“从你的羊群里牵一头最老的出来，我就可以向你展示一下我的草药的魔力。”美狄亚说。

一只老山羊被带到了她面前，她把山羊放进一口装满水的大锅里面。她在水面上撒了一些有魔法的草药。嚯！大锅里的水一下子沸腾了，一只活蹦乱跳的小羊羔从蒸汽和泡泡中冒了出来。

国王珀利阿斯让美狄亚也把他变得年轻。美狄亚说，这只有国王的女儿可以做到，但她非常乐意把神奇的草药卖给他们。但是她给他们的草药根本没有什么魔法，国王珀利阿斯被他自己的女儿烧死在了沸腾的大锅里。

这下约尔科斯的王位是伊阿宋的了，但是美狄亚再次犯下了可怕的罪行。她骗了无辜的女孩，让她们杀死了自己的父亲。众神都不再喜欢她，她由一个可爱的年轻女巫变成了一个邪恶的巫婆。约尔科斯的人都拒绝让她做他们的王后，并且让另一个人替代伊阿宋做了国王。伊阿宋失去了王位，同时也失去了对美狄亚的爱恋。他忘记了自己曾经发誓至死不渝地爱她，也忘了她是为他才犯下的罪行。他让美狄亚离开他，让他好去娶科林斯的公主，并且继承公主父亲的王位。

美狄亚心中充满了鄙夷和愤怒，她变得越来越像一个邪魔巫师。为了报复伊阿宋，她送了一条有魔法的裙子给他的新娘。这是一件漂亮的长裙，但是新娘一穿上它，便化为一团火焰，整个王宫也变成了一片火海。随后，美狄亚驾着一辆由两条龙拉的马车消失在一片黑色的云团里。

伊阿宋再也没有找到过快乐，因为他背弃了自己对美狄亚的神圣誓言，赫拉因而也不再青睐他。他不再美貌，好运和朋友都弃他而去。有一天，孤独而被人遗忘的伊阿宋坐在那曾经满载荣耀的船——阿耳戈号的阴影里，这艘船如今在科林斯的海滩上腐烂着。突然，船首上的神像木落下来，掉在他头上，把他砸死了。

金羊毛被挂在特尔斐的阿波罗神庙中，作为一个奇迹供所有的希腊人瞻仰，同时也让人们永远都记得伊阿宋和阿耳戈英雄的伟大事迹。

捕猎卡吕冬野猪
The Calydonian Boar Hunt

卡吕冬（Calydonia）的梅利埃格（Meleager）是曾与伊阿宋一起远航的阿耳戈英雄之一。他那高超的掷矛技术无人能敌。但是面对在他父亲的王国里横冲直撞的可怕野猪时，他也无能为力。有一天，国王在向众神献祭时唯独忘记了阿尔忒弥斯。愤怒的女神派了一头有史以来最大的野猪来报复他。这头野猪长着象牙般粗壮的獠牙和钢铁般坚硬的猪毛。梅利埃格邀请了阿耳戈英雄和希腊所有伟大的运动员来卡吕冬围捕这头可怕的野兽。谁能射杀这头卡吕冬野猪，谁就将获得无限的荣耀。

很多英雄都参与了捕猎行动，其中有一个叫阿塔兰忒（Atalanta）的姑娘。

她是全希腊跑得最快的人，同时也是一名出色的女猎手。很多男人都抱怨起来，不愿意和一个姑娘一起狩猎，但是梅利埃格坚持说，这位姑娘比他们所有的人跑得都快，当然应该欢迎她前来参加这场围猎。男人们虽然仍有些不满，也只好让步。

一连几天，英雄们都在卡吕冬王宫里宴饮，然后向众神献上了丰厚的祭品，便出发去捕猎了。他们把野猪赶出巢穴，它一冲出来，长矛和箭矢就从四面八方射来。一阵喧嚣之后，有七个人已经倒在地上死去了，有的是被野猪杀死的，有的死于他们激动的同伴的箭下。只有阿塔兰忒一个人始终保持着冷静的头脑。她飞速地从这里跑到那里，终于找到一个绝佳的射击地点，然后她飞快地射出了一箭。一个英雄刚好在狂奔的野猪前面被绊倒，阿塔兰忒的这支箭射中了野猪，救了他的命。紧接着梅利埃格向前跃出一步，用尽平生之力掷出了他的长矛。这头野兽翻滚了几下，倒在地上死了。

梅利埃格把猪皮和獠牙都给了阿塔兰忒。这些战利品属于她，梅利埃格说，因为正是她阻止了野猪的进攻。男人们又一次提出了抗议，因为眼看着一个姑娘拿走了所有的荣誉，这让他们太失颜面了。梅利埃格的两个舅舅嘲讽地说他肯定是爱上了这个姑娘。“等你的妻子知道了可有你好看的！”他们不怀好意地笑着说。

梅利埃格狂怒之下将他的长矛掷向正在嘲笑他的舅舅们，把他们都杀死了。梅利埃格的母亲听说她的儿子把她的兄弟都杀害了，也火冒三丈。她跑到藏宝箱前，拿出一块已经烧焦一半的木柴。这是一块维系着梅利埃格生命的神奇木柴。

梅利埃格出生时，这根木柴正在壁炉中燃烧。命运三女神前来探望这个婴儿，他母亲无意中听到她们说，真是太可惜了，这根木柴一烧完，这个漂亮的小孩就要死了。梅利埃格的母亲赶紧抓起这根木柴，将火熄灭，并把它和自己最珍贵的珠宝藏在一起。这样梅利埃格才得以活下来，并成为一个伟大的英雄。

现在，王后怒火中烧，将这根旧干柴扔进了火中。就在它燃起火焰并化为一团灰烬之时，梅利埃格也感到一阵烧灼之痛贯穿全身，倒地身亡了。

对卡吕冬野猪的围捕以盛宴开始，却以葬礼结束。只有阿塔兰忒是开心的，她在与希腊最伟大的英雄们的比赛中赢得了自己的战利品。

爱情之果和纷争之果
The Apples of Love and the Apple of Discord

阿塔兰忒奔跑起来的样子是那么优雅，很多男子都因此爱上了她，但是她和阿尔忒弥斯一样，不爱任何男子。

阿塔兰忒一出生，她的父亲就狠心地将她遗弃在荒野里，因为他想要的是一个儿子。但是她并没有死掉。一头母熊听到了她的哭声，温柔地将她衔回了自己的洞穴，哺育她并把她和自己的幼崽一起抚养长大。

几年后，一位猎人看到一个女孩儿在树林中和野兽一起奔跑，感到十分惊奇，他设下陷阱抓住她并把她带回了家。不久，她就学会了说话并且举止也开始变得像人一样。她的养父对她那飞快的步伐感到非常骄傲。他带她去参加运动会，赢得了所有的比赛。她的声名传遍了希腊。这时，她的亲生父亲非常骄傲地宣称阿塔兰忒就是他失散多年的女儿。他是一个国王，而一个国王的女儿是不能到处乱跑，不嫁人的，所以这位国王开始为她物色合适的丈夫。但是阿塔兰忒并不想要一个丈夫。为了保持平静的生活，她说她只和在赛跑中赢了她的男子结婚。但是，任何一个和她比赛输了的男子都必须留下性命。她想这足以吓跑所有追求者。可她是那样迷人，所以还是有很多追求者想试试他们的运气，最终都丢了性命。

有一天，一个名叫墨拉尼昂（Melanion）的年轻王子来追求她。他比其他人都英俊潇洒。他知道自己跑不过阿塔兰忒，所以他向阿芙洛狄忒献祭，请求她的帮助。爱神很想看到所有美丽的女子都结婚，她给了墨拉尼昂三个金苹果，并告诉他该怎么做。

比赛开始时，阿塔兰忒确信自己会取胜，就让墨拉尼昂先跑。结果，当她追上来时，墨拉尼昂丢了一个金苹果在她脚边。苹果散发出美丽的光芒，阿塔兰忒情不自禁地停下来捡它。不一会儿，阿塔兰忒又追了上来，墨拉尼昂又丢出第二个苹果，这次他丢得远了点，她只好离开跑道去追那个苹果。当墨拉尼昂再次听到身后传来她轻捷的脚步声时，便把第三个苹果远远地丢进了灌木丛中。阿塔兰忒又跑去找那个苹果，当她找到时，墨拉尼昂已经越过了终点线。墨拉尼昂终于赢得了阿塔兰忒，他们结了婚。阿塔兰忒非常珍视自己的金苹果，并且爱上了自己聪明的丈夫。他们幸福地生活了好多年，从未忘记向将他们撮合到一起的阿芙洛狄忒供奉祭品。可是他们没有给予宙斯应有的尊重。宙斯就把他们变成了一对狮子，以示惩罚。从此，他们就像狮子一样肩并肩地穿行在森林里。

珀琉斯（Peleus）是塞萨利的国王。他一生都得感谢阿塔兰忒，因为当他在卡吕冬野猪前被绊倒时，是阿塔兰忒及时地射出一箭救了他。他曾经是阿耳戈英雄之一，也是希腊最伟大的运动员之一，诸神对他青眼有加。宙斯把美丽的海中女神西蒂斯赐予他做妻子，所有的神祇都被邀请前去参加婚礼。只有纷争女神厄里斯没有受到邀请。她非常生气，当每个人都欢享宴饮之际，她扔了一个金苹果在众多宾客之中，喊道："最美的女神将得到它！"

赫拉、阿芙洛狄忒和雅典娜都认为自己是最美的，于是都跑去捡。厄里斯扔出去的不是代表爱情的苹果，而是导致纷争的苹果，三个女神为谁该得到这个金苹果而争吵起来。婚礼在不愉快的气氛中终止了，在愈演愈烈的争吵中，女神们离开婚宴回到了奥林匹斯山。

新娘西蒂斯因为嫁给了一个凡人而闷闷不乐，因为这样一来她的孩子将无法像她一样永生。没有神敢跟她结合，因为有一则神谕预示她将为自己的丈夫生下一个儿子，这个儿子会比他的父亲更伟大。当然，珀琉斯则认为自己是最幸运的人。

西蒂斯给她的丈夫生了很多的孩子。为了让他们获得永生，她把他们放在圣火上炙烤，以去除他们的凡性，但是这些孩子没有一个能经受得起这种折磨，都没能活下来。最后，她生了一个比其他几个都健壮的男孩，他承受住了火的考验，她几乎要成功地除掉他的凡性了，但恰在这时珀琉斯冲进她的房间，将孩子一把夺走了。西蒂斯非常伤心和失望，她回到大海里再也没有回来。这个小男孩被半人半马族的喀戎抚养长大，成长为希腊有史以来最伟大的战士。他全身刀枪不入，除了脚后跟，因为那是他母亲将他放在圣火上炙烤时手握着而没被烤过的地方。他就是阿喀琉斯（Achilles）。

与此同时，奥林匹斯山上的纷争一直没有停息。三位女神的争吵仍在继续，没有一个神敢说她们当中到底谁最漂亮。

有一天，宙斯俯瞰大地时，目光落到了特洛伊（Troy）王子帕里斯（Paris）身上。他与大多数特洛伊王族的人一样，长得极为英俊。他的叔公伽倪墨德当年也是一个非常好看的男孩，以至于当时宙斯变幻成一只老鹰，把他从他父亲那儿偷偷地抓到奥林匹斯山上，做他的司酒少年。帕里斯的另一个亲戚，安喀塞斯（Anchises）也非常英俊，连阿芙洛狄忒都爱上了他。她把自己变成一个公主的模样，和他结了婚，还为他生了一个儿子，名叫埃涅阿斯（Aeneas）。

帕里斯的相貌比他所有的亲族还要出众。宙斯想，像他这般英俊的人物应该是美的最佳裁判者。他让赫尔墨斯把三位女神带下山，到离特洛伊很近的艾达山（Mount Ida）去找在那里为王室放牧的帕里斯，让他给她们做个评判。

当三位光芒四射的女神站在他面前时，帕里斯盯着她们，惊讶得一句话也说不出来。赫尔墨斯把金苹果递给他，让他把这苹果送给她们中最美丽的一位。

“把它给我，”有着雪白臂膀的赫拉说，“整个亚洲都会成为你的国土。”

“选我，”长着灰色眼睛的雅典娜说，“你将会成为最睿智的人。”

“把苹果给我，世间最美丽的女人将属于你。”阿芙洛狄忒说。

帕里斯还年轻，他喜欢美貌胜过权力和智慧，他把苹果给了阿芙洛狄忒。

阿芙洛狄忒高兴地接过苹果，压根儿就没想到世上最美的女人海伦（Helen）——斯巴达（Sparta）的王后，已经有了丈夫。

缪斯女神为特洛伊的海伦那绝世的美貌唱起了美妙的颂歌。海伦是宙斯的女儿，她的美貌自她出生之时就已经是一个传奇。宙斯化身为一只天鹅从奥林匹斯山上飞下来，追求她的母亲勒达（Leda）。

勒达生下了两个蓝色的蛋，当这两个蛋被孵化时，海伦和她的兄弟波吕丢刻斯（Pollux）从其中一个蛋中破壳而出。他们是宙斯的孩子，可获永生。而从另一个蛋里孵出来的是他们同母异父的兄妹——克吕泰涅斯特拉（Clytemnestra）和卡斯托耳（Castor），他们是勒达和她凡间的丈夫——国王廷达柔斯（Tyndareus）的孩子。

卡斯托耳和波吕丢刻斯从小就形影不离，他们两个都成长为了不起的运动健将。卡斯托耳以擅长驯马而闻名于世，波吕丢刻斯则成为著名的拳击手。他们保护着彼此直至死亡。他们并肩作战，波吕丢刻斯后来去了奥林匹斯山，而卡斯托耳因为是凡人，则去了地府。他们非常想念彼此，宙斯也很同情他们，便允许波吕丢刻斯把他一半的神性给他的兄弟。从此，这对幸福的双胞胎就相随相伴，一半时间住在奥林匹斯山上，另一半时间住在哈得斯的地府。

海伦和克吕泰涅斯特拉这两姐妹在她们凡间的父亲——国王廷达柔斯的王宫里长大。克吕泰涅斯特拉不久就与伟大的迈锡尼国王阿伽门农（Agamemnon）结了婚。但是海伦有那么多的追求者，廷达柔斯也不知道该选择谁。他怕一旦把她许给一个人，其他被拒绝的人会聚集起来攻打他。他的王宫被海伦的追求者包围着，更多的追求者还在不断赶来。在他们中间有个叫奥德修斯

（Odysseus）的年轻王子。他很聪明，当他看到那么多的追求者时，便撤回了自己的求婚。他知道，在像海伦这样迷人的女子身上，战争永远不会止息。他转而向他温柔的表妹珀涅罗珀（Penelope）求婚，并且向廷达柔斯国王提供了解决这个问题的方法。他必须让所有的追求者都接受他为海伦选中的丈夫，并且发誓一旦有人想夺走她，所有的人都必须帮助这个人把海伦赢回来。追求者都同意了。每个人都希望自己就是国王所选中的那个人，他们都发了誓。廷达柔斯最终把海伦嫁给了斯巴达的墨涅拉厄斯（Menelaus），其他的追求者都毫无怨言地离开了。

当阿芙洛狄忒把她许诺给帕里斯时，海伦已经作为斯巴达的王后幸福地生活了很多年。她那世间最美女人的名声也四处传播。特洛伊人恳求帕里斯忘掉阿芙洛狄忒的承诺，否则肯定会有可怕的灾难降临到他们头上。但是帕里斯根本听不进这些忠告，他穿越爱琴海，去将海伦从墨涅拉厄斯国王身边偷走并带回特洛伊。

帕里斯进入斯巴达王宫，海伦正安详而幸福地坐在那儿，在侍女们的环绕中，编织着最好的羊毛。当她抬头看到帕里斯时，厄洛斯将爱情之箭射向她的心房。她毫不犹豫地收拾好珍爱之物，与帕里斯私奔去往特洛伊。

一阵清风将他们带到了海上，但当他们正要驶向深海时，紫红色的水域变得平滑如镜、波澜不惊，和善的老海神涅柔斯从海洋深处升起。他警告他们赶紧回去，否则可怕的灾难将会降临到他们和亲人的头上。但是海伦和帕里斯眼里只有彼此，根本听不进他的劝告。

他们在特洛伊上岸，特洛伊人高兴地出来迎接她。他们为世间最美的女人如今成为特洛伊的海伦而自豪。

但是，墨涅拉厄斯可不是个肯善罢甘休的人。他才不管是不是女神把他的王后许诺给了帕里斯呢。他向海伦当年的追求者们提起了他们曾经立下的誓言。这些人都全副武装地加入了他的队伍。不久，一支庞大的希腊舰队就抵达了特洛伊，他们要把海伦带回斯巴达。特洛伊人拒绝放弃海伦，况且特洛伊城被阿波罗和波塞冬筑起的高墙环绕着，要想攻克它也绝非易事。经过很长时间的谈判，双方决定让帕里斯和墨涅拉厄斯单独决斗，海伦将属于胜利者。帕里斯不是勇士，他只喜欢躺在丝质的枕头上沉醉地看着海伦美丽的眼睛。但是，阿芙洛狄忒来解救他了。她把他藏在云团中。由于墨涅拉厄斯根本找不到他的对手，决斗的办法行不通，双方的军队就只好正面交锋了。

整整十年，希腊人和特洛伊人都在为争夺海伦而征战。众神饶有兴致地看着这一切，甚至还参与到战事中去。赫拉因为帕里斯没有把苹果给她而耿耿于怀，站在了希腊人一边。智慧和正义之神雅典娜也对帕里斯心存愠怒，作为特洛伊城守护神的她竟也站到了希腊一边。阿瑞斯是哪儿打得最激烈就往哪儿跑，负伤后，他就会大声号叫来震慑两边的军队。甜美的阿芙洛狄忒也加入日益白热化的战斗，帮助她所青睐的帕里斯，而且还受了伤。“够了！”宙斯说，他命令所有的神都撤出这场战争。他们坐在特洛伊的城墙上，看着这些凡人会有什么结果。双方都有许多伟大的英雄倒下了。但是希腊人无法摧毁特洛伊巍峨的城墙，而只要西蒂斯那刀枪不入的儿子阿喀琉斯还在为希腊人而战，特洛伊人就也赶不走希腊人。尽管帕里斯并非伟大的射手，命运还是选择了他来结果伟大的英雄阿喀琉斯。阿波罗在别的神没注意到他时跑到帕里斯的身边，在他张弓搭箭之际给了他一些指点。这支箭射中了阿喀琉斯的脚踵，这是他身上唯一一个会受伤的地方。受了这致命的伤，阿喀琉斯倒在了地上。希腊人为他们的英雄阿喀琉斯的殒落而深感哀痛，他们要向帕里斯复仇。帕里斯在被赫拉克勒斯给菲罗克忒忒斯的毒箭射中后也倒下了。

不久，希腊人拆除营帐，登船离开了。他们在海岸上留下了一匹巨大的木马。特洛伊人以为他们终于战胜了希腊人。他们把木马当做战利品拉进城中。但是这匹木马是中空的，里面藏着许多希腊战士。到了深夜，他们爬出来把城门打开。原来，狡猾的希腊人并没有离开，他们躲在一个岛屿的后面。现在他们涌入城中，骄傲的特洛伊城被摧毁了。

海伦被凯旋之师带回了斯巴达，她美丽依旧，像以前一样坐在侍女中间，用深紫和浅紫的线在最好的羊毛料上刺绣。

在特洛伊王宫里，除了阿芙洛狄忒的儿子埃涅阿斯、他的父亲和他的小儿子之外再没有一个人。女神回来把他们带离这硝烟弥漫的废墟，去往安全之地了。

埃涅阿斯从一块大陆游荡到另一块大陆，最后来到了意大利。在那儿他建立了一个王国。诸神宠爱地看着他，因为命中注定他的子孙将建立起伟大的城市罗马。

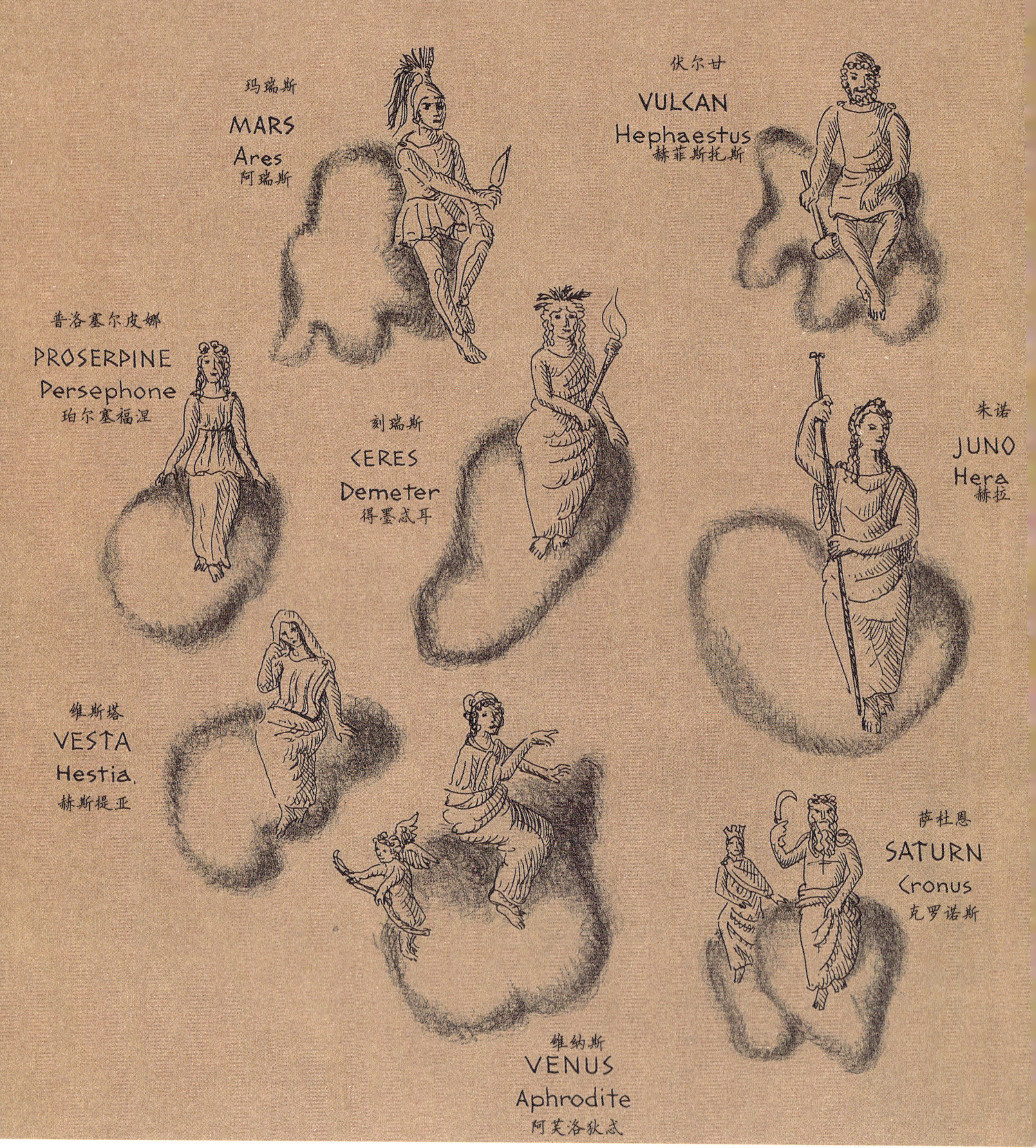

后来确实如此。罗马人为奥林匹斯山诸神建起了恢宏的神庙，这些神庙或许没有希腊的神庙美，但更为奢华，诸神的荣耀也更胜以往。他们被赋予了希

腊名字之外的罗马名字。但他们还是一样的神，虽然今天我们更熟悉的是他们的罗马名字。

Scorpion
Serpent holder
Cup
Hydra
Hercules
Eagle
Lyre
Dragon
Lion
Big Bear
Little Bear
Dolphin
Swan
Cepheus
Crab
Twins
Andromeda
Perseus
Ram
Bull
Whale

万事都有终了时，宙斯和奥林匹斯山诸神的统治也是。他们的辉煌如今在世间所余只是破败的殿宇和庄严的塑像。缪斯的歌声也归于沉寂，但她们的歌咏流传至今，诸神挂在天上的星座仍在深蓝的天穹中闪烁。

D'AULAIRES' BOOK OF GREEK MYTHS

INGRI D'AULAIRE
&
EDGAR PARIN D'AULAIRE

IN OLDEN TIMES

When men still worshiped ugly idols, there lived in the land of Greece a folk of shepherds and herdsmen who cherished light and beauty. They did not worship dark idols like their neighbors, but created instead their own beautiful, radiant gods.

The Greek gods looked much like people and acted like them, too, only they were taller, handsomer and could do no wrong. Fire-breathing monsters and beasts with many heads stood for all that was dark and wicked. They were for gods and great heroes to conquer.

The gods lived on top of Olympus, a mountain so high and steep that no man could climb it and see them in their shining palace. But they often descended to earth, sometimes in their own shapes, sometimes disguised as humans or animals.

Mortals worshiped the gods and the gods honored Mother Earth. They had all sprung from her, for she was the beginning of all life.

GAEA, MOTHER EARTH

GAEA, the Earth, came out of darkness so long ago that nobody knows when or how. Earth was young and lonesome, for nothing lived on her yet. Above her rose Uranus, the Sky, dark and blue, set all over with sparkling stars. He was magnificent to behold, and young Earth looked up at him and fell in love with him. Sky smiled down at Earth, twinkling with his countless stars, and they were joined in love. Soon young Earth became Mother Earth, the mother of all things living. All her children loved their warm and bountiful mother and feared their mighty father, Uranus, lord of the universe.

THE TITANS

THE TITANS were the first children of Mother Earth. They were the first gods, taller than the mountains she created to serve them as thrones, and both Earth and Sky were proud of them. There were six Titans, six glorious gods, and they had six sisters, the Titanesses, whom they took for their wives.

When Gaea again gave birth, Uranus was not proud. Their new children were also huge, but each had only one glowing eye set in the middle of his forehead. They were the three Cyclopes and they were named Lightning, Thunder, and Thunderbolt. They were not handsome gods, but tremendously strong smiths. Sparks from their heavy hammers flashed across the sky and lit up the heavens so brightly that even their father's stars faded.

After a while Mother Earth bore three more sons. Uranus looked at them with disgust. Each of them had fifty heads and a hundred strong arms. He hated to see such ugly creatures walk about on lovely Earth, so he seized them and their brothers the Cyclopes and flung them into Tartarus, the deepest, darkest pit under the earth.

Mother Earth loved her children and could not forgive her husband for his cruelty to them. Out of hardest flint she fashioned a sickle and spoke to her sons the Titans:

"Take this weapon, make an end to your father's cruelty and set your brothers free."

Fear took hold of five of the Titans and they trembled and refused. Only Cronus, the youngest but the strongest, dared to take the sickle. He fell upon his father. Uranus could not withstand the weapon wielded by his strong son and he fled, giving up his powers.

Mother Earth made Pontus, the boundless seas, her second husband, and from this union sprang the gods of the watery depths. And from her rich ground grew an abundance of trees and flowers and, out of her crevices, sprites, beasts, and early man crept forth.

CRONUS was now the lord of the universe. He sat on the highest mountain and ruled over heaven and earth with a firm hand. The other gods obeyed his will and early man worshiped him. This was man's Golden Age. Men lived happily and in peace with the gods and each other. They did not kill and they had no locks on their doors, for theft had not yet been invented.

But Cronus did not set his monstrous brothers free, and Mother Earth was angry with him and plotted his downfall. She had to wait, for no god yet born was strong enough to oppose him. But she knew that one of his sons would be stronger than he, just as Cronus had been stronger than his father. Cronus knew it too, so every time his Titaness-wife Rhea gave birth, he took the newborn god and swallowed it. With all of his offspring securely inside him, he had nothing to fear.

But Rhea mourned. Her five sisters, who had married the five other Titans, were surrounded by their Titan children, while she was all alone. When Rhea expected her sixth child, she asked Mother Earth to help her save the child from his father. That was just what Mother Earth had been waiting for. She gave her daughter whispered advice, and Rhea went away smiling.

As soon as Rhea had borne her child, the god Zeus, she hid him.Then she wrapped a stone in baby clothes and gave it to her husband to swallow instead of her son. Cronus was fooled and swallowed the stone, and the little god Zeus was spirited away to a secret cave on the island of Crete. Old Cronus never heard the cries of his young son, for Mother Earth set noisy earth sprites outside the cave. They made such a clatter, beating their shields with their swords, that other sounds were drowned out.

ZEUS AND HIS FAMILY

ZEUS was tended by gentle nymphs and was nursed by the fairy goat Amaltheia. From the horns of the goat flowed ambrosia and nectar, the food and drink of the gods. Zeus grew rapidly, and it was not long before he strode out of the cave as a great new god. To thank the nymphs for tending him so well, he gave them the horns of the goat. They were horns of plenty and could never be emptied. From the hide of the goat he made for himself an impenetrable breastplate, the Aegis, and now he was so strong that Cronus could do nothing against him.

Young Zeus chose Metis, a Titan's daughter, for his first wife. She was the goddess of prudence, and he needed her good advice. She warned him not to try alone to overthrow his child-devouring father, for Cronus had all the other Titans and their sons on his side. First Zeus must also have strong allies.

Metis went to Cronus and cunningly tricked him into eating a magic herb. He thought that the herb would make him unconquerable. Instead it made him so sick that he vomited up not only the stone he had swallowed, but his five other children as well. They were the gods Hades and Poseidon and the goddesses Hestia, Demeter, and Hera, all mighty gods who right away joined forces with Zeus. When Cronus saw the six young gods rising against him, he knew that his hour had come and he surrendered his powers and fled.

Now Zeus was the lord of the universe. He did not want to rule alone. He shared his powers with his brothers and sisters. But the Titans and their sons revolted. They refused to let themselves be ruled by the new gods. Only Prometheus and his brother Epimetheus left the Titans to join Zeus, for Prometheus could look into the future and he knew that Zeus would win.

Zeus freed the monstrous sons of Mother Earth from Tartarus.

Gratefully the hundred-armed ones fought for him with all their strength, and the Cyclopes forged mighty weapons for him and his brothers.

They made a trident for Poseidon. It was so forceful that when he struck the ground with it, the earth shook, and when he struck the sea, frothing waves stood mountain high.

For Hades they made a cap of invisibility so he could strike his enemies unseen, and for Zeus they forged lightning bolts. Armed with them, he was the mightiest god of them all, nothing could stand against him and his thunderbolts. The Titans fought a bitter battle, but at last they had to surrender, and Zeus locked them up in Tartarus. The hundred-armed monsters went to stand guard at the gates to see that they never escaped. Atlas, the strongest of the Titans, was sent to the end of the world to carry forever the vault of the sky on his shoulders.

Angry with Zeus for sending her sons the Titans into the dark pit of Tartarus, Mother Earth now brought forth two terrible monsters, Typhon and his mate, Echidna, and sent them against Zeus. They were so fearful that when the gods saw them they changed themselves into animals and fled in terror. Typhon's hundred horrible heads touched the stars, venom dripped from his evil eyes, and lava and red-hot stones poured from his gaping mouths. Hissing like a hundred snakes and roaring like a hundred lions, he tore up whole mountains and threw them at the gods.

Zeus soon regained his courage and turned, and when the other gods saw him taking his stand, they came back to help him fight the monster. A terrible battle raged, and hardly a living creature was left on earth. But Zeus was fated to win, and as Typhon tore up huge Mount Aetna to hurl at the gods, Zeus struck it with a hundred well-aimed thunderbolts and the mountain fell back, pinning Typhon underneath. There the monster lies to this very day, belching fire, lava, and smoke through the top of the mountain.

Echidna, his hideous mate, escaped destruction. She cowered in a cave, protecting Typhon's dreadful offspring, and Zeus let them live as a challenge to future heroes.

Now at last Mother Earth gave up her struggle. There were no more upheavals, and the wounds of the war soon healed. The mountains stood firmly anchored. The seas had their shores. The rivers had their riverbeds and oxhorned river-gods watched over them, and each tree and each spring had its nymph. The earth again was green and fruitful and Zeus could begin to rule in peace.

The one-eyed Cyclopes were not only smiths but masons as well, and they built a towering palace for the gods on top of Mount Olympus, the highest mountain in Greece. The palace was hidden in clouds, and the goddesses of the seasons rolled them away whenever a god wanted to go down to earth. Nobody else could pass through the gate of clouds.

Iris, the fleet-footed messenger of the gods, had her own path down to earth. Dressed in a gown of iridescent drops, she ran along the rainbow on her busy errands between Olympus and earth.

In the gleaming hall of the palace, where light never failed, the Olympian gods sat on twelve golden thrones and reigned over heaven and earth. There were twelve great gods, for Zeus shared his powers, not only with his brothers and sisters, but with six of his children and the goddess of love as well.

Zeus himself sat on the highest throne, with a bucketful of thunderbolts beside him. On his right sat his youngest sister, Hera, whom he had chosen from all his wives as his queen. Beside her sat her son, Ares, god of war, and Hephaestus, god of fire, with Aphrodite, goddess of love, between them. Next was Zeus's son Hermes, the herald of the gods, and Zeus's sister Demeter, goddess of the harvest with her daughter, Persephone, on her lap. On the left of Zeus sat his brother Poseidon, the lord of the sea. Next to him sat the four children of Zeus: Athena, the twins Apollo and Artemis, and Dionysus, the youngest of the gods. Athena was the goddess of wisdom, Apollo, the god of light and music, Artemis, goddess of the hunt, and Dionysus, the god of wine.

Hestia, the eldest sister of Zeus, was goddess of the hearth. She had no throne, but tended the sacred fire in the hall, and every hearth on earth was her altar. She was the gentlest of all the Olympians.

Hades, the eldest brother of Zeus, was the lord of the dead. He preferred to stay in his gloomy palace in the underworld and never went to Olympus.

The gods themselves could not die, for divine ichor flowed in their veins instead of blood. Most of the time they lived happily together, feasting on sweet-smelling ambrosia and nectar, but when their wills clashed, there were violent quarrels. Then Zeus would reach for a thunderbolt and the Olympians would tremble and fall to order, for Zeus alone was stronger than all the other gods together.

•—• HERA

HERA, the beautiful queen of Olympus, was a very jealous wife. Even Zeus, who was afraid of nothing, feared her fits of temper. She hated all his other wives, and when Zeus first asked her to be his wife, she refused. Slyly Zeus created a thunderstorm, changed himself into a little cuckoo, and, pretending to be in distress, he flew into Hera's arms for protection. She pitied the wet little bird and hugged it close to keep it warm, but all of a sudden she found herself holding mighty Zeus in her arms instead of the bird.

Thus Zeus won Hera and all nature burst into bloom for their wedding. Mother Earth gave the bride a little apple tree that bore golden apples of immortality. Hera treasured the tree and planted it in the garden of the Hesperides, her secret garden far to the west. She put a hundredheaded dragon under the tree to guard the apples and ordered the three Nymphs of the Hesperides to water and care for the tree.

Zeus loved Hera dearly, but he was also very fond of rocky Greece. He often sneaked down to earth in disguise to marry mortal girls. The more wives he had, the more children he would have, and all the better for Greece! All his children would inherit some of his greatness and become great heroes and rulers. But Hera in her jealous rage tormented his other wives and children, and even Zeus was powerless to stop her. She knew how tricky Zeus could be and kept very close watch over him.

One day as Hera looked down on earth, she spied a small dark thundercloud where no cloud should have been. She rushed down and darted into the cloud. Zeus was there just as she had suspected, but with him was only a little snow-white cow. He had seen Hera coming and, to protect his newest bride Io from her wrath, he had changed the girl into a cow. Alas! The cow was as lovely as the girl, and Hera was not deceived, but she pretended to suspect nothing and begged Zeus to let her have the dainty cow. Zeus could not well refuse his queen such a little wish without giving himself away, and he had to give her the cow. Hera tied poor Io to a tree and sent her servant Argus to keep watch over her.

Argus had a hundred bright eyes placed all over his body. He was so big and strong that singlehandedly he had made an end to the monstrous Echidna, who had lived in a cave and had devoured all who passed by. He was Hera's faithful servant and the best of watchmen, for he never closed more than half of his eyes in sleep at a time.

Argus sat down next to the cow and watched her with all his eyes, and poor Io had to walk on four legs and eat grass. She raised her mournful eyes to Olympus, but Zeus was so afraid of Hera that he did not dare to help her. At last he could no longer bear to see her distress, and he asked his son Hermes, the craftiest of the gods, to run down to earth and set Io free. Hermes disguised himself as a shepherd and walked up to Argus playing a tune on his shepherd's pipe. Argus was bored, having nothing to do with all his eyes but watch a little cow, and he was glad to have music and company. Hermes sat down beside him, and after he had played for a while, he began to tell a long and dull story. It had no beginning and it had no end and fifty of Argus's eyes closed in sleep. Hermes droned on and on and slowly the fifty other eyes fell shut, one by one. Quickly Hermes touched all the eyes with his magic wand and closed them forever in eternal sleep. Argus had been bored to death.

Hermes then untied the cow, and Io ran home to her father, the river-god Inachos. He did not recognize the cow as his daughter, and Io could not tell him what had happened, all she could say was, "Mooo!" But when she lifted up her little hoof and scratched her name, "I-O," in the river sand, her father at once understood what had happened, for he knew the ways of Zeus. Inachos rose out of his river bed and rushed off to take revenge on the mighty thunder-god. He flew at Zeus in such a rage that to save himself Zeus had to throw a thunderbolt, and ever since the bed of the river Inachos in Arcadia has been dry.

Hera was furious when she saw that Argus was dead and the cow Io had been set free. She sent a vicious gadfly to sting and chase the cow. To be sure that her faithful servant Argus would never be forgotten, she took his hundred bright eyes and put them on the tail of the peacock, her favorite bird. The eyes could no longer see, but they looked gorgeous, and that went to the peacock's little head, and made it the vainest of all animals.

Pursued by the gadfly, Io ran all over Greece. Trying to escape from its tormenting sting, she jumped across the strait that separates Europe from Asia Minor, and, ever since, it has been called the Bosporus, the "cow ford."

But still the gadfly chased her all the way to the land of Egypt. When the Egyptians saw the snow-white cow, they fell to their knees and worshiped her. She became an Egyptian goddess, and Hera now permitted Zeus to change her back to her human shape. But first he had to promise never to look at Io again.

Io lived long as the goddess-queen of Egypt, and the son she bore to Zeus became king after her. Her descendants returned to Greece as great kings and beautiful queens. Poor Io's sufferings had not all been in vain.

•—• HEPHAESTUS

HEPHAESTUS, the god of smiths and fire, was the son of Zeus and Hera. He was a hard-working, peace-loving god and was very fond of his mother. Often he tried to soothe her temper with gentle words. Once he had even dared to step between his quarreling parents. He sided with Hera, and that made Zeus so angry that he seized his son by the legs and flung him out of Olympus. For a whole day, Hephaestus hurtled through the air. In the evening he fell on the island of Lemnos, with a thump so hard that the island shook. Thetis, a gentle sea goddess, found him all broken and bruised. She bound his wounds and nursed him back to health.

Zeus forgave him and Hephaestus returned to Olympus, but ever after, he walked like a flickering flame. His body was big and strong and his hands were wonderfully skilled, but his weak legs could not support him for long. He built for himself two robots of gold and silver to help him about. They had mechanical brains and could think for themselves. They even could speak with their tongues of silver. They also served him as helpers in his workshop on Olympus. It was there that Hephaestus made the twelve golden thrones of the gods and their marvelous weapons, chariots, and jewels.

He also had forges inside volcanoes on earth. His helpers there were the one-eyed Cyclopes. They worked his bellows and swung his heavy hammers. When Hephaestus was at work, the din of the hammers could be heard for miles and sparks flew out of the tops of the mountains.

All the Olympian gods were fond of Hephaestus and often went to his forge to admire his work. When Aphrodite, his lovely wife, came to his workshop to look at the matchless jewels he was fashioning for her, she daintly lifted her trailing garments out of the soot.

•—• APHRODITE

APHRODITE, the beautiful goddess of love, was the only Olympian who had neither mother nor father. Nobody knew from where she had come. The West Wind had first seen her in the pearly light of dawn as she rose out of the sea on a cushion of foam. She floated lightly over the gentle waves and was so lovely to behold that the wind almost lost his breath. With soft puffs, he blew her to the flowering island of Cythera, where the three Graces welcomed her ashore. The three Graces, goddesses of beauty, became her attendants. They dressed her in shimmering garments, bedecked her with sparkling jewels, and placed her in a golden chariot drawn by white doves. Then they led her to Olympus, where all the gods rejoiced in her beauty, seated her on a golden throne, and made her one of them.

Zeus was afraid that the gods would fight over the hand of Aphrodite, and, to prevent it, he quickly chose a husband for her. He gave her to Hephaestus, the steadiest of the gods, and he, who could hardly believe in his good luck, used all his skill to make the most lavish jewels for her. He made her a girdle of finely wrought gold and wove magic into the filigree work. That was not very wise of him, for when she wore her magic girdle no one could resist her, and she was all too irresistible already.

Aphrodite had a mischievous little son whose name was Eros. He darted about with a bow and a quiver full of arrows. They were arrows of love and he delighted in shooting them into the hearts of unwary victims. Whoever was hit by one of his arrows fell head over heels in love with the first person he saw, while Eros laughed mockingly.

Once a year Aphrodite returned to Cythera and dived into the sea from which she had come. Sparkling and young, she rose from the water, as dewy fresh as on the day when she had first been seen. She loved gaiety and glamour and was not at all pleased at being the wife of sooty, hardworking Hephaestus. She would rather have had his brother Ares for her husband.

•—• ARES

ARES, god of war, was tall and handsome but vain, and as cruel as his brother Hephaestus was kind. Eris, the spirit of strife, was his constant companion. Eris was sinister and mean, and her greatest joy was to make trouble. She had a golden apple that was so bright and shiny everybody wanted to have it. When she threw it among friends, their friendship came to a rapid end. When she threw it among enemies, war broke out, for the golden apple of Eris was an apple of discord.

When Ares heard the clashing of arms, he grinned with glee, put on his gleaming helmet, and leapt into his war chariot. Brandishing his sword like a torch, he rushed into the thick of battle, not caring who won or lost as long as much blood was shed. A vicious crowd followed at his heels, carrying with them Pain, Panic, Famine, and Oblivion.

Once in a while, Ares himself was wounded. He was immortal but he could not bear to suffer pain and screamed so loudly that he could be heard for miles. Then he would run home to Olympus, where Zeus in disgust called him the worst of his children and told him to stop his howling. His wounds, treated with the ointment of the gods, quickly healed, and Ares returned as good as ever and seated himself on his throne, tall, handsome, and boastful, the plume on his golden helmet nodding proudly.

Aphrodite admired him for his splendid looks, but none of the other gods were fond of him, least of all his half sister Athena. She loathed his vain strutting and senseless bloodshed.

•—• ATHENA

ATHENA, the goddess of wisdom, was the favorite child of Zeus. She had sprung fully grown out of her father's head.

Her mother was Metis, goddess of prudence, the first wife of Zeus. He depended on her, for he needed her wise council, but Mother Earth warned him that, were Metis to bear him a son, this son would dethrone him as Zeus had dethroned Cronus, his father who had dethroned his own father, Uranus. This must not happen, thought Zeus, but he could not do without her advice, so he decided to swallow her. Slyly, he proposed that they play a game of changing shapes, and Metis, forgetting her prudence, playfully turned herself into all kinds of animals, big and small. Just as she had taken on the shape of a little fly, Zeus opened wide his mouth, took a deep breath, and zip! he swallowed the fly. Ever after, Metis sat in his head and guided him from there.

Now it happened that Metis was going to have a daughter, and she sat inside Zeus's head hammering out a helmet and weaving a splendid robe for the coming child. Soon Zeus began to suffer from pounding headaches and cried out in agony. All the gods came running to help him, and skilled Hephaestus grasped his tools and split open his father's skull. Out sprang Athena, wearing the robe and the helmet, her gray eyes flashing. Thunder roared and the gods stood in awe.

Athena's constant companion was Nike, the spirit of victory. With Nike at her side, Athena led armies, but only those that fought for just causes. In time of peace she stood behind the artists of Greece and taught them the fine and useful arts. She had great pride in her own skills at the loom and the potter's wheel, but was happy to see her pupils excel as long as they showed her proper respect.

One of her pupils was Arachne, a simple country girl, who was wonderfully skilled at the loom. People came from far and wide to admire her weavings. Stupidly she boasted that she had learned nothing from Athena; indeed, that she was better than the goddess!

That hurt Athena's pride. Disguised as an old woman, she went to the girl and tried to talk sense into her.

"Your work is beautiful," she said, "but why compare yourself with the gods? Why not be contented to be the best among mortals?"

"Let the goddess Athena herself come and measure her skill against mine," Arachne answered haughtily.

Angrily Athena threw off her disguise and stood before the girl in all her glory.

"Vain girl," she said, "you may have your wish. Sit down at your loom and let us compete."

Athena wove the most beautiful tapestry ever seen, every thread and knot was perfect and the colors sparkled. It pictured the Olympian gods in all their glory and majesty.

Arachne's tapestry was also beautifully woven; Athena herself had to admit that the girl's craftmanship was flawless. But what kind of a picture had she woven? An irreverent scene making fun of Zeus and his wives!

In a wrath the goddess tore the tapestry to shreds and struck the girl with the shuttle. Immediately Arachne felt her head shrink almost to nothing, her nimble fingers change into long, spindly legs. Athena had turned her into a spider.

"Vainglorious girl, go on and spin your thread and weave your empty net forever," said Athena to Arachne, the spider. Athena was a just goddess and she could be very stern. She knew that the gods were great only as long as they were properly worshiped by mortals.

Athena was very fond of a certain city in Greece, and so was her uncle, Poseidon. Both of them claimed the city, and after a long quarrel they decided that the one who could give it the finest gift should have it.

Leading a procession of citizens, the two gods mounted the Acropolis, the flat-topped rock that crowned the city. Poseidon struck the cliff with his trident, and a spring welled up. The people marveled, but the water was salty as the sea that Poseidon ruled, and not very useful. Then Athena gave the city her gift. She planted an olive tree in a crevice on the rock. It was the first olive tree the people had ever seen. Athena's gift was judged the better of the two, for it gave food, oil, and wood, and the city was hers. From her beautiful temple on top of the Acropolis, Athena watched over Athens, her city, with the wise owl, her bird, on her shoulder, and under her leadership the Athenians grew famous for their arts and crafts.

•—• POSEIDON

POSEIDON, lord of the sea, was a moody and violent god. His fierce blue eyes pierced the haze, and his sea-blue hair streamed out behind him. He was called the Earthshaker, for when he struck the ground with his trident, the earth trembled and split open. When he struck the sea, waves rose mountain high and the winds howled, wrecking ships and drowning those who lived on the shores. But when he was in a calm mood, he would stretch out his hand and still the sea and raise new lands out of the water.

In the days of Cronus and the Titans, the sea was ruled by Nereus, son of Mother Earth and Pontus, the seas. Nereus was an old sea god with a long gray beard and a fishtail and was the father of fifty sea nymphs, the lovely Nereids. When Poseidon, the Olympian, came to take over the kingdom of the sea, kind old Nereus gave him his daughter Amphitrite for his queen and retired to an underwater grotto. He gave the new king and queen his palace at the bottom of the sea. It was made of the palest gold and lay in a garden of corals and shimmering pearls. There Amphitrite lived contentedly surrounded by her forty-nine Nereid sisters. She had an only son, whose name was Triton. He had a fishtail instead of legs, like his grandfather Nereus, and rode about on the back of a sea monster, trumpeting on a conch shell.

Poseidon was rarely at home. He was a restless god and loved to race the waves with his team of snow-white horses. It was said that he had created the horse in the shape of breaking waves. Like his brother Zeus, Poseidon had many wives and many children, but Amphitrite was not jealous like Hera.

One of the islands that Poseidon raised out of the sea was Delos. It was so newly created that it was still floating about on the water. The little island was barren. Nothing grew on it yet except a single palm tree. In its shade, the two great gods Apollo and Artemis were to be born.

Zeus had married the goddess Leto, and when Hera found out that Leto was expecting twins, she flew into a jealous rage and ordered all the lands in the world to refuse Leto shelter. Chased away from every land, poor Leto wandered from place to place and could not rest to give birth to her twins.

At last she came to Delos and the little island welcomed her. Since it was still floating and not quite land, it was free from Hera's bidding. Exhausted, Leto sank down in the shade of the palm tree, but still she could not give birth to her twins, for Hera forbade Ilithyia, the goddess of childbirth, to go to her. Without her help no child could be born. All the other goddesses felt sorry for Leto and tried to sway Hera by offering her a beautiful necklace. It was nine yards long, made of gold and amber, and Hera could not resist it. She let Ilithyia go, and Iris whisked her down the rainbow to Leto.

Leto's first child was Artemis, a girl as beautiful as the moon, with hair as dark as the night. She was to be the goddess of the hunt and all newborn creatures. Then Apollo came into the world. He was fair as the sun and he was to be the god of music, light, and reason.

Zeus was filled with joy at the sight of his beautiful twins and he gave them each a silver bow and a quiver full of arrows. The arrows of Artemis were soft as moonbeams and brought painless death, those of Apollo were hard and piercing as the rays of the sun.

Zeus blessed the little island and fastened it to the bottom of the sea. Grass and flowers burst forth from the barren ground, and Delos became the richest of all the Greek islands. Pilgrims flocked to it and loaded it with temples and treasures to honor Leto and her twins.

APOLLO

APOLLO grew rapidly, as all gods did, and when he was full grown, Zeus sent him off in a chariot drawn by white swans to win for himself the oracle of Delphi.

No place in Greece was as sacred as Delphi, on the steep slopes of Mount Parnassus. Sulphurous fumes rose from a deep cleft in the mountainside. A sibyl, the priestess of Delphi, sat on a tripod over the cleft and the vapors put her into a magic sleep. In her dreams the sibyl heard the voice of Mother Earth coming up from the depths, and repeated the mystic words she heard. Priests stood around the sibyl and explained the meanings of her muttered prophecies to the pilgrims who had come to the oracle of Delphi to learn about their future.

The oracle was guarded by the darksome dragon Python, who lay coiled around the sacred place. Old age had made him mean and so ill-tempered that the nymphs fled from the sacred spring nearby and the birds no longer

dared to sing in the trees.

The oracle had warned Python that Leto's son would one day destroy him. He had tried to devour Leto when she wandered about looking for a place to give birth to her children, but she had escaped. When the old black dragon saw radiant Apollo flying toward him in his golden chariot, he knew that his last hour had come. But he sold his life dearly. He unleashed his fury, spitting fire and venom, and his black scaly body did not stop its writhing and coiling until Apollo had shot him with a thousand of his silver shafts. In torrents did the dragon's venom flow down the mountainside, and the oracle of Delphi was Apollo's.

Now there was light and joy on the once-somber slopes of Mount Parnassus. The air was filled with sweet tunes as the birds in the sky and the nymphs of the sacred spring returned to sing Apollo's praise. The voice of the young god rose above all the others, for he was also the god of music.

•—• ARTEMIS

ARTEMIS, as a newborn goddess, went to her father, Zeus, and asked him to grant her a wish. She wanted to remain forever a wild young maiden hunting through the woods, and she asked him to promise never to make her marry. Zeus consented, and then she asked him for fifty fleet nymphs as companions and a pack of lop-eared hounds to hunt with. Her father gave her all she asked, and she herself caught four hinds with golden antlers and harnessed them to her silver chariot.

When the moon's magic light shone over echoing hills and wooded valleys, Artemis hunted with the nymphs and her hounds. After a wild hunt, the goddess loved to bathe in a quiet pool. Woe to the mortal who happened to see her then!

One night, quite by chance, a young hunter whose name was Actaeon came upon the pool in the woods where Artemis and her nymphs were bathing. He should have taken to his heels and run for his life, but instead, he stood spellbound by the sight of the goddess. Artemis was furious! While the nymphs flung a tunic over her shoulders, the goddess dipped her hand into the pool and threw a handful of water at Actaeon. The moment the silvery drops touched his forehead, antlers sprouted, and rapidly all of Actaeon changed into a stag. His own hounds leaped at him, and, to his horror, he could not utter a human sound to call them off. They brought him down, never knowing that the deer was their own master.

"No mortal shall live to boast that he has seen Artemis bathing, " said the goddess, and she picked up her bow and arrows and went on hunting with her nymphs. Artemis was a cold and pitiless goddess.

Apollo and Artemis, though different as day and night, were very fond of each other and they both adored their mother. No one could say a belittling word about gentle Leto without arousing the wrath of her twins.

There was a queen of Thebes whose name was Niobe. She was beautiful and she was rich and she was blessed with fourteen children. Zeus himself was her grandfather, and she was very proud.

"Why worship Leto?" she said to her people. "Build me a temple and worship me in her stead. I have seven sons and seven daughters, while she has only one of each."

When Apollo and Artemis heard this, they grew very angry. Niobe's disrespect could not go unpunished.

Apollo shot his hard arrows at Niobe's seven sons. By no fault of their own, they were torn from life in the prime of their youth. Then Artemis let fly her painless shafts at the seven daughters. Quietly, they lay down on their beds and died.

Niobe's proud heart was broken. She wept for so long that the gods at last took pity on her and changed her into an unfeeling rock. Still, inside the rock, a spring welled up and water like tears trickled down the face of the hard stone.

Apollo had many wives, but Zeus kept his promise to Artemis and never made her marry. Only once she promised her hand to a suitor, but that was a promise she had no intention of keeping. The suitor was Otus, a gigantic son of Poseidon.

Otus and his brother, Ephialtes, were almost sixty feet tall when they reached manhood, and still they went on growing. The gods watched them

with concern, for an oracle had predicted that neither gods nor mortals could kill the giant brothers. Mother Earth, however, watched them with pleasure. She was still angry with Zeus for keeping her sons, the Titans, in Tartarus, and she hoped that Otus and Ephialtes would grow big enough to overthrow him.

One night as the brothers slept with their ears to the ground, they heard Mother Earth whisper that such tall and handsome youths should not let themselves be ruled by Zeus. That was just what they had been thinking themselves, for they were vain, as many strong people are. They pulled up mountains, piled them on top of each other, and built a vast new mountain as high as Olympus. From the top they called to Zeus to surrender his powers to them and move out of his palace with the other Olympians. Artemis could stay and become his bride, shouted Otus, and Ephialtes would take Hera.

The two goddesses tossed their heads with scorn, and Zeus in a fury hurled thunderbolts at the ruffians. Zeus's thunderbolts glanced off harmlessly, and when Ares rushed out to fight them, they grabbed him and crammed him into a bronze jar and clamped the lid shut.

For once Zeus was really worried, but Apollo, the god of reason, said that if no one could kill them they must be tricked into killing each other. He persuaded Artemis to pretend that she was in love with Otus. Otus smirked when Apollo called to him that Artemis thought so much of him she had accepted his proposal and would wait for him on the island of Naxos. That made Ephialtes jealous. Why hadn't Hera fallen in love with him? Wasn't he as handsome as his brother? But he swallowed his pride and went to Naxos with his brother to meet the bride.

When Artemis saw the two brothers arriving, she quickly changed herself into a white deer and ran across their path. She darted to and fro between them and the brothers, who were eager huntsmen, threw their javelins at the deer. Cleverly, she dodged and the brothers fell to the ground, pierced by each other's javelins. Neither gods nor mortals could kill the giant brothers, but now they had put an end to each other and were thrown into Tartarus, tied back to back with writhing snakes.

All the gods thanked Artemis for saving them, and pulled Ares out of the jar where he had been crouching all the while, howling and screaming.

Orion was another giant son of Poseidon, but, unlike Otus and Ephialtes, he was modest. He was a great hunter, no beast could escape from his club and jeweled sword, but he never forgot to praise Artemis as the greatest of all hunters.

One day Orion, who could walk on water as if it were land, came to the island of Chios. The island was infested with lions, wolves, and boars who roared and howled so loudly at night that the King of Chios could not sleep. He promised Orion the hand of his daughter if he could rid the island of all the wild beasts. The king's daughter was beautiful, her father's greatest treasure, and Orion hunted as never before. Soon there was not a wild beast left, but the king did not want to part with his daughter, and claimed that he could still hear the howling of wolves at night. Orion grew angry and threatened to carry off the princess, but the king soothed him with honeyed words, sent for wine, and filled his cup so often that Orion drank too much and feel asleep. Stealthily the evil king crept up and put out both his eyes.

"Now see if you can carry off my daughter," he said.

Blind and helpless, Orion left Chios and staggered over the seas in search of the sun, which he knew could restore his eyesight, but he could not find his way. From afar he heard the Cyclopes' hammers and he followed the sound till he came to Hephaestus' forge on the island of Lemnos. The kind god took pity on him and lent him a Cyclops boy to show him the way to the East.

With the Cyclops on his shoulders to see for him, Orion walked on till he met the rising sun. The sun let its healing rays play over Orion's blind eyes, and his sight was restored. Then he rushed back to seek revenge on the false king. But when he arrived, the palace was empty, for the king had seen his huge, menacing shape against the sky and fled with his daughter.

Again Orion went hunting and soon forgot the king and the beautiful princess. He walked from island to island and after a while he came to the island of Crete. There he met the goddess Artemis. She was glad to see him, for he could hunt as well as she and was so very modest about it. Together they hunted wild goats and rejoiced in each other's company. Orion was the only man Artemis had ever favored, and her brother Apollo grew jealous. One day while Artemis was away, he sent an enormous scorpion to attack Orion. Orion's club and mighty sword were no avail against the scorpion's poisonous tail. He turned to flee, but as he did, the giant insect stung his heel.

Artemis was angry with her brother when she returned and found her companion dead. But she could not stay angry with her twin for long, and he helped her hang Orion's image in the skies as a constellation so the great hunter would never be forgotten.

Over the stormy winter sea the constellation of Orion glitters, enormous and menacing, and the dark clouds flee before him like wild animals. But in summer, when the constellation of the Scorpion rises over the horizon, Orion begins to sway and stagger, and then he, in his turn, flees and disappears into the ocean.

•—• HERMES

HERMES, merriest of the Olympians, was the god of shepherds, travelers, merchants, thieves, and all others who lived by their wits.

His mother Maia, a Titan's daughter, lived in a cave on lofty Mount Cyllene, a cave so deep that Hera never knew that Maia was one of Zeus's wives. Maia had therefore borne her son Hermes in peace.

Hermes was very precocious, even for a god. His mother had hardly wrapped him and put him into a basket when he began to think of mischief. As soon as she had fallen asleep, he wriggled out of his wrappings and tiptoed out of the cave. In the dark of night he toddled straight to the pasture where Apollo kept a large herd of white cows. Apollo liked music better than cows and he did not even notice that Hermes stole into the pasture and picked out the fifty best cows. To keep Apollo from knowing who had stolen his herd and which way they had been driven, Hermes slyly wrapped the hoofs of the cows with bark to disguise their prints, and tied brooms to their tails so they would erase their own tracks. To confuse Apollo even further, he drove the cows backward out of the pasture, and tied bundles of branches to his own little feet so it looked as if a giant had led something into the pasture, but nothing out. He hurried home to Mount Cyllene and hid the stolen cows in a grove. Two of them he sacrificed to the twelve Olympian gods, not forgetting to include himself as the twelfth! Then he took the entrails of the sacrificed cows, made seven strings of them, and strung them tautly across an empty tortoise shell. When he plucked the strings, they made lovely music. He had invented the first lyre. Pleased with himself, he hid the lyre under his arm and tiptoed back into the cave. He climbed into his basket, closed his eyes, and pretended to be sound asleep, but he did not fool his mother. She knew what he had been up to.

"Shame on you," she said, "sneaking out at night and stealing Apollo's cows."

"Why, Mother!" said Hermes. "I did what I had to do for you and for me. We don't want to live in this dark cave forever. Soon I will be seated on high Olympus as one of the twelve great gods, and you too will live there in glory as my mother." Then he pulled out his lyre and played his mother to sleep with a lullaby.

At dawn Apollo stormed into the cave where Hermes lay in his basket pretending to be asleep. But Apollo wasn't fooled. An oracle had told him who had stolen his herd, and he jerked little Hermes out of his crib and commanded him to return the cows at once.

"How could I have stolen your cows?" Hermes whimpered, "I am only a newborn babe. I don't even know what a cow is. Look for yourself and you can see that there is not a single cow hidden in this cave."

"You are not only a thief but a liar as well," raged Apollo, and chased Hermes out of the cave and straight up to Olympus.

All the gods burst out laughing when they saw innocent-looking little Hermes running with furious Apollo at his heels.

"Tell this thief and liar to give me back my cows at once," said Apollo to their father, Zeus.

"Tell my big brother to stop bullying me. I am a newborn and helpless infant. And I am not a liar," said Hermes. "There isn't a cow in my mother's cave."

"If they are not in the cave, then show Apollo where they are," said Zeus, and hid a smile in his beard. He was proud of both his sons and wanted them to be friends.

Hermes had to obey his father, and without any more tricks he led his brother to the woods where the cows were hidden. Apollo forgave him, but when he counted his cows and found that two were missing, his anger flared again. Hermes had expected this and quickly pulled out his lyre and began to play. Apollo listened spellbound to the beautiful sounds from the new musical instrument, and he quite forgot his anger. As the god of music, he must have the lyre and he offered Hermes his whole herd in exchange for the instrument.

Hermes drove a hard bargain and Apollo had to give him his magic wand as well. From then on the two brothers were the best of friends.

Never again did Hermes steal, though he was the god of thieves. He never told a lie, but he didn't always tell the whole truth. His mother, Maia, had no further reasons to be ashamed of him. As the mother of one of the twelve great Olympians, she moved up with him to the glory of Olympus.

Zeus was so delighted with Hermes' ready wit that he made him the herald of the gods. He gave him a golden hat with wings, a pair of winged sandals, and a cape under which he could hide his magic tricks. In a flash he could move from place to place. He put glib words on the tongues of politicians and helped merchants close good bargains. He was as popular among mortals as he was among the gods. Even Hera was fond of him. She had been really angry with him only once, and that was when he had killed her hundred-eyed servant, Argus. Then she was so furious that she demanded he be punished, and called all the great and minor gods to sit in council and judge him. Each god was given a pebble and told to cast his vote according to his decision. Those who found Hermes guilty of a crime were to throw their pebbles at Hera's feet, those who found him innocent were to throw their pebbles at his feet. Hermes talked well in his own defense. Was it a crime to bore someone to death? he asked. After all, that was what he had done to Argus. The gods applauded and so many threw their votes to Hermes that he was completely buried in a heap of pebbles.

Ever after, travelers put up piles of stones along the roads, and they have believed that Hermes stands inside, helping them find their way. These were the first cairns.

Hermes also guided those who set off on their last voyage. He touched the eyes of a dying man with his magic wand and led him down to Hades in the underworld.

•—• HADES

HADES, lord of the dead, was a gloomy god of few words. Mortals feared him so much that they did not dare mention his name, for they might attract his attention and he might send for them. Instead of Hades they called him the Rich One, and indeed, rich he was. All the treasures in the ground belonged to him. They also called him the Hospitable One, for in his desolate underground realm he always had room for another dead soul.

Hermes guided the souls of the dead down to the brink of the river Styx, a murky, stagnant river that flowed around the underworld. There Hermes left them in charge of the ferryman Charon. If they had money to pay for their fare, Charon set them across. If not, he refused to take them, for he was greedy. Those who could not pay had to wander about till they found the pauper's entrance to Hades. That is why, when a man died, his kin put a coin under his tongue.

Sooner or later, all mortals came to Hades. Once inside his realm, they whirled about forever like dry leaves in a cold autumn wind. Cerberus, the three-headed watchdog of the underworld, stood at the gates. He let the dead souls enter, but, once past his gnashing teeth and spiked tail, they could never go out again.

Hades lived in a dark and gloomy palace with his ice-cold queen, Persephone. She was beautiful, but as silent and somber as her husband, for she wasn't happy. She had not come to rule the joyless underworld of her own free will. She had been kidnaped by Hades.

•—• PERSEPHONE AND DEMETER

PERSEPHONE grew up on Olympus and her gay laughter rang through the brilliant halls. She was the daughter of Demeter, goddess of the harvest, and her mother loved her so dearly she could not bear to have her out of her sight. When Demeter sat on her golden throne, her daughter was always on her lap; when she went down to earth to look after her trees and fields, she took Persephone. Wherever Persephone danced on her light feet, flowers sprang up. She was so lovely and full of grace that even Hades, who saw so little, noticed her and fell in love with her. He wanted her for his queen, but he knew that her mother would never consent to part with her, so he decided to carry her off.

One day as Persephone ran about in the meadow gathering flowers, she strayed away from her mother and the attending nymphs. Suddenly, the ground split open and up from the yawning crevice came a dark chariot drawn by black horses. At the reins stood grim Hades. He seized the terrified girl, turned his horses, and plunged back into the ground. A herd of pigs rooting in the meadow tumbled into the cleft, and Persephone's cries for help died out as the ground closed again as suddenly as it had opened. Up in the field, a little swineherd stood and wept over the pigs he had lost, while Demeter rushed wildly about in the meadow, looking in vain for her daughter, who had vanished without leaving a trace.

With the frightened girl in his arms, Hades raced his snorting horses down away from the sunlit world. Down and down they sped on the dark path to his dismal underground palace. He led weeping Persephone in, seated her beside him on a throne of black marble, and decked her with gold and precious stones. But the jewels brought her no joy. She wanted no cold stones. She longed for warm sunshine and flowers and her golden-tressed mother.

Dead souls crowded out from cracks and crevices to look at their new queen, while ever more souls came across the Styx and Persephone watched them drink from a spring under dark poplars. It was the spring of Lethe, and those who drank from its waters forgot who they were and what they had done on earth. Rhadamanthus, a judge of the dead, dealt out punishment to the souls of great sinners. They were sentenced to suffer forever under the whips of the avenging Erinyes. Heroes were led to the Elysian fields, where they lived happily forever in never-failing light.

Around the palace of Hades there was a garden where whispering poplars and weeping willows grew. They had no flowers and bore no fruit and no birds sang in their branches. There was only one tree in the whole realm of Hades that bore fruit. That was a little pomegranate tree. The gardener of the underworld offered the tempting pomegranates to the queen, but Persephone refused to touch the food of the dead.

Wordlessly she walked through the garden at silent Hades' side and slowly her heart turned to ice.

Above, on earth, Demeter ran about searching for her lost daughter, and all nature grieved with her. Flowers wilted, trees lost their leaves, and the fields grew barren and cold. In vain did the plow cut through the icy ground; nothing could sprout and nothing could grow while the goddess of the harvest wept. People and animals starved and the gods begged Demeter again to bless the earth. But she refused to let anything grow until she had found her daughter.

Bent with grief, Demeter turned into a gray old woman. She returned to the meadow where Persephone had vanished and asked the sun if he had seen what had happened, but he said no, dark clouds had hidden his face that day. She wandered around the meadow and after a while she met a youth whose name was Triptolemus. He told her that his brother, a

swineherd, had seen his pigs disappear into the ground and had heard the frightened screams of a girl.

Demeter now understood that Hades had kidnaped her daughter, and her grief turned to anger. She called to Zeus and said that she would never again make the earth green if he did not command Hades to return Persephone. Zeus could not let the world perish and he sent Hermes down to Hades, bidding him to let Persephone go. Even Hades had to obey the orders of Zeus, and sadly he said farewell to his queen.

Joyfully, Persephone leaped to her feet, but as she was leaving with Hermes, a hooting laugh came from the garden. There stood the gardener of Hades, grinning. He pointed to a pomegranate from which a few of the kernels were missing. Persephone, lost in thought, had eaten the seeds, he said.

Then dark Hades smiled. He watched Hermes lead Persephone up to the bright world above. He knew that she must return to him, for she had tasted the food of the dead.

When Persephone again appeared on earth, Demeter sprang to her feet with a cry of joy and rushed to greet her daughter. No longer was she a sad old woman, but a radiant goddess. Again she blessed her fields and the flowers bloomed anew and the grain ripened.

"Dear child," she said, "never again shall we be parted. Together we shall make all nature bloom." But joy soon was changed to sadness, for Persephone had to admit that she had tasted the food of the dead and must return to Hades. However, Zeus decided that mother and daughter should not be parted forever. He ruled that Persephone had to return to Hades and spend one month in the underworld for each seed she had eaten.

Every year, when Persephone left her, Demeter grieved, nothing grew, and there was winter on earth. But as soon as her daughter's light footsteps were heard, the whole earth burst into bloom. Spring had come. As long as mother and daughter were together, the earth was warm and bore fruit.

Demeter was a kind goddess. She did not want mankind to starve during the cold months of winter when Persephone was away. She lent her chariot, laden with grain, to Triptolemus, the youth who had helped her to find her lost daughter. She told him to scatter her golden grain over the world and teach men how to sow it in spring and reap it in fall and store it away for the long months when again the earth was barren and cold.

•—• DIONYSUS

DIONYSUS, the god of wine, was the youngest of the Olympians. He was the only one of the twelve great gods whose mother was a mortal. His father was Zeus himself.

Jealous Hera hated his mother, the beautiful princess Semele, and one day when Zeus was away, the goddess disguised herself as an old crone and went to visit her. She talked about this and about that, pretending to be very friendly, and then she asked why Semele's husband was not at home, and what kind of man he might be.

"He is nobody less than mighty Zeus," Semele said proudly.

"How can you be so sure about that?" said the old woman. "I know many husbands who claim to be the lord of all creation. Do you have proof that he really is who he says he is? If I were you, I would ask him to show himself in all his splendor." Then she went away, and Semele was left alone, wondering.

When Zeus returned, Semele asked him to grant her a wish. Zeus, who loved her dearly, swore by the river Styx to fulfill any wish she might have.

"Then show yourself in all your splendor," said Semele. Zeus begged her to change her wish, for he knew that no mortal eyes could bear the sight of him when he revealed himself as the flashing thunder-god, a hundred times brighter than the sun. But Hera had planted the seed of suspicion so deep in Semele's heart that she refused to change her wish. Zeus had to keep his promise, for he had sworn by the river Styx, the most solemn oath of the gods.

He joined together the smallest storm clouds he could find, chose his tiniest lightning bolt, and showed himself to Semele as the mighty thunder-god. Even so, he was so brilliant that Semele caught fire and burned to cinders. Zeus could do nothing to save her. She went down to Hades as a fluttering ghost. Zeus barely managed to rescue her unborn son, and sewed him under the skin of his own leg, and when the child was ready to be born, he sprang forth as the immortal god Dionysus.

Zeus knew well enough who was the cause of Semele's death, and he gave her little son to Hermes and told him to hide the boy from Hera. Hermes carried Dionysus to the faraway valley of Nysa, and left him in the care of a band of Maenads, the nymphs of the valley. There Dionysus grew up with tigers and leopards for playmates.

Large bunches of purple grapes grew on the sunny slope of the valley of Nysa, and in time Dionysus invented the making of wine from their juice. As a young and beautiful god, dressed in flowing robes of royal purple, he went out into the world to teach men how to make wine. The Maenads went with him, and so did the leopards and tigers, and ever more followers joined him. Wherever he went he was worshiped as a new god, and his father, Zeus, watched him with pleasure.

Dionysus returned to Greece and traveled from island to island teaching the making of wine. One day as he was sleeping alone on a beach, a pirate ship sailed by. When the pirates saw the richly clad youth, they thought he was a prince and carried him off on their ship to hold him for ransom. He did not wake from his heavy slumber till the ship was far out at sea. With gentle words he tried to persuade the pirates to take him back; he was not a prince, he said, he was the god of wine, and his riches were not of this world. The pirates laughed scornfully and sailed on, paying him no heed.

Suddenly their laughter died, for out of the sea sprouted vines loaded with grapes. They grew, twining around the oars, winding up the mast, and spreading over the whole ship as though it were an arbor. Blood-red wine dripped down the sail and the air was filled with the sound of roaring tigers and braying asses. Dionysus himself seemed to grow till he filled the ship with his glory. Horrified, the sailors threw themselves into the sea, but they did not drown, for Dionysus was a kind god. He changed them into dolphins, and that is why dolphins are the most human of all creatures that live in the ocean.

Dionysus had brought much joy to mankind, and Zeus decided that the time had come to give him a golden throne on Olympus. Hera rose in anger and said she refused to share the hall with the son of a mortal woman, but Zeus pounded his indomitable fist and Hera sat silent.

There were only twelve thrones in the hall, so kind Hestia quietly rose from hers and said that Dionysus could have it. Her place was at the hearth, she said; she needed no throne.

Before seating himself on his throne Dionysus asked to see his mother for whom he had always longed. Zeus not only permitted him to see her, but let him go down to Hades and bring her up to the glory of Olympus, for she was now the mother of one of the great gods. Happily Dionysus entered the hall and seated himself on his golden throne. The air was filled with the music of flutes and tambourines. Never had there been such a din and merriment on Olympus. Zeus looked around with great content and beckoned to his cupbearer, Ganymede, bidding him fill the golden goblets with sweet nectar.

MINOR GODS, NYMPHS, SATYRS, AND CENTAURS

MINOR GODS AND GODDESSES also lived on Olympus besides the twelve great ones. The most powerful of them were the goddesses of destiny, Clotho, Lachesis, and Atropos. They were the three Fates and they decided how long a mortal would live and how long the rule of the gods should last. When a mortal was born, Clotho spun the thread of life, Lachesis measured a certain length, and Atropos cut the thread at the end of the life. They knew the past and the future, and even Zeus had no power to sway their decisions. Their sister, Nemesis, saw to it that all evil and all good on earth were justly repaid, and all mortals feared her.

•—• PROMETHEUS

Man's creator and his best friend was the Titan Prometheus. Zeus had given Prometheus and his brother, Epimetheus, the task of repopulating the earth after all living creatures had perished in the early battles of the gods. He gave the two brothers great measures of gifts to bestow upon their creations, and they went down to earth and began to make men and beasts out of river clay. Wise Prometheus modeled men with great care in the shape of the gods. Epimetheus rapidly made all kinds of animals and without any foresight he lavished the good gifts upon them. When Prometheus had finished shaping man, he found that there were few of the good gifts left. Animals could run faster, see, smell, and hear better, and had much more endurance. Besides, they were kept snug in their warm coats of fur, while men shivered in the cold nights.

Prometheus was sorry for mankind and he went to Zeus and asked him if he might have some of the sacred fire for his poor creations. But Zeus said no, fire belonged to the gods alone.

PROMETHEUS could not bear to see his people suffer and he decided to steal fire, though he knew that Zeus would punish him severely. He went up to Olympus, took a glowing ember from the sacred hearth, and hid it in a hollow stalk of fennel. He carried it down to earth, gave it to mankind, and told them never to let the light from Olympus die out. No longer did men shiver in the cold of the night, and the beasts feared the light of the fire and did not dare to attack them.

A strange thing happened: as men lifted their eyes from the ground and watched the smoke from their fires spiraling upward, their thoughts rose with it up to the heavens. They began to wonder and think, and were no longer earth-bound clods. They built temples to honor the gods and, wanting to share what they had with them, they burned the best pieces of meat on their altars.

Zeus was furious when he first saw the fires flickering on earth, but he was appeased when the savory scent of roast meat reached his nostrils. All the gods loved the smell of the burnt offerings; it spiced their daily food of ambrosia and nectar. But Prometheus knew how hard men worked to make their living and thought it a pity that they burned up the best parts of their food. He told them to butcher an ox and divide the meat in two equal heaps. In one were the chops and roasts, hidden under sinews and bones. In the other were scraps and entrails, covered with snow-white fat. Prometheus then invited Zeus to come down to earth and choose for himself which part he wanted for his burnt offerings. Zeus, of course, chose the best-looking heap, but when he discovered that he had been tricked he grew very angry.

Not only had Prometheus stolen the sacred fire and given it to men, he had also taught them to cheat the gods. He resolved to punish both Prometheus and his creations.

Cast in unbreakable irons, Prometheus was chained to the top of the Caucasus Mountains. Every day an eagle swooped out of the sky and ate his liver. At night his immortal liver grew anew, but every day the eagle returned and he had to suffer again.

Thus was Prometheus punished. But Zeus found a more subtle way to punish the mortals. He sent to earth a beautiful but silly woman. Her name was Pandora.

PANDORA

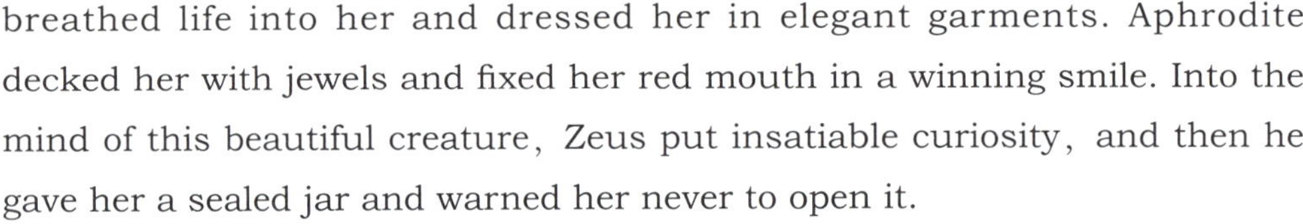

PANDORA was modeled by Hephaestus in the likeness of Aphrodite. He carved her out of a block of white marble, made her lips of red rubies and her eyes of sparkling sapphires. Athena breathed life into her and dressed her in elegant garments. Aphrodite decked her with jewels and fixed her red mouth in a winning smile. Into the mind of this beautiful creature, Zeus put insatiable curiosity, and then he gave her a sealed jar and warned her never to open it.

Hermes brought Pandora down to earth and offered her in marriage to Epimetheus, who lived among the mortals. Epimetheus had been warned by Prometheus never to accept a gift from Zeus, but he could not resist the beautiful woman. Thus Pandora came to live among mortals, and men came from near and far to stand awestruck by her wondrous beauty.

But Pandora was not perfectly happy, for she did not know what was in the jar that Zeus had given her. It was not long before her curiosity got the better of her and she had to take a quick peek.

The moment she opened the lid, out swarmed a horde of miseries: Greed, Vanity, Slander, Envy, and all the evils that until then had been unknown to mankind. Horrified at what she had done, Pandora clapped the lid on, just in time to keep Hope from flying away too. Zeus had put Hope at the bottom of the jar, and the unleashed miseries would quickly have put an end to it.

They stung and bit the mortals as Zeus had planned, but their sufferings made them wicked instead of good, as Zeus had hoped. They lied, they stole, and they killed each other and became so evil that Zeus in disgust decided to drown them in a flood.

But there was one man on earth who had not turned evil. He was a son of Prometheus. His name was Deucalion.

•—• DEUCALION

DEUCALION often went to the Caucasus Mountains to comfort his suffering father. He could not break the chains that bound him, but while he was there, he could keep away the eagle that tortured Prometheus. Deucalion was a good son, and his father was thankful for his help.

Prometheus, who could look into the future, knew that Zeus was planning to flood the earth. He told his son to build an ark and board it with Pyrrha, his virtuous wife.

Deucalion did as his father told him. He built a sturdy ark, and when Zeus let loose all the winds and opened wide the floodgates of the sky, he went aboard with Pyrrha. For nine days and nine nights it rained until the whole earth was flooded. Nothing but the highest mountain peaks remained above water and all mortals were drowned. Only Deucalion and Pyrrha were saved; they floated in their ark over the deep, dark waters.

On the tenth day, the rain stopped, and slowly dry land began to appear. Deucalion and Pyrrha stepped out of the ark and walked about on the desolate earth. Lonesome and forlorn, they came to a temple, grown over with seaweed, and entered it. The sacred fire on the altar had gone out, but they lit it again with the embers they had kept glowing aboard the ark, and lifted up their hands in prayer to the gods to thank them for saving their lives. Zeus was touched by their piety and felt sorry for them because they were so lonesome. He spoke to them and said: "Pick up the bones of your mother and throw them over your shoulders."

Deucalion understood that Zeus did not mean their mortal mothers, but their Mother Earth. Rocks were her bones. He told Pyrrha to pick up a handful of stones and throw them over her shoulder while he did the same. Behind Deucalion, a score of men sprang up, and there, behind Pyrrha, a score of women. This new race of mortals was called Deucalion's race.

The Deucalion race, made from stone, was hardier than the one made from clay. The new mortals withstood better the stings of Pandora's miseries, which of course, had flown high and dry during the flood, and plague mankind to this very day.

The winds had carried on as they wished when Zeus flooded the earth. They were powerful fellows, and when they stormed together, they brought confusion and destruction, whirling dust and water all the way up to Olympus. Zeus decided that they needed a dependable guardian who would keep them locked up and let out only one at a time. He chose Aeolus, a grandson of Deucalion and Pyrrha, to be the keeper of the winds and sent him to live with them and guard them in a hollow cliff, far out at sea.

The winds hated to be confined. They stormed and howled around Aeolus, trying to force their way out of the cavern, but Aeolus was steady and strong and kept them in hand. When Poseidon or one of the other gods called for a wind, Aeolus pierced the wall of the cliff with his spear and let the wind out. Then he plugged up the hole and kept it closed until it was time for the wind to return.

When Boreas, the North Wind, was called for, he rushed out, icy and wild, tearing up trees and piling up waves in front of him.

When Notus, the South Wind, was let out, he pressed himself groaning through the hole in the cliff. He was so heavy with moisture that water dripped from his tangled beard, and he spread a leaden fog over land and sea. Wanderers lost their paths and ships drifted helplessly about.

Zephyr, the West Wind, was gentler than his brothers. When he blew, he swept the sky clear of clouds and all nature smiled.

Eurus, the East Wind, was the least important of the brothers. He wasn't called for often.

•—• EOS

EOS, gentle dawn, was the mother of the four winds. While all creation slept, she rose from her pink pillows to announce the coming of a new day. She dipped her rosy fingers into a cup filled with dew and sprinkled the drops over flowers and trees. All nature awoke, rejoicing to see her.

One morning as Eos looked down on earth, her eyes fell on a young prince waking from his slumber. He was so handsome she could not take her eyes off him, and she wanted him for her husband. But how could she, who was a goddess, be married to a mortal whose life span was so short?

As soon as her morning duties were done, she went to Zeus and persuaded him to grant eternal life to the young prince, whose name was Tithonus.

She brought him with her to her palace in the east, and they spent many delightful years together.

But Eos had forgotten to ask that Tithonus be also given eternal youth, and slowly his strength left his once-supple limbs. He shriveled and shrank, and his manly voice changed to a feeble squeak. He shrank to a tiny, wizened old man, yet he could not die, for he had been given eternal life. He became so small and weak that Eos had to put him into a little basket and hide him in a corner of her palace. There, in his dark corner, he went on withering and shriveling till at last he turned into a grasshopper, chirping for all eternity.

But Eos stayed rosy and young, always a joy to behold when she came out to wake the sleeping world and announce the coming of her brother, the sun.

•—• HELIOS AND PHAËTHON

HELIOS, the sun, mounted his glowing chariot and drove out in great splendor as soon as Eos threw open the gates of his golden palace in the east. His radiance lit up the wide expanse of sky. So bright was he that only the gods could look straight at him without being blinded. Brilliant rays encircled his head, and his chariot glowed like fire.

With a strong hand, Helios guided his four fiery steeds up the vault of the heavens. The path was steep and narrow and the horses were wild, but Helios held them well on their course. At high noon, he stopped at the top of the sky and looked around, and nothing could escape his piercing gaze. Again he drove on and now he gave free rein to his steeds. Far to the west they could see his glittering evening palace, and, eager to reach their stables, they raced on the downhill course, faster and faster. They passed a great herd of white cows hurrying homeward to Helios' palace and met a large flock of sheep going out to pasture in the sky. For Helios owned a snow-white cow for each day of the year and a woolly sheep for each night.

The shadows grew long and dusk settled over the world when Helios and his foaming team arrived. His five daughters, the Heliades, awaited them. They unharnessed the tired horses and let them plunge into the ocean for a cooling bath. Then the horses rested in their stables and Helios talked with his daughters and told them all he had seen that day.

In the dark of the night, he boarded a vessel of gold with his team and sailed around the world, back to his palace in the east. The way was far shorter by sea than by air, so he had time to stay for a while in his morning palace too before he set out on another day's journey.

Helios had a son named Phaëthon. He was a mortal and very proud of his radiant father. One morning as Helios was about to set off on his daily journey across the sky, Phaëthon came to him and begged him to grant his dearest wish. Helios, who was very fond of his handsome son, rashly swore by the river Styx to give him any wish he might have, but when he heard Phaëthon's wish, he sorely regretted his oath. He tried in vain to make his son change his mind, for what Phaëthon wanted was to drive the sun chariot for one day, and Helios knew that no one but he himself could handle the spirited steeds.

Phaëthon was determined to have his wish, and Helios had to give in. Sadly, he put his golden rays on his son's head and rubbed divine ointment on his skin so he could withstand the searing heat of the chariot. He barely had time to warn him to stay well in the middle of the heavenly path when the gates of the palace were thrown open, and the rearing horses were brought forth. Phaëthon leaped into the chariot, grasped the reins, and the horses rushed out.

At first, all went well and Phaëthon stood proudly in the glowing chariot. But the fiery steeds soon felt that unskilled hands were holding the reins. They veered off the heavenly path and brushed by the dangerous constellations that lurked on both sides of it. The animals of the zodiac were enraged: the bull charged, the lion growled, the scorpion lashed out with its poisonous tail. The horses shied and Phaëthon was thrown halfway out of the chariot. Far down below he saw the earth and he grew so dizzy that he dropped the reins. Without a firm hand to guide them, the horses bolted. They raced so close to the earth that the ground cracked from the heat of the chariot and rivers and lakes dried up. Then upward they sped so high that the earth froze and turned to ice.

Zeus stood on Olympus and shook his head. He had to stop the careening chariot to save the earth from destruction, and he threw a thunderbolt at it. In a shower of sparks, the chariot flew apart and Phaëthon plunged into the river Po. On the riverbanks his sisters mourned so long that Zeus took pity on them and changed them into poplar trees and their tears into drops of golden amber.

Hephaestus had to work the whole night through to mend the broken chariot so Helios could drive it again the next day. Helios grieved over his lost son, and he never again allowed anyone to drive his chariot except for Apollo, the god of light.

•—• SELENE

SELENE, the moon, came out at night to light up the world while her brother, Helios, was resting. Slowly she drove her milk-white horses across the sky, and her pale moonbeams fell gently on the sleeping earth where all was peace and quiet.

One night Selene's soft light fell on Endymion, a young shepherd, who was sleeping beside his flock. She stopped to look at him. He was smiling in his sleep and was so young and handsome that she completely lost her heart to him. She drove through the night, but she could not get him out of her mind.

When her duties were over, she went to Zeus and asked him to grant Endymion eternal sleep so he would stay forever young and handsome. She had learned from her sister, Eos, not to ask for eternal life for a mortal and be left with a grasshopper on her hands.

Zeus granted Selene's wish and Endymion slept on and on, smiling in his sleep. He dreamed that he held the moon in his arms. But it was not a dream after all, for Selene bore her husband fifty daughters, all pale and beautiful as their mother and sleepy as their father.

In Selene's magic light, river-gods rose from silvery streams to inspect their river beds, and hills trembled under the hoofs of the wild centaurs. Laughing nymphs and bleating satyrs danced to the music of Pan, god of nature, master of them all.

•—• PAN

PAN, the great god of nature, was not a handsome god. He had goat's legs, pointed ears, a pair of small horns, and he was covered all over with dark, shaggy hair. He was so ugly that his mother, a nymph, ran away screaming when she first saw him. But his father, Hermes, was delighted with the strange looks of his son. He carried him up to Olympus to amuse the other gods and they all laughed and took him to their hearts. They called him Pan and sent him back to the dark woods and stony hills of Greece as the great god of nature. He was to be the protector of hunters, shepherds, and curly-fleeced sheep.

Pan was a lonely and moody god. When he was sad, he went off by himself and hid in a cool cave. If a wanderer happened to come upon him and disturb him in his retreat, he would let out a scream so bone-chilling that whoever heard it took to his heels and fled in a fear that they called panic.

But when Pan was in a good mood, and that was mostly on moonlit nights, he cavorted through glades and forests, and up steep mountain slopes playing on his shepherd's pipe, and nymphs and satyrs followed dancing behind him. Sweet and unearthly were the tunes that floated over the hills.

The satyrs much resembled their master, Pan, but they were mischievous and good for nothing except for chasing nymphs. Old satyrs, or sileni, were fat and too lazy to walk. They rode about on asses, but they often fell off, since they were fond of drinking wine.

The lightfooted nymphs always looked young, though some of them were very old in years. Their life span was so long that they were almost immortal: they lived ten thousand times longer than man. There were water nymphs and nymphs of mountains and glens. There were nymphs who lived in trees and nymphs who lived in springs.

When a tree grew old and rotted, the nymph who lived in it moved to another tree of the same kind. A wood chopper, about to fell a healthy tree, must remember first to ask permission of the tree nymph. If he did not, she might send out a swarm of bees to sting him, or she might turn the ax in his hands so he would cut his own leg instead of the tree trunk.

A thirsty hunter must never drink from a spring without asking the water nymph's permission. If he ignored the nymph, she might send a venomous water snake to bite him, or she might poison the water and make him sick.

River-gods, too, had to be asked before anyone took water from their rivers. They were usually helpful and friendly to men and willingly shared their water, but woe to the one who tried to carry off their waternymph daughters. They would rush out of their river beds and charge him in full river-god rage. They were dangerous opponents, for they grew oxhorns on their heads and could change their shapes at will. Zeus himself feared their rage, and Pan and the satyrs kept well out of their way, though Pan liked all nymphs and fell in love with many of them.

•—• ECHO

ECHO was one of the nymphs with whom Pan fell in love. She was a gay nymph who chattered and prattled all day long and never kept quiet long enough for Pan to win her with music and poetry.

One day Hera came down from Olympus to look for Zeus. She suspected that he was playing with the nymphs, but Echo detained her so long with idle chatter that Zeus, who really was there, was able to sneak away. Hera, in a rage, punished Echo by taking from her the gift of forming her own words. From then on poor Echo could only repeat the words of others.

Now at last Pan thought he could win her by his words. But before he had a chance, she had lost her heart to another. He was Narcissus, and he was so handsome that every girl and every nymph he met fell in love with him. Unfortunately, he liked nobody but himself.

Echo trailed silently behind Narcissus as he hunted in the woods, hoping to hear an endearing word from him that she could repeat. But he never so much as noticed her. At last toward nightfall, they came to a quiet pool, and as Narcissus was thirsty, he bent down to drink. Suddenly, he stopped and stared, for in the mirroring surface of the water he saw the handsomest face he had ever seen. He smiled and the handsome face smiled back at him. Joyfully he nodded and so did the stranger in the water.

"I love you," said Narcissus to the handsome face.

"I love you," repeated Echo eagerly. She stood behind him, happy to be able to speak to him at last.

But Narcissus neither saw nor heard her; he was spellbound by the handsome stranger in the water. He did not know that it was his own image that he had fallen in love with and he sat smiling at himself, forgetting to eat, forgetting to drink, until he wasted away and died. Hermes came and led him down to the realm of the dead, but where he had been sitting the lovely Narcissus flower sprang up. Echo stood beside the flower and grieved and pined until she too faded away.

Nothing was left of Echo but her voice, which to this day can be heard senselessly repeating the words of others.

Pan grieved for a while, but then another pretty nymph crossed his path and he forgot all about Echo. Her name was Syrinx.

SYRINX AND DAPHNE

SYRINX ran away from Pan; she thought he was so ugly. Pan chased after her, and, to escape from him, she changed herself into a reed. She stood among hundreds of other reeds on the riverbank, and Pan couldn't find her. As he walked through the reed patch, sighing and looking for her in vain, the wind blew through the reeds. They swayed and bent and made a plaintive whistling sound. Pan listened, enchanted. "Thus you and I shall always sing together," he said.

He cut ten reeds into unequal lengths, tied them together, and made the first panpipe. He called the new instrument his syrinx, for every time he played on it he thought he heard the melodious voice of his beloved nymph. Again Pan was lonesome and he retreated to his cool cave, deep in the woods, and scared away all passers-by with his unearthly screams.

Splendid Apollo himself fared no better than Pan when he fell in love with a nymph called Daphne. Daphne had a cold heart, she had vowed never to marry, and when Apollo wooed her, she would not listen to the sound of his golden lyre and ran away. As she fled, she was lovelier still, with her golden hair streaming behind her, and Apollo could not bear to lose her. He set off in pursuit, beseeching her to stop. Daphne ran toward the bank of a river that belonged to her father, the river-god Ladon, calling to him to save her from her pursuer. Ladon had no time to rise out of his river bed and come to his daughter's rescue, but the moment Daphne's toes touched the sand of the riverbank, he changed them into roots. Apollo, who was close at her heels, caught up with her, but the instant he threw his arms about her, her arms changed into branches, her lovely head into the crown of a tree, and she became a laurel. Still, inside the hard bark, Apollo could hear the beating of Daphne's frightened heart.

Apollo carefully broke off some twigs and made a wreath of the shining leaves.

"Fair nymph," he said, "you would not be my bride, but at least consent to be my tree and your leaves shall crown my brow."

Ever after, the greatest honor an artist or a hero could be given was to be crowned with a wreath from Apollo's sacred tree, the laurel.

Daphne would rather be an unmoving tree than the bride of the great god Apollo, but all the other nymphs loved to sit at his feet and listen to his enchanting music, and were very honored when he or any of the other great Olympian gods chose one of them as a bride.

•—• THE CENTAURS

THE WILD AND VULGAR CENTAURS did not honor any of the gods. They were half men and half horses, as cunning as wild men and as savage as untamed horses. They had inherited the worst dispositions of both.

The first centaurs had come tumbling out of a cloud that their father, Ixion, King of the Lapith people, had married, mistaking it for the goddess

Hera. Zeus had created the cloud to test the ungodliness of the wicked king who wanted to carry off Hera. Ixion was severely punished for his ungodliness. He was condemned to whirl about forever in the underworld, tied to a flaming wheel, but his offspring, the centaurs, remained on earth as a scourge to the Lapith people.

•—• CHIRON AND ASCLEPIUS

The centaurs lived without law and order, stormed over fields, trampled crops, and carried off the Lapith women, and they ate raw meat. The young centaurs were no better than their elders. They were poorly brought up by parents who kicked them and spanked them and left them to fend for themselves.

There was one centaur who was kind and wise and was fond of children. His name was Chiron. Though he looked like the other centaurs, he wasn't related to them at all. He was the son of Cronus the Titan and was immortal. Chiron was famous as the greatest teacher in Greece. Kings brought their small sons to him so he could raise them in the true spirit of heroes.

In his quiet cave on Mount Pelion, he taught them manly sports and how to use the healing herbs of the earth and how to read the stars in the sky. All his pupils returned to their homes exceeding their fathers in courage and knowledge.

One day Apollo brought to Chiron his little mortal son, Asclepius. His mother, a Lapith princess, had died, and Apollo asked Chiron to raise the boy.

ASCLEPIUS grew up in Chiron's cave, raised with loving care, and, being the son of Apollo, he soon surpassed his foster father in his knowledge of healing the sick.

When he was grown, he left Chiron's cave and went down from the mountain to help the people of Greece. He became the first great physician. People flocked to him from far and near, and many who came on crutches went away skipping and dancing. His patients adored him and showered treasures upon him, and it wasn't long before they worshiped him as a god and built temples in his honor. Asclepius put beds in his temples and they became the first hospitals. There he went about from bed to bed, pleased to be looked upon as a god, leaning on a staff entwined with sacred serpents. Serpents knew all the secrets of the earth and often told him the causes and cures for diseases. Sometimes he put his patients to sleep with a magic draught and listened to what they muttered in their dreams. Their words often revealed to him what caused their ailments, and he could then find a cure for them.

Asclepius had a wife and seven children, and all the children followed in their father's footsteps. His sons were his assistant physicians his daughters were his nurses. Hygeia, one of his daughters, washed and scrubbed her patients from morning to night, and it was a marvel to see how fast they regained their health. Before Hygeia's time, it was thought that soap and water would kill the sick.

Asclepius grew famous, rich, and pink-faced, and as time went on, he grew so skilled in his art that he could even bring the dead back to life. The Fates became upset and complained to Zeus that they measured and clipped the threads of life in vain. Hades too was angry, for he was being cheated out of dead souls. Apollo pointed out to Zeus how much good his son was doing for mankind, and for a while Zeus was lenient. But when Asclepius accepted gold for bringing the dead back to life, Zeus hurled a thunderbolt at him.

Nothing but a small heap of ashes was left of Asclepius, the first great doctor. But his temples and his teachings of medical science remained, and the gods put his image among the stars as a constellation.

Apollo was furious with Zeus for killing his son and wanted revenge.

He did not dare to raise his hand against his mighty father, but he slew the Cyclopes who had given Zeus the thunderbolt. Zeus, in his turn, had to revenge the Cyclopes. He punished Apollo by making him serve for a year as a slave on earth.

Apollo found a good master and suffered no hardship. But the gods on high Olympus missed him and his music, the nine Muses most of all.

•—• THE NINE MUSES

THE NINE MUSES were daughters of Zeus and the Titaness Mnemosyne. Their mother's memory was as long as her beautiful hair, for she was the goddess of memory and knew all that had happened since the beginning of time. She gathered her nine daughters around her and told them wondrous tales. She told them about the creation of earth and the fall of the Titans, about the glorious Olympians and their rise to power, about Prometheus, who stole the heavenly fire, about the sun and the stars, and most of all about the greatness and wisdom of their father, Zeus. The nine Muses listened to her with wide, sparkling eyes and turned her stories into poems and songs so they would never be forgotten.

Apollo, the god of music, trained them and taught them to sing harmoniously together. He led the choir of Muses through the halls of Olympus and over the slopes of Mount Parnassus, and their music rang so pure and fine that even the songbirds fell silent to listen.

Each of the Muses had her own special art. Calliope, the Muse of heroic poetry, was the first among them. She had a mortal son named Orpheus, and he sang almost as beautifully as the Muses themselves. When he was grown, he left his mother and his eight loving aunts and went to live in his father's kingdom of Thrace to bring the joy of music to earth. His voice rang so pure and true that the fiercest warriors put down their swords and savage beasts lay spellbound at his feet. Trees pulled up their roots and moved closer to listen, and even hard rocks rolled up to him.

Orpheus' music was joyful and gay, for he was in love with Euridice, a sweet young maiden, and she loved him in return. On the day of their wedding, his songs swelled out, filled with happiness as his bride danced on light feet through the meadow. Suddenly, she trod on a snake and sank to the ground, dead of its poisonous bite. Hermes gently closed her eyes and led her away to the underworld. No more songs came from Orpheus' throat, no more tunes rang out from his lyre. All joy had gone out of his life. He had to have his Euridice back.

Weeping and grieving, Orpheus wandered about searching for an entrance to Hades, and when at the end of the world he found it, he did what no living man had ever done before: he went down to the realm of the dead to beg for the return of his beloved. His music had power to move hard rocks; it might also move the cold heart of Hades. Hope gave him back his songs, and, playing and singing, he walked down the dark, steep path.

His silvery voice floated down through the dark like a gentle summer breeze and its magic moved the iron gates of Hades. They sprang open and let him in, and Cerberus, the three-headed watchdog, lay down at his feet and let him pass. The whole dark underworld stilled and listened to Orpheus' music as he entered the realm of the dead singing about his great love, begging to have his Euridice back. The fluttering souls hushed. Those condemned to eternal pains stopped groaning, and their torturers, the avenging furies, the Erinyes, dropped their whips and wept tears of blood.

Hades, the pitiless king of the dead, sat on his black marble throne with Queen Persephone at his side. Even he was so moved by the music that tears rolled down his sallow cheeks and cold Persephone sobbed. Her heart was so touched that she turned to her husband and begged him to let Euridice go back to the sunny world above. Hades gave his consent, but he made one condition: Orpheus must not look at his bride before they reached the realm of the living. She would walk behind him, but if he turned, and looked at her, she must return to the underworld.

Overcome with joy, Orpheus started up the dark path, and as his music faded into the distance, gloom again descended over the underworld. The way was long, and as Orpheus walked on and on, doubt began to creep

into his mind. Had Hades deceived him? Were the sounds he heard behind him really Euridice's footsteps? He had almost reached the upper world, and could already see a dim light ahead, when he could bear his doubts no longer. He had to turn and see if she really was there. He saw her sweet face, but only for an instant, for again Hermes appeared at her side. He turned her about and led her back to the dark gloom below. Faintly, Orpheus heard her whisper farewell. He had lost her forever through his lack of faith.

Orpheus never again found joy on earth. He wandered into the wilderness to grieve in solitude. He sang, but now his songs were so mournful that tears trickled down the cheeks of wild beasts and the willows wept.

A band of wild nymphs stormed through the woods shouting to Orpheus to join them. They yelled and carried on so loudly that they could not hear his silvery voice and were not touched by its magic. They wanted him to dance with them, but he had no heart for their revelry, and in a fury they threw themselves over him. They tore him to pieces and tossed his body into a river. The river stopped its gurgling to listen, for the haunting voice of Orpheus still issued forth from his dead lips as he floated down to the open sea.

The Muses grieved over him. They searched the sea till they found his body on the shores of the island of Lesbos. There they gave him a proper funeral, and at last he could rejoin his beloved Euridice as a flitting ghost in the underworld.

MORTAL DESCENDANTS OF ZEUS

THE MUSES sang not only of the gods and of the spirits sprung from Mother Earth, but also of great kings and heroes, descended all from mighty Zeus. The tales of heroes and brave men still ring in our ears as we listen to the Muses sing.

•—• EUROPA AND CADMUS

JOYOUSLY the Muses sang about lovely Europa, chosen by Zeus to be the first Queen of Crete. Her father, King Agenor of Tyre, was a descendant of Io, the girl who had fled to Egypt in the shape of a white cow.

Zeus had been looking far and wide for a maiden worthy of being Queen of Crete, the island where he had been raised. One day his eyes fell on Europa, and her beauty quite captured his heart.

Changing himself into a snow-white bull, he trotted about in the meadow by the sea where Europa was playing with her maidens. At first she was afraid of the strange bull who suddenly stood beside her, but as he looked at her with big, soft eyes, she lost her fear. She tied a wreath of flowers around his broad neck and gently patted his glistening sides. The bull knelt down at her feet, and trustingly she climbed up on his back and asked him to take her for a ride. He walked up and down the beach with her, and Europa laughed and clapped her hands and called to her maidens to come and see the marvelous bull she had found. But suddenly the bull turned and rushed away over the sea with her. Her maidens cried out in terror and the king came running out of his palace, just in time to see the bull and his daughter disappear beyond the horizon.

Trembling, Europa clung to the horns of the bull. But to her surprise, not a drop of water touched her toes, for Nereids swimming all about smoothed the waves with their hands and made the sea a polished road for the bull to run on. Then the bull turned his head and spoke. He was not a bull, he said, but Zeus himself, and he had come to earth to make her his bride and the Queen of Crete.

When Zeus arrived in Crete with Europa, he put a royal crown of jewels on her head as a token of his love, and she lived in Crete in glory and delight to the end of her days. She had three sons: Minos and Sarpedon, who became great kings, and Radamanthus who was so wise that after his death he was made a judge in the underworld.

When Zeus returned to Olympus, he ordered his son Hephaestus, the smith, to make a bronze robot that would watch over Crete and Europa. Three times a day, Talos, the robot, walked with clanking steps around the shores of the island, and whenever an enemy ship approached, he hurled rocks at it and sank it.

The king of Tyre had sent his three sons to search for their kidnaped sister. Two of the brothers soon gave up, but Cadmus, the third brother, sailed on to Greece with his men. There he went to the oracle at Delphi and asked where Europa could be found. His sister was well and happy, he was told, and he must give up the search for her. Instead, he should stay in Greece and found a new kingdom; a snow-white cow would lead him to a good site for a walled city.

Cadmus left Delphi, and indeed, before long, he met a white cow. He followed her uphill and downhill, over mountains and through valleys, and at last the cow lay down on top of a knoll in the middle of a wide plain. Cadmus saw with pleasure that it was a perfect site for a walled city. He sent one of his men for water from a nearby bubbling spring. The man did not return. Cadmus sent another man to look for him. He did not return either, and, one after another, Cadmus sent off all his men, but not one of them came back. At last, he went himself to see what had happened and found a dragon guarding the spring. The monster had devoured all his men, and now it was so sluggish and sleepy that Cadmus easily slayed it. But that did not bring his men back to life and Cadmus could not build a walled city all alone. He sacrificed the white cow to the gods and begged them for help. Athena answered his plea. "Plow a field," she told him. "Pull out the dragon's teeth and sow them in the furrows."

This advice sounded strange, but Cadmus did as he was told. As soon as the dragon's teeth were sown, up shot a host of fierce warriors. They rushed at Cadmus, waving their swords and the terror-struck hero gave himself up for lost. Again, Athena called to him: "Throw a rock among them!" He did, and at once the warriors flew at one another, each accusing his neighbor of having thrown the rock. They fought furiously till only five were left, and they were badly wounded. Cadmus nursed them back to health and they became his faithful men and helped him to build Thebes, the great walled city with seven gates.

Cadmus became a great king and the gods favored him. Zeus gave him Harmonia, a daughter of Aphrodite, for his queen. The gods gave the bride a magic necklace to keep her beautiful and young and Thebes, ruled by Cadmus and his descendants, became one of the greatest Greek cities.

•—• TANTALUS AND PELOPS

THE MUSES sang about Tantalus, condemned to suffer forever in the underworld. He stood in water up to his neck, but could never quench his thirst, for whenever he bent to drink, the water receded. Above his head hung branches loaded with fruits, but whenever he tried to pick one, the branch bent out of his reach.

Tantalus was a son of Zeus, and he had been so favored by the gods that he had been invited to feast with them on high Olympus. In return,

he had asked the gods to come to dine in his palace in Asia Minor. He was a king of vast riches, but nothing he owned seemed good enough to set before his exalted guests. His son, Pelops, was his greatest treasure, and, wanting to give the gods his best, Tantalus decided to sacrifice him. He made a stew of him and set the dish before the gods. But the Olympian gods detested human sacrifice. Outraged, they threw Tantalus to the punishing grounds in the underworld and brought Pelops back to life. But one of his shoulder bones was missing, and the gods replaced it with a piece of ivory. They all gave him rich gifts. Poseidon gave him a team of fast horses and told him to set off and win himself a new kingdom.

In Greece there was a beautiful princess whose name was Hippodamia. She was the daughter of Oenomaüs, the King of Elis, and whoever married her would inherit his kingdom, but her father loved her so dearly that he could not bear to part with her. He had a team of horses given to him by Ares, the god of war, whose son he was, and whenever a suitor came to ask for his daughter's hand, Oenomaüs challenged him to a chariot race. If the suitor won, he would win the princess; if he lost, he would lose his head. No horses on earth could outrun the horses of Ares, and the heads of twelve suitors already hung at the gates of the palace. When Pelops arrived in Elis to woo the princess, Oenomaüs did not know that Pelops also had a team of magic horses, and the King looked forward to nailing the thirteenth head on the gates! But Hippodamia fell in love with the young prince and wanted to save his life. She asked her father's stable boy to fix the king's chariot so that Pelops would win. The stable boy, eager to please her, did more than he was asked to do. He took out the wooden pins that held the wheels to the axle, and replaced them with pins of wax.

Never had there been such a race! The fiery horses ran neck to neck, and the king, to his surprise, could not pull ahead, no matter how hard he swung the whip. Then suddenly the wax pins gave way. The wheels of the chariot flew off and the king was thrown to his death.

Pelops married Hippodamia and became the King of Elis. He flung the faithless stable boy into the sea, and gave the old king a magnificent funeral feast inviting heroes from all over Greece to take part in athletic games in his honor and offered fabulous prizes to the winners, for Pelops had brought with him the great riches of his father, Tantalus. The games were held on the plain of Olympia, in Elis, and were to be repeated every four years. They were called the Olympic games.

•—• DANAÜS, PERSEUS, AND THE GORGON

LOUD was the song of the Muses about Danaüs, first of a line of great kings and heroes.

King Danaüs of Libya had fifty daughters, his brother, King Aegyptus, had fifty sons. The fifty sons wanted to marry the fifty daughters, but they were rough and rowdy and King Danaüs did not want them for sons-in-law. He feared that they might carry off his daughters by force, so secretly he built a ship with fifty oars and fled with his daughters. The fifty princesses pulled at the oars and rowed the ship across the wide sea. They reached Argos, in Greece, and when the people there saw the king standing in the prow of a gorgeous ship rowed by princesses, they were awed. They were certain that Danaüs had been sent by the gods, and made him their king.

Danaüs was a good ruler, and peace and happiness reigned in Argos until one day another splendid ship arrived. And who should be at the oars but King Aegyptus' fifty sons, who had come to claim their brides. Danaüs did not dare to oppose them and had a lavish wedding feast prepared. But secretly he gave each of his fifty daughters a dagger and ordered them all to kill their husbands as soon as they were alone. Forty-nine of the brides obeyed him. But Hypermnestra, the eldest, fell in love with Lynceus, her prince, and fled with him. In vain did Danaüs try to find new husbands for his widowed daughters; nobody dared to marry them. The forty-nine Danaides had to live a life without joy, and when they died and came to the underworld, they were sentenced to carry water forever in sieves, trying in vain to fill a bath and wash off their sins.

When King Danaüs grew old, there was no heir to his throne, and he had to send for Hypermnestra and Lynceus, who were living in great happiness. They became King and Queen of Argos, and their son became King after them. When he died, his son, Acrisius, inherited the throne. Acrisius, however, had no son. He had only a beautiful, golden-haired daughter whose name was Danaë, but her beauty brought no joy to her father. He wanted a son and heir to his kingdom. When an oracle told him that he would die by the hand of his daughter's son, he put Danaë in a sealed chamber that had neither windows nor doors, only an opening in the roof. There no suitor could see her beauty and she would remain unwed and childless. But Acrisius forgot to reckon with Zeus. The thunder-god spied the lonesome maiden through the opening in the roof, and in the shape of a golden shower he descended to her. No longer was Danaë lonesome, for now she was the happy bride of Zeus. But when her father heard the cries of an infant from her chamber he broke through the walls in a rage, intending to kill his grandson. When he learned that Zeus was the child's father he did not dare to lay hands on him. Instead, he put Danaë and her son, Perseus, in a chest and threw it into the sea. If they drowned, Poseidon would be to blame.

Zeus gently steered the chest to the shore of an island, and a fisherman who was casting his nets hauled it in. Great was his surprise when he saw what the chest contained. When Danaë had told him her story, he took her and little Perseus to his hut and cared for them as if they were his own, for he was a kind old man and childless.

In his humble hut Perseus grew into a fine and valiant youth, proud of being the son of Zeus and the beautiful Danaë. But Danaë's beauty attracted the eye of the ruthless king of the island. He wanted her for his queen. In vain did Danaë turn him away. She was the bride of Zeus and swore that she could marry no other. The king pursued her and would have carried her off by force if Perseus had not protected her. The scheming king decided to get rid of Perseus, and he let it be known that he was going to marry a princess from a neighboring island. As was the custom, all the men in the kingdom brought him gifts. Only Perseus was so poor that he had nothing to give. So he offered his services to the king instead. This was just what the king had expected. "Slay the monster Medusa and bring me her head," he said. No man who had ever set out to kill Medusa had come back, and the king was sure that now he was forever rid of Perseus.

Medusa was one of three horrible Gorgon sisters, so gruesome that all living creatures turned to stone at the sight of them. They lived on an island far out at sea, but nobody knew just where.

Perseus bid his mother good-bye and set out to search for Medusa. He went over land and over sea asking his way, but nobody could tell him where the Gorgons lived. As he stood at a crossroad wondering which way to go, Athena and Hermes suddenly appeared. Zeus had sent them to help him. They could tell him the way to the island of the Gorgons, but he needed more help than that. Athena lent him her shield, polished as brightly as a mirror. Hermes lent him his sword, which was so sharp that it could cut through the hardest metal, and he also needed three magic things owned by the nymphs of the north, they told him, but even the gods did not know where these nymphs lived. That was a secret closely guarded by the three Gray Sisters, and they would never willingly reveal it, for they were the Gorgons' sisters. But Hermes offered to take Perseus to them and find a way to get the secret out of them. He took Perseus under his arm, swung himself into the air, and flew off, swifter than the wind. They flew far, far to the west and at last they came to a land where the sun never shone and everything was as gray as dusk. There sat the three Gray Sisters. Their hair was gray, their faces were gray, and they had only one gray eye between them, which they took turns looking through. As one of the sisters was handing the eye to another, Perseus sprang forward and snatched it.

"Now I have your eye," cried Perseus. "You will never get it back unless you tell me the way to the nymphs of the north."

The three Gray Sisters wailed and begged for their eye, but Perseus would not give it back, and so they had to tell him the way. Again Hermes took him under his arm and flew with him far, far to the north, beyond the North Wind, where the sun never set. The nymphs of the north received them kindly, and when they heard why Perseus had come, they gladly lent him the three things he needed; a pair of winged sandals to carry him through the air, a cap to make him invisible and a magic bag to hold whatever was put into it. Now he was ready to slay the Medusa, said Hermes. He showed him the way and wished him good luck. Wearing the winged sandals, Perseus flew far to the west. When he came to the island of the Gorgons he did not look down. He looked, instead, into Athena's polished shield, and shuddered at the sight he saw mirrored there. The three Gorgon sisters were lying on the shore, fast asleep. Long yellow fangs hung from their grinning mouths, on their heads grew writhing snakes instead of hair, and their necks were covered with scales of bronze. Around them stood the strangest stones; it was easy to see that they had once been men.

Looking into the mirroring shield, Perseus swooped down, and with one deft stroke he cut off the Medusa's head. Out from the monster's severed neck sprang a beautiful winged horse, the Pegasus. He neighed and the other two Gorgons awoke. Quickly Perseus threw Medusa's head into the magic bag and swung himself into the air. Wailing, the two Gorgon sisters took to the air on heavy wings in groping pursuit. They could not find him, for he had put on the magic cap of invisibility.

On his way home, as he flew over the coast of Ethiopia, Perseus saw, far below, a beautiful maiden chained to a rock by the sea. She was so pale that at first he thought she was a marble statue, but then he saw tears trickling from her eyes. He swooped down and tore at her chains, trying to break them.

"Flee!" she said. "Or you too will be devoured by the sea monster!" But Perseus refused to leave and she told her sad story: Her name was Andromeda and she was the daughter of King Cepheus and Queen

Cassiopeia. Her mother was very vain and had boasted unwisely that she was even lovelier than the Nereids. Poseidon could not tolerate having a mortal compare herself to the goddesses of the sea, and as punishment he sent a sea monster to ravage the kingdom of Ethiopia. To appease the angry god and save his kingdom, her father had to sacrifice her, his only daughter, to the monster. And there she stood, chained to the cliff, waiting to be devoured. She had begged the prince to whom she was engaged to save her, but he had fled in fear.

"I shall save you and you shall be mine," said Perseus.

As he spoke, a horrible sea monster came from the sea, its huge mouth opened wide to swallow Andromeda. But Perseus sprang into the air, dived at the monster and drove his sword deep into its throat. The monster bellowed, lashed its tail wildly, and rolled over on its back. It sank and the sea was tinted red by its blood. Ever since, that stretch of water has been called the Red Sea.

No sooner was the monster dead than Andromeda's cowardly suitor returned with many warriors to claim her for his bride. Now he was bold and menacing and King Cepheus did not dare to oppose him.

"Andromeda, shield your eyes!" cried Perseus, and with that he lifted the head of the Medusa out of the bag. The suitor and his men stared in horror and whips!, they were changed into stones! Unfortunately, the king and the queen had also looked at the Gorgon's head and they too turned into stone. But since a son of Zeus was going to marry their daughter, the gods took pity on them and hung Cepheus and Cassiopeia in the sky as constellations.

Perseus lifted Andromeda into his arms and flew homewards. But when he arrived at the fisherman's hut, he learned that Danaë and the fisherman had gone into hiding. As soon as the king of the island had gotten rid of Perseus, he had tried to carry Danaë off. To save her, the kind old fisherman had fled with her. When Perseus heard that, he made straight for the king's palace.

"Here is the head you wanted!" he shouted, and pulled Medusa's head out of the bag. Startled, the king and his men looked up, and there they sat, turned into statues of stone, some of them with their mouths still open in astonishment.

The people of the island rejoiced at being rid of the tyrant, and as soon as the fisherman and Danaë came out of hiding, they made the fisherman their new king. He gave Perseus and Andromeda the grandest of wedding feasts and everybody was happy.

Perseus did not keep the Gorgon's head, it was much too dangerous for a mortal to own. He gave it to Athena when he returned her shield and the other magic objects he had borrowed.

Perseus thought that his grandfather Acrisius would be happy to see him now that he was a hero, and he set sail for Argos with Danaë and Andromeda. But when the old king learned that his grandson was approaching he fled, for he still remembered the oracle's warning, and so Perseus became king of Argos.

Perseus ruled wisely and well, his mother and his wife always at his side. Since he was a great athlete, he also took part in games all over Greece. One day, a sudden gust of wind changed the course of a discus he had thrown, and it killed an old man who was watching the games. Who should that old man be but Acrisius, his grandfather! Thus the words of the oracle came true.

After that, Perseus no longer wanted to live in his grandfather's city, Argos. So he founded instead the splendid fortified city of Mycenae, not far away, and many great kings and heroes were descended from him and Andromeda.

When at last Perseus and Andromeda died, Zeus put them, too, in the sky as constellations.

CLEVER AND VAINGLORIOUS KINGS

•—• KING MIDAS

WHEN PERSEUS gave Athena the Gorgon's head, she fastened it on her breastplate, and it made her still more powerful. She also fetched two of Medusa's bones, and from them she made herself a double flute. She could not understand why Hera and Aphrodite burst out laughing every time she played on it, for she was very pleased with the music she made. But one day she saw her own image in her polished shield. With puckered lips and puffed cheeks she did not look at all like her stately self. In disgust she threw the flute down to earth and put a curse on it.

Marsyas, a satyr who was capering about in the Phrygian woods, found the flute and began to play on it. When he discovered he could play two melodies at the same time, he was wild with joy. He hopped through the woods, playing on his double flute, boasting that now he could make better music than Apollo himself.

Apollo frowned when he heard that a satyr dared compare himself to him, the god of music, and he stormed down from Olympus to the Phrygian woods. He found Marsyas who was so delighted with his own music that he even challenged Apollo to a contest.

"You shall have your contest," said Apollo, "but if I win, you shall lose your hide."

The nine Muses, of course, were to be the judges, and Marsyas insisted that King Midas of Phrygia also be a judge.

KING MIDAS was a kind but rather stupid man who had always been a friend to the Phrygian satyrs. One morning his servants had found an old

satyr sleeping in the king's favorite flower bed. Midas had spared the satyr from punishment and let him go. This old satyr was a follower of Dionysus, and the god had rewarded Midas for his kindness by granting him a wish. Shortsightedly, King Midas wished that everything he touched would turn to gold. His golden touch made him the richest man on earth, but he almost starved to death for even his food and drink turned to gold. And when his little daughter ran to him to hug him, she too turned into gold! Midas had to beg Dionysus to undo his wish and make everything as it had been before.

Now again, King Midas showed poor judgment. The nine Muses all agreed that Apollo was by far the better musician, but Midas voted for the Phrygian satyr. Apollo disdainfully turned his lyre upside down and played just as well as before. He ordered Marsyas to turn his flute and do the same. Not a sound came from Marsyas' flute however hard he blew, and even Midas had to admit that the satyr's flute was inferior to Apollo's lyre. So Marsyas lost the contest and Apollo pulled off his skin and made a drum of it. Then he turned to King Midas and said, "Ears as stupid as yours belong to an ass. Ass's ears you shall have from now on!"

Ever after, King Midas went about with a tall, peaked cap on his head to hide his long ears. His subjects thought he had started a new fashion, and it wasn't long before all the Phrygians wore tall, peaked caps.

The king's barber was the only one who knew what Midas was hiding. He had been forbidden to breathe a word about it and he almost burst from having to keep such an important secret. When he could bear it no longer he ran out to a lonesome field, dug a hole in the ground, and whispered into it, "King Midas has ass's ears!" He quickly covered up the hole and thought the secret was safe. But the nearby reeds had heard and as they swayed in the wind they whispered, "Midas has ass's ears, Midas has ass's ears," and soon the secret spread all over the world.

King Midas was so ashamed that he left his throne and hid deep in the woods where no one could see him.

•—• SISYPHUS

SISYPHUS of Corinth was the cleverest king who ever lived. He was so cunning that he fooled even the gods.

One day Sisyphus saw the river-god Asopus, who was looking for his daughter, Aegina. Sisyphus, who noticed everything that was happening in his kingdom, went after him and said, "I'll tell you what has become of your daughter if you'll give my city a spring." For the only thing his great city lacked was a good supply of fresh water.

Asopus hated to part with any of his water. He twisted and squirmed, but at last he struck the ground, and a crystal clear spring bubbled forth.

"It is Zeus himself who has carried off your daughter," said Sisyphus. "I saw him hurry by with her," and he pointed out to Asopus the way Zeus had taken. The river-god rushed off in a fury and soon caught up with the elopers. Zeus, taken by surprise, had no thunderbolt at hand, so, to save himself and the nymph from the river-god's rage, he changed himself into a rock and her into the island Aegina.

Sisyphus had his spring of water, but Asopus lost his daughter, and Zeus was furious with Sisyphus for meddling in his affairs. He asked Hades to take him to the underworld and punish him severely. Hades was glad to do his brother Zeus a favor and he went himself to fetch Sisyphus. When the sly king saw the lord of the dead in person, he pretended to be very honored. But why, he asked, had not Hermes, whose office it was to guide dead souls to the underworld, come for him? While Hades searched for a suitable answer, Sisyphus deftly wound a chain around him. And there stood the lord of the dead, chained to a post like a dog.

As long as Sisyphus kept Hades tied up, nobody could die. The Fates got the threads of life tangled and the whole world was in confusion. Finally the gods threatened to make life so miserable for Sisyphus that he would wish he were dead, and Sisyphus then had to let Hades go. Again people could die and life could go on normally. The very first soul to be claimed was, of course, that of Sisyphus himself. This time Hermes came for him.

The wily king, who had expected this, had told his loving wife not to give him a funeral feast, and not to put a coin under his tongue. So he arrived in the realm of the dead as a poor beggar. Hades was shocked! After all, Sisyphus was a king and entitled to a funeral feast and a golden coin under his tongue to pay for his passage across the Styx. His wife had to be punished, or she might set a bad example for others. He sent Sisyphus back to earth and told him to teach his wife respect. "Fooled him again!" said Sisyphus when he rejoined his devoted wife. They lived happily for many long years, till at last he died of old age and went to Hades for good. There he was given a task that kept him too busy to think up new tricks. He had to push a boulder up a steep hill, but every time he had almost reached the top, the boulder slipped from his hands and rolled all the way to the bottom again.

•—• BELLEROPHON

BELLEROPHON, a grandson of Sisyphus, was a great tamer of horses. He would have given all he owned for a ride on the winged horse Pegasus, who had sprung out of Medusa's neck. Pegasus had flown to Greece, where the nine Muses had found him and tended him. They were the only ones who could come close enough to touch him, for Pegasus was wild and swift.

One night, Bellerophon fell asleep in Athena's temple. He dreamed that the goddess gave him a golden bridle that would make the flying horse tame. And when he awoke, he really held a golden bridle in his hand.

Not long thereafter, Pegasus flew over Corinth, saw the clear spring that Sisyphus had won from the river-god, and stopped to drink. Carefully Bellerophon tiptoed up to the winged horse and flung the bridle over his head. The horse neighed, looked at Bellerophon, and suddenly he was so tame that Bellerophon could mount him. Never had there been such a horse and such a horseman. They galloped through the air, over land and over sea, faster than the wind.

On the back of his flying horse, Bellerophon set off to fight the Chimera, a fire-breathing beast that was ravaging the kingdom of Lycia in Asia Minor. The Chimera was more fearful than a nightmare. She was lion in front, serpent in back, and goat in between. She spat fire from all her three heads and her hide was so tough that no weapon could pierce it. Swooping down as close as he dared without singeing the coat of his flying horse, Bellerophon went at the monster with a lump of lead stuck to the end of his spear. The Chimera hissed like a serpent, bleated like a goat, and as she opened wide her lion's jaws to roar, he thrust the lump of lead down her throat. Her flaming breath melted the lead and it trickled into her stomach and killed her.

The people of Lycia, who had been hiding in fear behind bolted doors, now dared to come out, and the king of the country was so thankful that he gave Bellerophon the hand of his daughter. When the old king died, Bellerophon inherited the kingdom. He became a great king, loved by his people, feared by his neighbors and all the monsters lurking nearby. But his fame went to his head and he grew so vain that he thought he was as great as the gods. He even held himself equal to Zeus. He soared ever higher on his flying horse, and at last he tried to enter Olympus itself. There pride took a spill. Pegasus threw him and Bellerophon fell to earth, landing in thistle thorns in a distant country. Torn and lame, he wandered about as an unknown beggar until he died. Pegasus entered Olympus alone and Zeus made the handsome winged horse the carrier of his thunderbolts.

•—• MELAMPUS

MELAMPUS, a cousin of Bellerophon, won glory and fame and one third of a kingdom, all because he was kind to animals. Once when he was a child, he found a dead mother snake on the road. He did not kick it into a ditch, but gave it a proper funeral, picked up the little motherless snakes, and reared them tenderly. In gratitude they licked his ears so clean that he could understand the language of all animals, crawling and flying. From their talk he learned the secrets of the earth and grew wise beyond measure.

Once he was thrown into prison for trying to steal some cows from a neighboring king, and one night as he lay on his cot, he heard a family of termites talking inside the roof beam. "Brother," said one termite to another, "if we go on chewing all night, the roof will collapse before morning."

Melampus jumped up and hammered at the door. He demanded to be moved at once, for the roof would soon fall in. The jailer laughed, but Melampus made such a fuss that he was finally moved. Just then the roof did cave in. Everybody marveled, and the king called for him and told him that, if he could find a cure for his sick son, he could have the cows he had tried to steal. The young prince had been sick since he was a child, and no one knew what ailed him.

Melampus slaughtered an ox and spread the meat on the ground. Right away, two vultures swooped down and began to gorge themselves. When they had eaten their fill, one of the vultures said to the other, "I haven't been so full since that time when the king sacrificed a ram to the gods. I remember how terrified the little prince was when he saw his father with a bloody knife in his hand. He screamed so loudly that his father threw away his knife and ran to comfort him. The knife stuck in the tree over yonder and wounded the tree nymph. She cast a spell on the boy and he has been sick ever since. Now the bark has closed over the knife, but if the king knew what I know, he would dig out the rusty blade, make a brew from the rust, and give it to the prince to drink."

Melampus at once dug out the blade and made a rusty brew. The sickly prince drank it and right away he was so fit that he bounded over a field of barley without bending a stalk. Melampus won great fame as a healer and from all corners of Greece, kings sent for him to cure their sick.

The King of Tiryns had three lovely daughters who suddenly went quite out of their minds and thought they were cows. The king sent for Melampus, who said that he would cure them if the king would give him a third of his kingdom. That was far too much, thought the king, and Melampus went away. The princesses grew worse and ran all over the kingdom mooing like cows. The king again sent for Melampus. This time Melampus came with his brother and now he wanted a third of the kingdom for his brother, too! The king had to agree, for it was very embarrassing to him that his daughters ran around shouting, "We are cows, we are cows!"

Melampus hired some fast runners and sent them after the crazy girls. They had to run halfway across Greece before they could catch them and bring them back. Melampus forced them to drink a draught of magic herbs, and that cured all of them except one, poor girl, who died of exhaustion.

The king, who had to part with two-thirds of his kingdom, thought that he might as well give Melampus and his brother each a princess in the bargain, and they all lived happily thereafter.

•—• HERACLES

PROUDLY did the Muses sing of Heracles, often called Hercules, the strongest man who ever lived on earth and the greatest of all the descendants of Danaüs. His mother was Princess Alcmena, granddaughter of Perseus and Andromeda, and famed for her beauty and virtue.

His father was Zeus, so Hera, of course, hated Alcmena and pursued Heracles with her wrath. When he was an infant the goddess sent two spotted serpents into his cradle, but little Heracles simply grasped them in his powerful hands and squeezed the life out of them. He grew stronger every day, but his trouble was that he did not know his own strength.

Being of noble birth, he had to learn to sing and play the lyre, but Heracles would much rather wrestle and fight. One day his music teacher Linus scolded him for singing out of tune. In a fit of fury Heracles banged his lyre over the teacher's head, harder than he had meant, and the blow killed the poor man. Heracles was too strong to have around a palace so he was sent into the mountains as a shepherd. There he could use his tremendous strength on prowling beasts. Soon he had rid the countryside around Thebes of lions and wolves, and the fame of his strength spread far

and wide. He came back from the mountains as a hero, and the King of Thebes regarded him so highly that he gave him his daughter in marriage. Hera did not like this at all, and she made Heracles insane. Raving mad, he swatted down his own children, mistaking them for wild beasts. When he regained his senses, he was horrified at what he had done, and went to the oracle of Delphi to learn what he must do to atone for his crime. He was told that he must serve for ten years as the slave of his cousin Eurystheus and perform ten labors for him.

Hera was pleased, for Eurystheus, the King of Mycenae, was a weak little man who hated his strong cousin Heracles. With her help the king would surely think of the hardest tasks for Heracles to perform.

For his first four labors Eurystheus sent Heracles to rid the nearby countryside of dangerous beasts and monsters.

In the valley of Nemea dwelt a monstrous lion whose hide was so tough it could not be pierced by any weapons. It was one of Echidna's dreadful offspring, which Zeus had let live as a challenge to future heroes.

Heracles chased it out of its lair, seized it in his bare hands, and squeezed it to death. Then he skinned the beast with its own claws, and with the impenetrable skin of the Nemean lion slung over his head and shoulders, he reported back to Eurystheus, his first labor performed.

In the swamps of Lerna there lived a nine-headed Hydra, another of Echidna's brood. This monster was so poisonous that the fumes from its breath alone were enough to kill whatever came close to it.

Heracles filled his enormous lungs with air, held his breath, and ran at the Hydra. Swinging his club, he knocked off its heads, and one after the other they rolled to the ground. But no sooner had he knocked off one head than a new one grew in its place. He half turned around and let out enough air to call to his charioteer to bring a firebrand and sear the necks. Then no new heads could sprout. When Hera saw that Heracles was winning over the Hydra, she sent a giant crab to pinch his heel. With a mighty kick Heracles sent the giant crab flying as he knocked off the last of the heads. Then he dipped his arrows in the Hydra's blood, making them so poisonous that a mere scratch from them was deadly, and he returned to Mycenae, his second labor performed.

On the slopes of Mount Erymanthus roamed a wild and dreadful boar, with tusks as sharp as swords. Eurystheus sent Heracles to bring this beast back alive.

With loud yells, Heracles chased the boar out of its lair and drove it ahead of him all the way to the top of the snow-capped mountain. The heavy beast sank into the snow and it was easy for Heracles to catch and subdue it. He pushed, dragged, and rolled it all the way down to the gates of Mycenae. When Eurystheus saw the fearful boar, he dived into an urn and barely dared to peek out.

Then Eurystheus sent Heracles to rid the Stymphalian Lake of a swarm of dangerous birds. They had feathers of brass so sharp that, when one of them fell to the ground, it killed whomever it hit. But they could not penetrate Heracles' lion skin, and he made such a din, with a huge rattle, that the birds took fright and flew away, never to return.

Eurystheus was distressed to see with what great ease Heracles had performed his first four labors. Now he sent him to bring back alive one of the sacred hinds of Artemis. He hoped that Heracles would harm the creature with his brute strength and thereby earn the wrath of the goddess. But Heracles pursued the swift deer with great patience over hills and dales. The year was almost over when at last he caught the deer. With great care he carried it back to Mycenae.

Next, to humble his strong cousin, Eurystheus ordered Heracles to clean the stables of King Augeas, who lived across the mountains to the west. King Augeas had huge herds and his stables and barnyards had not been cleaned for years. Heaps of dung rose mountain high. No man alive could clean his stables in a year, thought Eurystheus. But Heracles with tremendous strength changed the course of two rivers. The waters flooded through stables and barnyards and washed them clean in less than a day.

Eurystheus now, on the advice of Hera, sent Heracles far afield for his last four labors. He must travel way to the east and fetch back to Mycenae the golden girdle of Hippolyta, Queen of the Amazons. The Amazons were a tribe of wild and warlike women who rode better and fought harder than any men. Eurystheus was sure that even Heracles would be overwhelmed by the furious women. But when Heracles arrived in Amazon land, the proud queen was so taken by the sight of his bulging muscles that she gave him her belt without a fight. She would gladly have given him her hand in the bargain, but Hera, in the disguise of an Amazon, spread the rumor that Heracles had come to kidnap Hippolyta. The Amazons threw themselves upon Heracles, but for once they had found their master! Heracles swung his mighty club, and the little Amazon husbands, who were spinning and cooking and tending the babies, were amazed to see their dangerous wives subdued by a single man.

In triumph, Heracles returned to Mycenae with Hippolyta's belt. He could not bring the queen, she had been killed in the fight.

Far to the north there lived a king whose name was Diomedes. He was a very inhospitable king and had trained his four mares to devour all strangers who came to his land.

Now Eurystheus sent Heracles to capture the four man-eating mares and bring them back alive.

Heracles traveled to the north, slew King Diomedes, and threw him to his own mares. When the mares had eaten the evil king, they were so tame that they let Heracles drive them back to the gates of Mycenae.

Then Eurystheus sent Heracles south to catch a fierce, fire-breathing bull on the island of Crete. The Cretans, who were great bullfighters, could not catch the bull, but Heracles seized the charging bull by the horns without heeding the flames from its nostrils, flung it to the ground, and returned to Mycenae, bringing the subdued beast. Eurystheus was glad he had a safe urn to hide in.

For his tenth labor, Heracles was sent to an island far out in the ocean, to bring back a huge herd of red cows. They belonged to Geryon, a monster with three bodies on one pair of legs.

Heracles walked off with a powerful stride and soon reached the end of all land in the west. The only boat he could spot was the golden vessel of Helios, the sun. Heracles aimed his mighty bow at the sun and threatened to shoot him from the sky if he did not lend it to him. Helios did not dare to refuse, and he let Heracles take his golden boat.

Before he sailed off, Heracles pulled up two huge crags and set them down, one on each side of the strait that separates Europe from Africa. There they stand to this day, called the Pillars of Hercules.

When Heracles was out at sea and the waves rose high around him, he aimed a poisoned arrow at the waves, threatening to shoot them if they did not still at once. The waves flattened in fear and Heracles sailed on to Geryon's island. He began at once to load the herd of red cows, and Geryon's watchman and his two-headed dog rushed at him. With one swing of his mighty club Heracles did away with them both. Then Geryon himself came running to attack him, his three huge bodies swaying on his thin legs. Calmly Heracles lifted his bow, took careful aim, and sent a poisoned arrow through all of the monster's three bodies. As time was getting short, Heracles rowed back as fast as he could with the herd. When he arrived at the mainland, Hera sent a swarm of gadflies to sting the cows and they scattered all over Europe. Still, Heracles managed to round them up and bring them to the gates of Mycenae just before the year was up. There, Eurystheus sacrificed the cows to Hera, and, gratified, the goddess whispered into his ear that he must demand two more labors from Heracles, for his charioteer had helped him to singe the heads of the Hydra, and not he but the waters of two rivers had washed the Augean stables clean.

Heracles scowled but he bowed his head in submission, for he had won much glory on his ten labors and hoped to win some more.

For his eleventh labor, Heracles was sent to find Hera's secret garden of the Hesperides and pick three golden apples from the little apple tree that Mother Earth had given Hera for her wedding gift. Nereus, the Old Gray Man of the Sea, was the only one on earth who knew where the garden was, but he would not reveal the secret. When Heracles seized him to squeeze the secret out of him, Nereus tried to escape by changing himself into all kinds of animals. But Heracles held on to him and at last Nereus had to tell him that the garden of the Hesperides lay west of the setting sun, not far from where the Titan Atlas stood, holding up the sky.

On his way to the garden, Heracles heard the groans of the Titan

Prometheus, who was chained to the Caucasus Mountains. Heracles was in a hurry, but he felt sorry for the Titan and took time off to tear apart his chains. Zeus, impressed by the strength of his son, let him do it. In gratitude Prometheus warned Heracles not to pick the golden apples himself, or he would die. They were apples of immortality and could be picked only by a god.

Heracles traveled over land and over sea, and at last he came to the garden of the Hesperides. Nearby stood the Titan Atlas, and Heracles offered to hold up the sky for him if he would pick three golden apples from Hera's tree. Atlas said he would be glad to be rid of his heavy burden for a while, but he feared the dragon Ladon, which lay under the tree watching it with all the eyes of his hundred heads. A hundred-headed dragon could not frighten Heracles. He drew his bow and shot it. Then he took the sky on his shoulders, and Atlas reached out and picked the apples. The three little nymphs who tended the tree wept bitter tears, but they could not stop Atlas, now that the watchful dragon was dead.

Heracles' knees started to buckle, so heavy was the weight of the sky, but Atlas stretched himself, enjoying his freedom.

"I might as well take these apples to Eurystheus myself," said the Titan, and started to walk away. Heracles well understood that Atlas had no intention of ever coming back, but he pretended to agree.

"Very well," he said, "just hold the sky while I make a pad of my lion skin, the sky is hard on my shoulders."

This sounded reasonable to Atlas. He put down the golden apples and braced himself against the vault of the sky.

"Thank you for picking the apples," said Heracles, and hurried homeward.

On his way to Mycenae, Heracles was stopped by the giant wrestler Antaeus. He lived in a hut beside the road, and forced all travelers to wrestle with him. He was a son of Mother Earth and could not die as long as he touched her, so he always won and had built his hut of the skulls and bones of his victims. When Heracles threw the giant to the ground, thinking he was dead, but saw him springing up revived, he understood what was happening. Seizing Antaeus, he held him in the air until he had squeezed all life out of him.

Heracles hurried on to Mycenae and gave the golden apples to Eurystheus. But Eurystheus did not dare to keep them. He gave them to Athena, who took them back to Hera's garden, where they belonged.

For his twelfth labor Heracles had to go to the underworld, capture Cerberus, the snarling, three-headed watchdog of Hades, and bring him to Mycenae.

Heracles searched far and wide till at last he found an entrance to the underworld near Helios' evening palace, far to the west. Setting his face in a terrible scowl, he walked straight down to Hades. The fluttering souls trembled and Hades himself was so frightened at the sight that he told him to take the dog, only please not to treat it too roughly. Cerberus growled and lashed out with his spiked tail, but Heracles threw his arms around him and squeezed him till the dog's three tongues hung out. Whining, Cerberus let Heracles drag him to the upper world and all the way to the gates of Mycenae. When Eurystheus saw the fearful hound, once again he dived into the urn and cowered there, not daring to make a sound. Heracles did not know what to do with the dog, so he dragged Cerberus all the way back down to Hades.

Now Heracles was free. He had performed not only ten but twelve labors. He had atoned for his sins and Zeus was very pleased with his strong son. He was pleased with Hera, too, for she had unknowingly helped Heracles win more glory and fame than any other hero on earth. Admired by everyone, Heracles traveled all over Greece, performing more heroic deeds and making many friends.

But Hera, still relentless, again made him insane and he swatted men down like flies. When he recovered his senses, he once more had to atone for his sins, and this time it was his father, Zeus, who meted out his punishment, seeing to it that there was no glory to be won.

Zeus sentenced Heracles to serve for three years as the slave of Queen Omphale of Lydia. She dressed him in woman's clothes and made the strongest man in the world sit at her feet, spinning and sewing with his huge hands, while she herself donned his lion skin and brandished his club. Heracles grumbled and groaned, but he did as he was ordered. When his three years at last were over, he had learned his lesson of humility.

Again he performed heroic deeds and his friends were glad to see him back. One of his great friends was Admetus, King of Thessaly, under whom Apollo once had served when he was a slave on earth. To thank Admetus for his kindness, Apollo had persuaded the Fates not to cut his thread of life when his time to die had come, as long as Admetus could find someone else willing to die in his stead. That would be easy, thought the king. His faithful men were always saying that his life was dearer to them than their own. King Admetus had always been afraid of dying early, for he was very happy with his beautiful queen, Alcestis. The king and the queen were both fond of Heracles and always welcomed him warmly. But one day when Heracles came to the palace, King Admetus greeted him alone. He looked sad and downcast. When Heracles asked him what was wrong, he said nothing except that a woman of the household had died and he must go to her funeral. And he left Heracles alone with the servants. They too looked sad. They waited on him in silence and did not answer his questions. Heracles ate, drank, and made merry alone and at last he grew impatient, grasped one of the servants, and forced him to speak. The servant told him that the time had come for Admetus to die, and he had turned to his men and asked one of them to die in his stead. But now not one of them had been willing. Admetus then went to his parents, who were old and weary of life, and asked them to die in his stead. They too refused. But when he returned to his palace, he found Queen Alcestis setting off for the realm of the dead. She loved him so much, she said, she would gladly give her life for him, and the king was so fond of his own life that he let his queen depart. Now the king and all the household were mourning for Alcestis.

Heracles shed big tears when he heard this sad story, but, being a man of action, he seized his club and strode off to the underworld to force Hades to give Alcestis back. Such a loving wife should not be allowed to die.

Heracles did not have to use his club. Cerberus slunk out of the way as he stormed into the palace of Hades. The lord of the dead, himself, had a cold, unloving queen and he was so moved when Heracles told him of Alcestis' devotion that he let her go.

Heracles brought Queen Alcestis back to King Admetus and the grief in the palace changed to great joy. Now they all ate, drank, and made merry together and Alcestis grew famous far and wide as the most devoted wife who ever lived.

Heracles too wanted a wife and he chose Deianira, a Caledonian princess, for his bride. Deianira had already been promised to the river-god Achelous, but she dreaded the thought of being married to a river-god, who could change his shape at will. She would never know in which shape her husband would come home at night. She would rather marry the great hero Heracles. The two suitors agreed to wrestle, the victor to have the Princess Deianira. Of course, Heracles won. The river-god rushed at him in the shape of a bull, and Heracles seized him by a horn, wrenched it off, and threw him to the ground before he had time to change into something else. So Heracles and Deianira were married and were very happy together.

One day as they were out traveling, they came to a swollen stream. Heracles forded it with ease, but Deianira was afraid and stood on the bank. Along came the centaur Nessus and politely offered to carry her across. But Nessus, like all centaurs, was fond of pretty girls and before he had reached midstream he had made up his mind to carry her off. Once on the other side, he galloped off with her. Deianira screamed for help, Heracles shot a poisoned arrow at the centaur and Nessus fell to the ground. Before he died he whispered to Deianira, "Take some of my blood and save it. If you ever fear that you are losing your husband's love, paint some of the blood on his tunic and he will love you again."

Deianira carefully saved the drops of blood, for she knew well that many a girl would like to steal her magnificent husband.

One day as Heracles was away at war, he won a great victory and sent a messenger home for his best tunic. He wanted to celebrate with his men, but Deianira thought he wanted to make himself handsome for a girl. She painted some of Nessus' blood on the tunic. As soon as Heracles put it on, he felt as though a thousand fires were burning him. It was not a love potion that Nessus had given Deianira, but the deadly poison of the Hydra from Heracles' arrow, mixed with Nessus' blood. Heracles was so strong that the poison could not kill him, but his sufferings were unbearable. He ordered his men to build a funeral pyre, spread his lion skin over the top, and lay down on it. Then he gave his bow and deadly arrows to his young friend, Philoctetes, as a parting gift. As the flames rose around him, a loud thunderclap was heard, and Heracles, by the order of Zeus, rose up to Olympus, reclining on his lion skin.

The gods all welcomed Heracles and were glad to have him with them, for the Fates had predicted that Olympus would be attacked by a fearful enemy and the Olympians could be saved only if the strongest man ever born fought on their side. The prediction soon came to pass. In a last effort to defeat the mighty thunder-god Zeus, Mother Earth had given birth to fifty snake-legged giants, who surrounded Olympus and tried to storm the palace. They seemed unconquerable, for, like Antaeus, whom Heracles had fought on earth, they sprang up again revived as soon as they touched Mother Earth. Heracles knew what to do, and with his help the gods won over the giants and cast them down into the dismal pit of Tartarus. Heracles was now the hero of Mount Olympus, beloved by all the gods. Even Hera begged him to forgive her and gave him her daughter Hebe, goddess of eternal youth, for his Olympian bride. From then on Heracles lived in eternal bliss, forever a joy to the gods. His father Zeus was very pleased.

•—• THESEUS

THE MUSES sang of Heracles and his labors, and they also sang of the island of Crete, ruled by King Minos, the son of Zeus and Europa. His queen, Pasiphaë, a daughter of the sun-god Helios, had a golden glimmer in her eyes like all the descendants of the sun, and was accustomed to great magnificence. King Minos wanted his queen to live in a palace as splendid as her father's, and he ordered Daedalus, an Athenian architect and inventor of marvelous skill, to build the great palace of Cnossus.

The palace rose up story upon story, over a forest of columns. Winding stairs and intricate passageways connected the many halls and courtyards. Pictures were painted on the walls of the great halls, fountains splashed in the courtyards, and the bathrooms even had running water. Bulls' horns of the purest gold crowned the roofs, for the Cretans worshiped the bull, since Zeus, in the shape of a bull, had brought Europa to the island. Here the king and the queen and all their court lived in great splendor and happiness until one day Poseidon sent a snow-white bull from the sea. Since the island of Crete was completely surrounded by his domain, the sea, he too wanted to be honored, and ordered King Minos to sacrifice the bull to him. But Queen Pasiphaë was so taken by the beauty of the white bull that she persuaded the king to let it live. She admired the bull so much that she ordered Daedalus to construct a hollow wooden cow, so she could hide inside it and enjoy the beauty of the bull at close range.

Poseidon was very angry, and for punishment he made the bull mad. It ravaged the whole island, and though the Cretans were great bullfighters, no one could subdue the beast until Heracles had come to capture it for one of his labors.

To punish the king and queen, Poseidon caused Pasiphaë to give birth to a monster, the Minotaur. He was half man, half bull, and ate nothing but human flesh. Such a fearful monster could not go free, and the clever Daedalus constructed for him a labyrinth under the palace. It was a maze of passageways and little rooms from which nobody could ever hope to find his way out. There the Minotaur was shut in, and as long as he was provided with victims to devour, he kept quiet. When he was hungry, he bellowed so loudly that the whole palace shook. King Minos had to wage war with the neighboring islands so he could supply the Minotaur with the prisoners of war for food. When a son of Minos visited Athens and was accidently killed, King Minos used this as an excuse to threaten to sack the city unless seven

Athenian maidens and seven Athenian youths were sent to Crete to be sacrificed to the Minotaur every nine years.

To save his city, Aegeus, the King of Athens, had to consent, for Minos was much stronger than he. The people of Athens grumbled, for, while King Aegeus was childless and had nothing to lose, they had to see their sons and daughters sacrificed to the cruel Minotaur.

Two times nine years had passed and the king was growing old. For the third time a ship with black sails of mourning was due to depart, when word came to the king that a young hero, Theseus, from Troezen, was making his way to Athens, destroying all the monsters and highwaymen he met on the road. When King Aegeus heard that, his old heart beat faster. Once in his youth he had visited Troezen and had been secretly married to Princess Aethra. He did not bring Aethra back to Athens with him, but before he left, he said to her, "Should you bear me a son and should he grow up strong enough to lift this boulder under which I hide my sword and golden sandals, send him to me, for then he will be the worthy heir to the throne of Athens." King Aegeus in those days was known for his great strength.

Theseus, the young hero, arrived in Athens and went straight to the king's palace. Tall and handsome, he stood before Aegeus with the sandals and the sword, and the king was overjoyed. At last he had a son who was a hero as well. The king happily proclaimed Theseus the rightful heir to the throne of Athens and he became the hero of all Athens when he offered to take the place of one of the victims who were to be sent to Crete. Old King Aegeus begged his son not to go, but Theseus would not change his mind. "I shall make an end of the Minotaur and we shall return safely," he said. "We sail with black sails, but we shall return with white sails as a signal of my success."

The ship sailed to Crete and the fourteen young Athenians were locked in a dungeon to await their doom. But King Minos had a lovely daughter, Ariadne, as fair a maiden as eyes could see. She could not bear the thought that handsome Theseus should be sacrificed to the ugly Minotaur. She went to Daedalus and begged for help to save him. He gave Ariadne a magic ball of thread and told her that at midnight, when the Minotaur was fast asleep, she must take Theseus to the labyrinth. The magic ball of thread would roll ahead of him through the maze and lead him to the monster, and then it was up to Theseus to overpower the beast.

In the dark of the night, Ariadne went to Theseus' prison and whispered that, if he would promise to marry her and carry her away with him, she would help him. Gladly Theseus gave his word, and Ariadne led him to the gate of the labyrinth, tied the end of the thread to the gate so he would find his way back, and gave him the ball. As soon as Theseus put the ball of thread on the ground, it rolled ahead of him through dark corridors, up stairs, down stairs, and around winding passageways. Holding on to the unwinding thread, Theseus followed it wherever it led him, and before long he heard the thunderous snoring of the Minotaur, and there, surrounded by skulls and bleached bones, lay the monster fast asleep.

Theseus sprang at the Minotaur. It roared so loudly that the whole palace of Cnossus shook, but the monster was taken by surprise, and so strong was Theseus that, with his bare hands, he killed the cruel Minotaur.

Theseus quickly followed the thread back to Ariadne, who stood watch at the gate. Together they freed the other Athenians and ran to their ship in the harbor. Before they sailed, they bored holes in all of King Minos' ships so he could not pursue them. Ariadne urged them to hurry, for even she could not save them from Talos, the bronze robot who guarded the island. If he should see their ship leaving, he would throw rocks at it and sink it. Should one of them manage to swim ashore, Talos would throw himself into a blazing bonfire until he was red hot. Then he would burn the survivor to ashes in a fiery embrace. They could already hear his clanking steps, when just in time they hoisted their sail and a brisk wind blew them out to sea. In their rush they forgot to hoist the white sail of victory instead of the black sail of mourning.

Theseus' heart was filled with joy. Not only had he saved the Athenians from the Minotaur, he was also bringing a beautiful bride home to Athens. But in the middle of the night the god Dionysus appeared to him and spoke: "I forbid you to marry Ariadne. I myself have chosen her for my bride. You must set her ashore on the island of Naxos."

Theseus could not oppose an Olympian god. When they came to Naxos, he ordered everyone to go ashore and rest. There Ariadne fell into a heavy slumber, and while she slept, Theseus led the others back to the ship and they sailed off without her.

Poor Ariadne wept bitterly when she awoke and found herself deserted. Little did she suspect that the handsome stranger who came walking toward her was the god Dionysus and that it was he who had ordered Theseus to abandon her. The god gently dried her tears and gave her a drink from the cup in his hand and right away the sadness left her. She smiled up at the god and he put a crown of sparkling jewels on her head and made her his bride. They lived happily together for many years and their sons became kings of the surrounding islands. Dionysus loved Ariadne greatly, and when she died he put her jeweled crown into the sky as a constellation so she would never be forgotten.

Theseus, in his grief at having lost Ariadne, again forgot to hoist the white sail. When King Aegeus saw the black-sailed ship returning from Crete, he threw himself into the sea in despair.

Theseus inherited his father's throne and he and all of Athens mourned the loss of the old king and in his honor named the sea in which he had drowned the Aegean.

King Minos was beside himself with fury when he discovered that his daughter had fled with the Athenians. He knew that no one but the brilliant Daedalus could have helped Theseus unravel the mystery of the labyrinth, so Daedalus was kept a prisoner in the palace and treated very harshly. Daedalus could not bear to be locked up and let his talents go to waste. Secretly he made two sets of wings, one pair for himself and one pair for his son, Icarus. They were cleverly fashioned of feathers set in beeswax. He showed his son how to use them and warned him not to fly too high or the heat of the sun would melt the wax. Then he led him up to the highest tower, and, flapping their wings, they flew off like two birds. Neither King Minos nor Talos, the robot, could stop their flight.

Young and foolish, Icarus could not resist the temptation to rise ever higher into the sky; the whole world seemed at his feet. He flew too close to the sun and the wax began to melt. The feathers came loose, the wings fell apart, and Icarus plunged into the sea and drowned. Sadly Daedalus flew on alone and came to the island of Sicily. His fame had flown ahead of him and the King of Sicily welcomed him warmly, for he too wanted a splendid palace and bathrooms with running water.

As soon as King Minos' ships were mended, he set off in pursuit of Daedalus, the cunning craftsman. He sailed east and he sailed west, and when he came to the Sicilian shore and saw the wondrous palace going up, he had no doubts who was building it. But the king of Sicily hid Daedalus and denied that he had him in his service. Slyly King Minos sent a conch shell up to the palace, with a message that, if anyone could pull a thread through the windings of the conch, he would give him a sack of gold as a reward. The King of Sicily asked Daedalus to solve the problem. Daedalus thought for a while, then he tied a silken thread to an ant, put the ant at one end of the conch shell and a bit of honey at the other end. The ant smelled the honey and found its way through the conch, pulling the thread along with it. When King Minos saw this, he demanded the immediate surrender of Daedalus, for now he had proof that the King of Sicily was hiding him. Nobody but Daedalus could have threaded the conch!

The King of Sicily had to give in. He invited Minos to a feast, promising to surrender Daedalus. As was the custom, King Minos took a bath before the feast. But when he stepped into the fabulous bath that Daedalus had built, boiling water rushed out of the tap and scalded him to death. And Daedalus remained for the rest of his life at the court of the King of Sicily.

After the death of King Minos there was peace between Crete and Athens, and Theseus married Phaedra, Ariadne's younger sister. He became the greatest king Athens ever had, and his fame as a hero spread all over Greece. Another great hero, Pirithoüs, King of the Lapith people in northern Greece, was his inseparable friend. The first time the two heroes had met, they faced each other in combat. But each was so impressed by the other that instead of fighting, they dropped their weapons and swore eternal friendship. Together they performed many great deeds, and when Pirithoüs married a Lapith princess, Theseus, of course, was invited to the wedding feast. The centaurs were invited too, for though wild and lawless they were nonetheless distant relatives. At first they behaved quite mannerly, but as the wine jugs were passed around, they became boisterous and rowdy. Suddenly a young centaur sprang up, grasped the bride by the hair, and galloped away with her. At that, the other centaurs each grasped a screaming girl and took to the hills.

Theseus and Pirithoüs with their men set off in swift pursuit and soon caught up with the centaurs. There was a brutal battle, for the wild centaurs tore up big trees and swung them as clubs. But in Theseus and Pirithoüs they had found their masters. They were chased out of Greece, and the victorious heroes, with the bride and the other Lapith girls, returned to the feast.

Pirithoüs lived happily for a while, then he became a widower and asked his friend Theseus to help him win a new bride. Theseus vowed to help him, but shuddered when he heard that Pirithoüs wanted no one less than Persephone, the queen of the dead. She was unhappy with Hades, he said. Since Theseus had promised to help his friend, and a promise could not be broken, he descended to the underworld with Pirithoüs. They forced their way past Cerberus and entered the gloomy palace. Hades glowered at the two heroes, who had dared to enter his realm, but he listened politely while they stated their errand. "Sit down on that bench, " he said, "so we can discuss the matter." Grim Hades smiled as the two friends sat down, for it was a magic bench from which no one could ever rise. There they were to sit forever with ghosts and bats flitting about their heads.

A long time later Heracles came to Hades on an errand, and pitied the two heroes trying vainly to get up from the bench. He took hold of Theseus and tore him loose with a mighty tug. But when he tried to free Pirithoüs there came a loud earthquake. The gods did not allow Heracles to set him free, for he had shown too great irreverence by daring to want a goddess for a wife. Theseus returned to Athens wiser but thinner, for a part of him had remained stuck to the bench. Ever since, the Athenians have had lean thighs.

•—• OEDIPUS

ONE DAY a blind old man came to Theseus and asked for permission to stay in his kingdom and die in peace. No one dared let him stay in their country, for he was pursued by the avenging furies, the Erinyes. Homeless he wandered about. The old man, whose name was Oedipus, then told Theseus his sad story.

His misfortunes had started before he was born. His father, King Laius of Thebes, had been told by the oracle of Delphi that the child his queen, Jocasta, was carrying was fated to kill his father and marry his mother. This must never happen, thought the king, so when Oedipus was born he ordered a servant to take the child away and abandon him in the mountains. But destiny had willed it differently. A shepherd from the neighboring kingdom of Corinth heard the child's cries. He picked up the little boy and carried him to his king. The King and Queen of Corinth were childless and happily they adopted the handsome little boy. They loved him dearly and he never knew that he was not their real son. Without a care in the world he grew to manhood, and one day went to Delphi to find what the future had in store for him. Great was his horror when he heard the words of the oracle! He was destined to kill his father and marry his mother.

This must never happen, thought Oedipus. He took destiny in his own hands and fled across the mountains, never to see his dear parents again.

On a narrow mountain path, he met the chariot of a haughty lord. "Give way for our master's chariot," shouted the servants, and tried to push Oedipus off the path. Angrily Oedipus fought back and in the struggle the lord and all his servants were killed, except for one who escaped. Oedipus continued on his way and came to the city of Thebes. But its seven gates were closed. Nobody dared to enter or leave, for a monster, the Sphinx, had settled on a cliff just outside the city wall. This winged monster with a woman's head and a lion's body challenged all who passed by to solve her riddle. If they couldn't, she tore them to pieces. Nobody yet had solved the riddle of the Sphinx.

"What creature is it that walks on four feet in the morning, on two at noon, and on three in the evening," she asked with a sinister leer when she saw Oedipus.

"It is man," Oedipus answered. "As a child he crawls on four. When grown, he walks upright on his two feet, and in old age he leans on a staff."

The Sphinx let out a horrible scream. Her riddle was solved and she had lost her powers. In despair she threw herself to her death. The gates of Thebes burst open and the people crowded out to thank the stranger who had freed them. Their old king had recently been killed, leaving no son to inherit the throne and when they heard that Oedipus was a prince from Corinth, they asked him to marry their widowed queen and become their king. To be sure, Queen Jocasta was much older than Oedipus, but she was still beautiful, for she wore a magic necklace that the gods had given Harmonia, the first Queen of Thebes. Those who wore that necklace stayed young and beautiful all their lives. Thus Oedipus became King of Thebes, and he ruled the city justly and wisely for many years.

One day the news reached him that the King of Corinth had died the peaceful death of old age, and while he mourned his father, he was glad that he had been spared from a terrible destiny. Shortly afterward, a pestilence broke out in Thebes and people died in great numbers. Oedipus sent for a seer and asked how he could save his people. The pestilence would last until the death of the old king had been avenged, said the seer. Oedipus swore that he would find the man who had killed the old king, and put out his eyes. He sent his men to search till they found the one surviving servant of King Laius' party. When he was brought before King Oedipus, the servant recognized him at once as the slayer of the old king! And now the whole terrible truth came out, for he was also the selfsame servant who had abandoned the infant Oedipus in the mountains, and had known all the while that the child had been found and adopted by the King of Corinth.

In despair Queen Jocasta went to her room and took her own life and Oedipus in horror put out his own eyes and left Thebes, a broken old man. His daughter Antigone went with him, and they wandered from place to place, turned away from every city, till, at last, they came to Athens.

"Not cursed but blessed will be the place where you lie down and close your eyes," said Theseus when he had heard the story. "No man could have tried harder than you to escape his destiny."

The avenging Erinyes, who had been chasing him, now dropped their whips, and Oedipus could die in peace.

His two sons, Eteocles and Polynices, had no regard for the sufferings of their father. They stayed in Thebes and fought over the throne. At last they agreed to take turns being king, one year at a time. Eteocles ruled Thebes first, and when his year was up he refused to give up the throne.

Polynices left Thebes in a rage, taking with him the magic necklace of Harmonia, vowing to return with an army and take his rightful throne by force.

He went to his father-in-law, the King of Argos, and tried to persuade him to send an army to Thebes. The king had an aging and very vain sister who had great influence over him. Polynices promised her the magic necklace of Harmonia, which would make her young and beautiful again, if she could persuade her brother to go against Thebes. So great are the powers of a vain woman that, not only the King of Argos and his men, but seven armies of brave men set forth with Polynices to storm the seven gates of Thebes, most of them never to return.

Neither could the seven armies storm the seven gates of Thebes, nor could the Thebans drive the attackers away. So it was decided that the two brothers should fight in single combat, the winner to be king.

Eteocles gave his brother a mortal wound, but Polynices, before he fell, dealt him a deadly blow in return. Side by side they lay dead on the field, and all the bloodshed had been in vain.

The son of Eteocles became King of Thebes, and Harmonia's necklace, which had brought so much misfortune, was hung up in a temple in Delphi, so no woman would ever wear it again.

THE GOLDEN FLEECE

THE MUSES SANG about handsome Jason and his quest for the Golden Fleece.

Jason of Iolcus was as strong and well bred as he was handsome, for he had been raised by the wise centaur Chiron. Jason's father had brought the boy to the centaur and had asked him to bring him up, for he feared that his own brother, Pelias, who had taken from him the throne of Iolcus, might harm his heir. In Chiron's lonely mountain cave young Jason was raised to be a hero, skilled in all manly sports. When he was grown he left his foster father to go to Iolcus and reclaim his father's throne.

Hera, who was paying a visit to earth, saw the handsome youth as he walked down from the mountain. His golden hair hung to his shoulders and his strong body was wrapped in a leopard skin. Hera was taken by his fine looks. She quickly changed herself into an old crone and stood helplessly at the brink of a swollen stream as if she did not dare to wade across. Jason offered politely to carry her and lifted her on his strong shoulders. He started to wade and at first she was very light. But with each step she grew heavier, and when he reached midstream, she was so heavy that his feet sank deep into the mud. He lost one of his sandals, but struggled bravely on, and when he reached the other side, the old crone revealed herself as the goddess Hera.

"Lo," she said. "You are a mortal after my liking, I shall stand by you and help you win back your throne from your uncle Pelias." This was a promise the goddess gladly gave, for she had a grudge against Pelias, who had once forgotten to include her when he sacrificed to the gods.

Jason thanked her and went on his way in high spirits. When he arrived in Iolcus, people crowded around him, wondering who the handsome stranger might be, but when King Pelias saw him, his cheeks paled. An

oracle had predicted that a youth with only one sandal would be his undoing. Pelias feigned great friendship when Jason said who he was and why he had come, but underneath he held dark thoughts and planned to do away with his guest. Pelias feasted Jason and flattered him and promised him the throne as soon as he had performed a heroic deed to prove himself worthy of being a king.

"In the kingdom of Colchis, at the shores of the Black Sea," said Pelias, "on a branch in a dark grove, there hangs a golden fleece shining as brightly as the sun. Bring the fleece to me and the throne shall be yours."

The Golden Fleece was once the coat of a flying ram, sent by Zeus to save the life of young Prince Phrixus of Thessaly. The crops had failed and Phrixus' evil stepmother had convinced his father that he must sacrifice his son to save his country from famine. Sadly the king built an altar and put his son on it, but Zeus hated human sacrifice, and as the king lifted his knife, a golden ram swooped down from the skies and flew off with Phrixus on his back. They flew far to the east and landed in the kingdom of Colchis. The King of Colchis understood that Phrixus had been sent by the gods. He gave him his daughter in marriage and sacrificed the ram. Its glittering fleece was hung in a sacred grove and it was the greatest treasure of the country.

King Pelias was certain that Jason would not return alive, for he knew that the warlike king of Colchis would not part with the fleece and that a never-sleeping dragon was guarding it. But Pelias did not know that Jason had Hera's help.

"Give me timber and men to build for me a sturdy ship and I shall sail off at once," said Jason. The king gave him what he asked for and a great ship, the Argo, was built. It was the most seaworthy ship ever seen. Athena, herself prodded by Hera, put a piece of sacred oak in its prow. The oak had the power to speak in time of danger and advise Jason what to do.

With a ship like that it was not hard for Jason to gather a crew of heroes. Even Heracles came with his young friend Hylas. Calaïs and Zetes, winged sons of the North Wind, joined, and Orpheus came along to inspire the crew with his music. Soon each of the fifty oars of the ship was manned by a hero who swore to stand by Jason through all dangers.

Before they set sail, the heroes who called themselves the Argonauts, sacrificed richly to the gods and made sure to forget no one. Poseidon was in a good mood. He called for the West Wind and under full sail the Argo sped toward the east. When the wind grew tired and died down, the Argonauts put out their oars and rowed with all their might. Orpheus beat out the time with his lyre and the ship cut through the waves like an arrow. One after the other the heroes grew tired and pulled in their oars. Only Heracles and Jason were left rowing, each trying to outlast the other. Jason finally fainted, but just as he slumped forward, Heracles' huge oar broke in two, so equal glory was won by them both.

The Argonauts landed at a wooded coast so Heracles could cut himself a new oar. While Heracles searched for a suitable tree, his young friend Hylas went to a pool to fill his jar with fresh water. When the nymph of the pool saw the handsome boy bending down, she fell in love with him. She pulled him down with her to the bottom of the pool and Hylas vanished forever without leaving a trace.

Heracles went out of his mind with grief when he could not find his friend. He ran through the woods, calling for Hylas, beating down whatever was in his way. The Argonauts, brave as they were, all feared Heracles when he was struck with folly. They hastily boarded the ship and sailed away without him.

On toward the east the Argonauts sailed until they came to a country ruled by a king who was known for his knowledge and wisdom. They went ashore to ask the way to Colchis, but the king was so weak that he could barely answer their questions. He was so thin that only his skin held his bones together. Whenever food was set before him, three disgusting Harpies, fat birds with women's heads, swooped down and devoured it. What they did not eat they left so foul and filthy that it was not fit to be eaten. No one in his kingdom could keep the Harpies away.

The Argonauts felt sorry for the starving king. They told him to have his table set, and when the Harpies swooped down again, Zetes and Calaïs, the sons of the North Wind, took to their wings. They could fly faster than the Harpies, and when they caught them, they whipped the evil pests so hard that they barely escaped with their lives. The Harpies flew to the south, never to be seen again. At last the famished king could eat in peace. He could not thank the Argonauts enough and told them how to set their course and what dangers they would encounter. No ship had yet been able to reach the shores of Colchis, he said, for the passage to the Black Sea was blocked by two moving rocks. The rocks rolled apart and clashed together, crushing whatever came between them. But if a ship could move as fast as a bird in flight, it might get through. He gave Jason a dove and told him to send the bird ahead of the ship. If the dove came through alive, they had a chance, he said. If not, they had better give up and turn back.

The Argonauts took leave of the king and sailed toward the clashing rocks. From afar they could hear the din and the heroes trembled, but as the rocks rolled apart, Jason released the dove and the bird flew between them like a dart. Only the very tips of its tail feathers were clipped off when the rocks clashed together.

"All men to the oars!" Jason shouted. Orpheus grasped his lyre and played and his music inspired the heroes to row as never before. The Argo shot ahead like an arrow when the rocks rolled apart, and only the very end of its stern was crushed as they clashed together. Again the rocks rolled apart and stood firmly anchored. The spell was broken, and from then on ships could safely sail in and out of the Black Sea.

The Black Sea was a dangerous sea to sail upon, and Hera had her hands full, guiding the Argonauts through perils. But with her help Jason brought his ship safely through raging storms, past pirate shores and cannibal island, and the Argonauts finally arrived in Colchis.

Aeëtes, King of Colchis, a son of Helios, the sun, was a very inhospitable king. In fact he was so inhospitable that he killed all foreigners who came to his country. When he saw the Argo landing he was furious, and when Jason led his men to his palace and said that they were all great heroes and had come to offer the king their services in return for the Golden Fleece, he fumed with rage. "Very well, "he said to Jason. "Tomorrow, between sunrise and sunset, you must harness my firebreathing bulls, plow up a field, and sow it with dragon's teeth as Cadmus did at Thebes. If you succeed, the

Golden Fleece is yours. But if you fail, I shall cut out the tongues and lop off the hands of you and all your great heroes." King Aeëtes knew well that no man could withstand the searing heat that blew from the bulls' nostrils. What he did not know was that Hera was helping Jason.

Hera knew that the king's daughter, Medea, who stood at her father's side with modestly downcast eyes, was the only one who could save Jason. She was a lovely young sorceress, a priestess of the witch-goddess Hecate, and must be made to fall in love with Jason. So Hera asked Aphrodite to send her little son Eros to shoot one of his arrows of love into Medea's heart. Aphrodite promised Eros a beautiful enamel ball, and he shot an arrow into Medea's heart just as she lifted up her eyes and saw Jason. Her golden eyes gleamed; never had she seen anyone so handsome. She just had to use her magic and save him from her cruel father; there was nothing she would not do to save Jason's life. She went to Hecate's temple and implored the witch-goddess to help her and, guided by the witch-goddess, she concocted a magic salve so powerful that for one day neither iron nor fire could harm the one who was covered with it.

In the dark of the night, Medea sent for Jason. When he came to the temple, she blushingly told him that she loved him so much she would betray her own father to save him. She gave him the magic salve and told him to go up to the fire-breathing bulls without fear. Jason took the young sorceress in his arms and swore by all the gods of Olympus to make her his queen and love her to his dying day. Hera heard him and nodded, very pleased.

When the sun rose in the morning, Jason went straight up to the fire-breathing bulls. They bellowed and belched flames at him, but with Medea's salve he was invulnerable and so strong that he harnessed the bulls and drove them back and forth till the whole field was plowed. Then he seeded the dragon's teeth, and right away a host of warriors sprang up from the furrows. As Cadmus had done, he threw a rock among them and watched from afar as they killed one another. Before the sun had set, they all lay dead.

Jason had fulfilled his task, but King Aeëtes had no intention of keeping his part of the bargain. He called his men together and ordered them to seize the Argo and kill the foreigners at daybreak. In secrecy, Medea went to Jason and told him that he must take the Golden Fleece, now rightfully his, and flee from Colchis before dawn. Under cover of night she led him to the dark grove where the Golden Fleece, shining like the sun, hung on a branch of a tree. Around the trunk of the tree lay coiled the never-sleeping dragon. But Medea chanted incantations and bewitched the dragon. She stared at it with her golden eyes and it fell into a deep magic sleep. Quickly Jason took the Golden Fleece and ran with Medea to the waiting Argo, and quietly they slipped out to sea.

At daybreak, when the king's men were to attack the ship, they found it was gone. So were the Golden Fleece and the king's daughter, Medea. Red-faced with fury, Aeëtes set off in pursuit with his great fleet of Colchian warships. He wanted the Golden Fleece back and he wanted to punish his daughter. The fastest of his ships, steered by one of his sons, soon overtook the Argo.

The Argonauts thought themselves lost, but again Medea saved them. She called to her brother, who stood at the helm of his ship, and pretended to be sorry for what she had done. She said she would go home with him if he would meet her alone on a nearby island. At the same time, she whispered to Jason to lie in wait and kill her brother when he came. She knew that her father would have to stop the pursuit to give his son a funeral.

Hera and all the gods looked in horror at Medea, stained with her brother's blood. No mortal could commit a worse crime than to cause the death of his own kin. Zeus in anger threw thunderbolts. Lightning flashed, thunder roared, and the sea foamed. Then the sacred piece of oak in the bow of the Argo spoke. "Woe," it said, "woe to you all. Not a one among you will reach Greece unless the great sorceress Circe consents to purify Medea and Jason of their sin."

Tossed about by howling winds and towering waves, the Argonauts sailed in search of Circe's dwelling. At long last, off the coast of Italy, they found her palace. Medea warned the Argonauts not to leave the ship, for

Circe was a dangerous sorceress who amused herself by changing men who came to her island into the animal nearest the nature of each man. Some became lions, some rabbits, but most of them were changed into pigs and asses. Medea took Jason by the hand so no harm would befall him, and went ashore.

Circe was Medea's aunt. Like all the descendants of Helios, the sun, she had a golden glint in her eyes, and the moment she saw Medea, she recognized her as her kin. But she was not happy to see her niece, for through her magic she knew what Medea had done. Still she consented to sacrifice to Zeus and ask him to forgive Medea and Jason for their crime. The scented smoke of her burnt offering of sweet meats and cakes reached Zeus and put him in a good humor. He listened to Circe's words and again smiled down upon Medea and Jason.

They thanked Circe and rushed back to the ship. The Argonauts rejoiced. Now they could set sail for Greece. But still they had to pass through dangerous and bewitched waters. Soon they came to the island of the Sirens. The Sirens were half birds, half women, not loathsome like the Harpies, but enchanting creatures. They sat on a cliff, half hidden by sea spray, and sang so beautifully that all sailors who heard them dived into the sea and tried to swim to them, only to drown or pine to death at the Sirens' feet. When the alluring voices of the Sirens reached the ears of the Argonauts, Orpheus grasped his lyre and sang so loudly and sweetly that all other sounds were drowned out, and not one of the Argonauts jumped overboard.

After a while the Argo had to sail through a narrow strait that was guarded by two monsters. On one side lurked the monster Scylla. From her waist up she looked like a woman, but instead of legs, six furious, snarling dogs grew out from her hips, and they tore to pieces whatever came close to them. The monster Charybdis lived on the other side of the strait. She was forever hungry and sucked into her gullet all ships that ventured within her reach.

Helplessly, the Argo drifted between the two monsters, and the Argonauts again gave themselves up for lost, when up from the bottom of the sea rose the playful Nereids. They had come at Hera's bidding and they lifted up the Argo and threw it from hand to hand over the dangerous waters until it reached the open sea beyond. Poseidon called for the West Wind and the Argo sped homeward under full sail.

A loud cheer rang out from the valiant crew when they sighted the shore of Greece. They had been away for many long years and were homesick. But as the Argo neared the port of Iolcus, the ship was hailed by a fisherman who warned Jason that King Pelias had heard of his safe return and had made plans to kill him. Jason was downcast at his uncle's treachery, but Medea, her eyes flashing, asked to be set ashore alone. Once again she wanted to save his life.

Disguised as an old witch, she entered Iolcus, saying that she had magic herbs to sell that would make old creatures young again. The people crowded around her, wondering from where the witch had come. King Pelias himself came out from his palace and asked her to prove that what she said was true, for he felt he was growing old.

"Bring me the oldest ram in your flock and I will show you the magic of my herbs," said Medea.

An old ram was brought to her and she put it into a caldron full of water. On top she sprinkled some of her magic herbs, and lo! the water in the caldron boiled and out of the steam and bubbles sprang a frisky young lamb.

Now King Pelias asked Medea to make him young too. She answered that only his daughters could do that, but she would gladly sell them her magic herbs. But the herbs she gave them had no magic at all, and so King Pelias found his death in the boiling caldron at his own daughters' hands.

Now the throne of Iolcus was Jason's, but again Medea had committed a terrible crime. She had tricked innocent daughters into killing their own father. The gods turned from her and she changed from a lovely young sorceress into an evil witch. The people of Iolcus refused to accept her for their queen and took another king in Jason's stead. With the loss of his throne, Jason also lost his love for Medea. He forgot that he had sworn to love her till his dying day and that she had committed her crimes for his sake. He asked her to leave so he could marry the Princess of Corinth and inherit her father's kingdom.

Medea, scorned and furious, turned more and more to evil sorcery. To revenge herself on Jason, she sent a magic robe to his new bride. It was a beautiful gown, but the moment the bride put it on she went up in flames and so did the whole palace. Then Medea disappeared into a dark cloud, riding in a carriage drawn by two dragons.

Jason found no more happiness, for when he broke his sacred oath to Medea, he lost Hera's good will. His good looks left him and so did his luck and his friends. Lonesome and forgotten, he sat one day in the shade of his once glorious ship, the Argo, now rotting on the beach of Corinth. Suddenly the sacred piece of oak in the prow broke off, fell on him, and killed him.

The Golden Fleece was hung in Apollo's temple in Delphi, a wonder for all Greeks to behold and a reminder of the great deeds of Jason and the Argonauts.

THE CALYDONIAN BOAR HUNT

MELEAGER of Calydonia was one of the heroes who had sailed with Jason on the Argo. No one could throw a spear with greater skill than he. Still he was powerless to stop a fearful boar that was ravaging his father's kingdom. The king, one day, had forgotten to include Artemis when he sacrificed to the gods, and in revenge the angry goddess sent the biggest boar ever seen. The boar had tusks as big as an elephant's and bristles as sharp as steel. Meleager sent for the Argonauts and all the great athletes of Greece and asked them to come to Calydonia and hunt down the monstrous beast. Great glory awaited the one who could destroy the Calydonian Boar.

Many heroes came to the hunt, and also a girl whose name was Atalanta. She was the fastest runner in Greece and a great huntress as well. When some of the men grumbled at hunting with a girl, Meleager ruled that a girl who could outrun them all would certainly be welcome to join the chase. Still grumbling, the men had to give in.

For days the heroes feasted at the Calydonian court. Then they offered rich sacrifices to the gods and went off to the hunt. They drove the boar out of its lair, and as it charged, spears and arrows flew wild. When the dust settled, seven men lay dead, some killed by the boar, some by the arrows of their excited companions. Atalanta alone kept a cool head. She ran swiftly hither and thither till she could take good aim, and then she let an arrow fly. The arrow stopped the boar just in time to save the life of a hero who had stumbled in front of the onrushing beast. Quickly Meleager leaped forward and hurled his spear with all his might. The beast rolled over and lay dead.

Meleager offered the hide and the tusks to Atalanta. These trophies were hers, he said, for it was she who stopped the boar. Again the men protested, for it hurt their pride to see a girl walk off with all the glory. Meleager's two uncles teased him and said that he must be in love with the girl. "Just wait till your wife finds out about this!" they said, smiling maliciously.

In a rage Meleager hurled his spear at his taunting uncles, killing them both. When Meleager's mother heard that her son had slain her two brothers, she, too, flew into a rage. She ran to her treasure chest and took out a half-charred log. It was a magic log that held Meleager's life.

This log had been burning in the hearth when Meleager was born. The three Fates had come to see the infant, and the mother had overheard them say it was a pity that the handsome child would die as soon as the log had burned up. Quickly the mother had seized the log, beaten out the flames, and had hidden it among her dearest treasures. Thus Meleager had lived to become a great hero.

Now in her fury, the queen flung the old dry log into the fire. As it burst into flames and was consumed, Meleager felt a searing pain shoot through his body and fell dead.

The Calydonian Boar Hunt, which had begun with a feast, ended with a funeral. Only Atalanta was happy. She had won her trophies in competition with the greatest heroes of Greece.

THE APPLES OF LOVE AND THE APPLE OF DISCORD

ATALANTA, like Artemis, loved no men, though many men fell in love with her because she was so graceful when she ran.

When she was born her father had cruelly abandoned her in the wilderness, for he had hoped for a son. But she did not perish, for a she-bear heard her cries and carried her gently to her den, nursed her, and raised her with her cubs.

Years later, an astonished huntsman saw a girl racing with wild beasts through the woods. He caught her in a snare and brought her home with him. Soon she learned to talk and act like a human, and her foster father was very proud of her fleetness of foot. He took her to athletic games and she won all the races. Her fame spread over Greece, and now her real father proudly reclaimed her as his long-lost daughter. He was a king and a king's daughter could not be allowed to run about unmarried, so he began to search for a suitable husband for her. But Atalanta did not want a husband. To be left in peace, she said she would only marry a man who could beat her in a running race. However, anyone who raced her and lost would forfeit his life. That would scare all suitors away, she thought. But she was so lovely that many suitors tried their luck anyway and they all lost their lives.

One day a young prince whose name was Melanion came to court her. He was smarter than the others. He knew that he could not outrun Atalanta, so he sacrificed to Aphrodite and prayed for her help.

The goddess of love, who wanted to see all pretty girls married, gave Melanion three golden apples and told him what to do.

When the race began, Atalanta, certain that she would win, let Melanion have a head start. When she caught up with him, Melanion threw a golden apple at her feet. It glittered so beautifully that she had to stop and pick it up. Soon she overtook him again and Melanion threw the second apple, this time a bit farther away. She left the track and made a dash for the apple. When again Melanion heard her light footsteps behind him, he threw the third apple far into the bushes. Atalanta just had to have that one too, and before she found it, Melanion had crossed the finish line. So he had won her and they were married and Atalanta treasured her golden apples and loved her clever husband dearly. They lived happily for many years and never forgot to honor Aphrodite, who had brought them together. But they did not show proper respect to Zeus and he changed them into a pair of lions for punishment. For the rest of their lives they ran as lions hunting, side by side through the woods.

Peleus, a young king of Thessaly, had Atalanta to thank for his life, for it was he who had stumbled in front of the Calydonian Boar when she stopped it with her arrow. He had also been one of the Argonauts and was one of the greatest athletes in Greece, a favorite of the gods. Zeus gave him a beautiful Nereid, Thetis, for his bride, and all the gods came to the wedding. Only Eris, the spirit of strife, had not been invited. She was furious, and while everybody was making merry she threw a golden apple among the guests and shouted, "The fairest of the goddesses shall have it!"

Hera, Aphrodite, and Athena rushed to pick it up, each one thinking herself the fairest. It was not a golden apple of love that Eris had thrown, but the apple of discord, and the three goddesses began to quarrel about who should have it. The wedding broke up on a sour note, and in heated dispute the goddesses retired to high Olympus.

Thetis, the bride, was not happy at being married to a mortal, for her children would not be immortal, as she was. No god had dared to marry her, for an oracle had predicted that she would bear her husband a son who would become greater than his father. Peleus, of course, thought himself the most fortunate of men.

In time, Thetis bore her husband many children. Trying to make them immortal, she held them over sacred fire to burn away their mortality, but none survived the ordeal. At last, she gave birth to a boy sturdier than the others. He withstood the fire, and she had almost succeeded in making him immortal, when Peleus rushed into her room and snatched the child away. Thetis was so hurt and disappointed that she went back to the sea and never returned. The little boy was brought up by Chiron, the wise centaur, and he grew to be the greatest warrior that Greece has ever known. He was invulnerable except for his heel by which his mother held him over the fire. His name was Achilles.

Meanwhile discord reigned on Olympus. The three goddesses quarreled on, and none of the gods dared to say which of them was the fairest.

One day as Zeus looked down on earth, his eyes fell on Paris, a prince of Troy. He was overwhelmingly handsome, as were most men in the royal house of Troy. His grand-uncle Ganymede was such a goodlooking boy that Zeus, in the shape of an eagle, had stolen him from his father and carried him to Olympus to be his cupbearer. Anchises, another relative of Paris, was so exceedingly handsome that Aphrodite herself fell in love with him. She took on the shape of a princess so she could marry him and bore him a son whose name was Aeneas.

But Paris outshone all his relatives, and someone as handsome as he must be the best judge of beauty, thought Zeus. He told Hermes to lead the three goddesses down to Mount Ida near Troy, where Paris was herding the royal sheep and cows, and let Paris judge between them.

Paris stared in speechless wonder when the three radiant goddesses appeared before him. Hermes gave him the golden apple and told him to award it to the most beautiful of them.

"Give it to me," said white-armed Hera, "and all of Asia shall be your kingdom."

"Choose me," said gray-eyed Athena, "and you shall be the wisest of men."

"The most beautiful woman on earth shall be yours if you give me the apple," said Aphrodite.

Paris was young and loved beauty more than power or wisdom, and so he gave the apple to Aphrodite.

Aphrodite happily took the golden apple, and did not give it a thought that the most beautiful woman on earth, Helen, Queen of Sparta, already had a husband.

LOVELY was the song of the Muses about the great beauty of Helen of Troy. She was a daughter of Zeus and her beauty had been a wonder to all from the time she was born. Zeus in the disguise of a swan had flown down from Olympus to court her mother, Leda, and Leda had laid two blue eggs. When the eggs were hatched, Helen and her brother, Pollux, came out from one of them. They were the children of Zeus and immortal. From the other egg came their half sister and brother, Clytemnestra and Castor, children of Leda's mortal husband, King Tyndareus.

Castor and Pollux were inseparable from the time they were born, and both grew up to be great athletes. Castor won fame as a tamer of horses, Pollux as a boxer. They protected each other to the last breath. When side by side they fell in battle, Pollux went to Olympus, while Castor, being mortal, was sent to Hades. They missed each other so much that Zeus took pity on them. He allowed Pollux to give his brother half of his immortality and from then on the Heavenly Twins always stayed together, half the time on Olympus, the other half in Hades' realm.

The two sisters, Helen and Clytemnestra, grew up at the court of their mortal father, King Tyndareus. Clytemnestra soon was given in marriage to Agamemnon, the great King of Mycenae. But Helen had so many suitors that Tyndareus did not know whom to choose. He feared that if he gave her hand to one the crowd of rejected suitors would fall upon him. His palace was besieged by Helen's admirers and ever more came. Among them was Odysseus, a wise young prince. When he saw all the suitors, he withdrew his proposal, for he knew that there would always be fighting over a woman as lovely as Helen. Instead he asked for the hand of her gentle cousin, Penelope, and he advised King Tyndareus how to solve his problem. He must ask all the suitors to accept the one he chose for Helen's husband and swear to stand by and help to win her back should anyone try to steal her. The suitors agreed. Each one hoped that the choice would fall on him, and they all took the oath. Tyndareus then gave Helen's hand to Menelaus of Sparta, and all the other suitors left without grumbling.

Helen had been the Queen of Sparta for many happy years and her fame as the most beautiful woman on earth had spread all over, when Aphrodite promised her to Paris. The Trojans begged Paris to forget Aphrodite's promise, or a terrible misfortune would surely befall them. But Paris ignored their warnings and sailed across the Aegean Sea, to steal Helen from King Menelaus and bring her back to Troy.

Helen sat serene and happy, surrounded by her ladies, weaving and sewing her finest wools, when Paris entered the palace in Sparta. Just as she looked up and saw him, Eros shot an arrow of love into her heart. She gathered her treasures without hesitation and eloped with him for Troy.

A brisk wind carried them out to sea, but before they had sailed far, the wine-dark waters grew glassy and calm, and Nereus, the kind old man of the sea, rose from the depths. He warned them to return or dire woe would befall them and their kin. But Helen and Paris had eyes and ears only for each other and did not hear his warning.

They landed in Troy and the Trojans received her with great joy, proud that the most beautiful woman on earth was now Helen of Troy.

But Menelaus was not a man to stand idly by, whether or not his queen had been promised to Paris by a goddess. He reminded Helen's old suitors of their oath. They joined him with all their warriors, and it was not long before a huge Greek fleet arrived in Troy to fetch Helen back to Sparta. The Trojans refused to give Helen up, and Troy was hard to conquer, for it was surrounded by a high wall built by Apollo and Poseidon. After long talks, it was decided that Paris and Menelaus should fight in single combat and Helen would go to the winner. Paris was no warrior. He preferred to rest on silken pillows and gaze into Helen's beautiful eyes. But Aphrodite came to his rescue and hid him in a cloud and since Menelaus could not find his opponent, the duel was undecided. Then the two armies clashed together.

For ten long years, the Greeks and the Trojans fought over Helen. The gods watched with great interest and even took part in the fighting themselves. Hera, angry with Paris for not giving the apple to her, fought for the Greeks. Wise and just Athena was also annoyed with Paris, so even though she was protectress of Troy, she fought for the Greeks. Ares fought wherever the battle was hottest, and when he himself was wounded, he frightened both armies with his howls. Sweet Aphrodite herself entered the raging battle to help her darling Paris and she also was wounded. "Enough!" called Zeus, and he ordered all the gods to withdraw from the battle. They sat on the walls of Troy and watched the mortals decide the outcome for themselves.

Many great heroes fell on both sides, but the Greeks could not storm the mighty walls of Troy and the Trojans could not put the Greeks to flight as long as Achilles, the invulnerable son of Thetis, fought for them. Though Paris was no great marksman, fate had chosen him to slay the great hero Achilles. Apollo, unseen by the other gods, ran to Paris's side and guided his hand as he drew taut his bow. The arrow struck Achilles in the heel, his only vulnerable spot. Mortally wounded, he fell to the ground. The Greeks mourned greatly the loss of their hero Achilles, and took their revenge on Paris. He fell, pierced by one of the poisoned arrows that Heracles had given to Philoctetes.

Shortly afterward, the Greeks broke camp, boarded their ships, and sailed away. They left on the shore a large wooden horse. The Trojans thought they had finally routed the Greeks, and in triumph, they pulled the horse into their city as a trophy. But the horse was hollow and filled with Greek warriors. In the dark of the night, they crept out and opened wide the city gates. The wily Greeks had not left, but had been hiding behind an island. Now they came pouring into the city and proud Troy was destroyed.

Helen was brought back to Sparta in triumph to sit among her ladies as lovely as ever, embroidering in lavender and purple threads on the finest wools.

Of the royal house of Troy no one but Aphrodite's son Aeneas, his father, and his young son remained. The goddess returned to take them out of the smoking ruins and lead them to safety.

Aeneas wandered from land to land, till at last he came to Italy, where he founded a kingdom. The gods looked on him with favor, for it was fated that his descendants should build the mighty city of Rome.

So it came to pass! The Romans built huge temples to the Olympian gods, not so beautiful as the Greek ones, but much more luxurious, and the glory of the gods became greater than ever. They were given Roman names instead of their Greek ones, but they were still the same gods and it is under their Roman names that we know them best today.

EVERYTHING must come to an end, and so did the rule of Zeus and the other Olympian gods. All that is left of their glory on earth are broken temples and noble statues. Also the Muses fell silent, but their songs live on to this very day, and the constellations put up by the gods still glitter on the dark blue vault of the sky.

图书在版编目（CIP）数据

多莱尔的希腊神话书：汉、英 /（美）英格丽·多莱尔,（美）爱德加·帕林·多莱尔著绘；熊裕译. — 北京：北京联合出版公司, 2021.1
ISBN 978-7-5596-4417-6

Ⅰ. ①多… Ⅱ. ①英… ②爱… ③熊… Ⅲ. ①神话-作品集-古希腊-汉、英 Ⅳ. ①I545.73

中国版本图书馆CIP数据核字(2020)第130374号

多莱尔的希腊神话书
作者：[美] 英格丽·多莱尔 爱德加·帕林·多莱尔
译者：熊裕

出 品 人 赵红仕
责任编辑 管 文
特约编辑 朱 岳
统筹策划 周丽华
装帧设计 丁威静
选题策划 全本书店

北京联合出版公司出版（北京市西城区德外大街 83 号楼 9 层 100088）
北京联合天畅文化传播公司发行 北京中科印刷有限公司印刷 新华书店经销
字数 250 千字 787 毫米 ×1092 毫米 1/16 19 印张 2021年1月第1版 2021年1月第1次印刷
ISBN 978-7-5596-4417-6
定价:150.00 元